Data Modeling with ERwin

M. Carla DeAngelis

SAMS

201 West 103rd St., Indianapolis, Indiana, 46290 USA

Data Modeling with ER*win*

Trademarks

All terms mentioned in this book that are known to be trademarks or service marks have been appropriately capitalized. Sams cannot attest to the accuracy of this information. Use of a term in this book should not be regarded as affecting the validity of any trademark or service mark.

Warning and Disclaimer

Every effort has been made to make this book as complete and as accurate as possible, but no warranty or fitness is implied. The information provided is on an "as is" basis. The author and the publisher shall have neither liability nor responsibility to any person or entity with respect to any loss or damages aris-ing from the information contained in this book or from the use of the pro-grams accompanying it.

ASSOCIATE PUBLISHER
Bradley L. Jones

EXECUTIVE EDITOR
Chris Webb

DEVELOPMENT EDITOR
Thomas Cirtin

MANAGING EDITOR
Charlotte Clapp

PROJECT EDITOR
Elizabeth Roberts

COPY EDITOR
Kris Simmons
Mary Ellen Stephenson

INDEXER
Eric Schroeder

PROOFREADER
Maryann Steinhart

TECHNICAL EDITOR
William Copper

TEAM COORDINATOR
Meggo Barthlow

MEDIA DEVELOPER
Jason Haines

INTERIOR DESIGNER
Anne Jones

COVER DESIGNER
Anne Jones

COPYWRITER
Eric Borgert

PRODUCTION
Timothy Osborn

Contents at a Glance

Contents

PART III   Creating the Logical Model

9   Developing the Logical Data Model   171

10   Building Logical Relationships   201

About the Author

M. Carla DeAngelis, vice president and data architect for Bank of America, has more than 10 years' experience in software engineering. She holds a degree in computer science, with minors in mathematics and English, from Weber State University in Ogden, Utah. Ms. DeAngelis has performed logical and physical data modeling using ER*win* for some of Bank of America's most business-critical projects.

Prior to starting at Bank of America, she worked as a consultant for companies such as 3M, Armstrong Flooring, Blue Cross/Blue Shield, Rayonier, and Xerox. Ms. DeAngelis was awarded the 3M Information Technology Partners in Quality award, among many other awards and commendations.

Dedication

This book is dedicated to Bob (my husband and best friend), Shannon, Bob, RJ, Jake, Vanessa, Bobby, Kit, Gabriel (my wonderful family), and my dear friends.

Acknowledgments

I thank God for all His blessings in my life. I particularly thank my loving family and wonderful friends. Special thanks to Karen Armel, Maureen Page, Gina Gioia, Debbie Clark, Jan Hathaway, and Linda Harrington for always being there for me.

Thanks to Dr. Joe Schmuller for believing in me and encouraging me.

I want to thank the people at Sams Publishing who made this book possible: Tom Cirtin, my development editor, has a special gift for helping a first-time author over the rough spots. Elizabeth Roberts, my production editor, kept things moving. Kris Simmons, my copy editor, has an eagle eye for detail. William P. Copper, my technical editor, kept me on my toes. Chris Webb, my acquisitions editor, taught me to love deadlines. I also thank all the other fine people who helped make this book a reality.

I want to thank my employer, Bank of America, for providing a work environment that offered me the opportunity to develop in my area of expertise. I also want to thank my peers and colleagues at Bank of America. This intelligent, talented group creates an environment that promotes critical thinking and innovative solutions.

I must also thank my peers and colleagues at PathTech Software Solutions, Inc. The opportunity to work in PathTech's unique environment presented an invaluable growth experience. Special thanks to my brilliant friend Mark Weaver.

I give particular thanks to Clive Finklestein, the father of information engineering, for introducing me to modeling from the business perspective and using data-dependency analysis and data clustering for model analysis.

And special thanks to Michael Riengruber and William Gregory for introducing me to the concept of model reviews.

I want to thank the authors who wrote the books that taught me modeling concepts and techniques, which are listed in "References" at the end of this book. This book represents the *gestalt* of their teachings and my experience.

Tell Us What You Think!

As the reader of this book, *you* are our most important critic and commentator. We value your opinion and want to know what we're doing right, what we could do better, what areas you'd like to see us publish in, and any other words of wisdom you're willing to pass our way.

We welcome your comments. You can email or write us to let us know what you did or didn't like about this book—as well as what we can do to make our books stronger.

Please note that we cannot help you with technical problems related to the topic of this book, and that due to the high volume of mail we receive, we might not be able to reply to every message.

When you write, please be sure to include this book's title and author as well as your name and phone or fax number. We will carefully review your comments and share them with the author and editors who worked on the book.

Email: feedback@samspublishing.com

Mail: Sams Publishing
201 West 103rd Street
Indianapolis, IN 46290 USA

Introduction

In 1993, as a programmer on a team, I was assigned the task of producing the data model. The reason for selecting me was simple: I had used the company's data modeling tool. I had never really modeled before, but because I had been programming against databases for quite some time, I felt that I could do a good job.

Well, the truth is I finally did get a model produced. But it was definitely not a quality model, and in fact, it had a very short life. The team wrote the code and created the tables. I used the tool provided to me, more or less, to document the database structure. Back then, I didn't understand the role of data modeling in the development process and I wasn't really sure where to begin or what to produce. I needed something to guide me through the process of creating a logical and physical data model using a visual data modeling tool such as ER*win*.

ER*win* and Data Modeling

ER*win* is a visual data modeling tool that supports logical and physical data modeling. ER*win*, originally developed by LogicWorks, is owned by Computer Associates. Computer Associates offers a suite of complementary tools that work well with ER*win*. Check out the Computer Associates Web site for additional information on ER*win* (`www.cai.com/erwin`). Some of the benefits of using ER*win* are

- An easy-to-use visual environment makes it simple for good modelers to design logical and physical data models.
- Modeling provides an opportunity for increased productivity among development teams by supporting the sharing and reuse of data models.
- Using ER*win* decreases development time by automating the creation of physical data structures.
- ER*win* improves data model completeness and accuracy by providing a facility for automatically synchronizing the model and physical database.
- ER*win* provides support for the development and use of enterprise data modeling standards.

ER*win* supports the design of large, complex enterprise models by dividing them into smaller, more manageable subject areas. Stored displays allow multiple views of the same subject area to meet the needs of user communities, as well as development teams. ER*win* data models can be edited, viewed, and printed in a variety of ways. RPTwin, which comes bundled with ER*win*, is an easy-to-use report writer and browser. RPTwin contains a set of predefined common reports, as well as custom reporting options that allow modelers to define the appearance and contents of data model reports.

Who Should Use This Book?

Data Modeling with ERwin is intended for use by novice modelers who are interested in producing quality logical and physical data models using ER*win*. To use this book effectively, you need a basic understanding of databases and good problem-solving skills. A fairly good understanding of Windows 95/98 will be helpful, and a working knowledge of at least one DBMS platform is a real plus.

Facilitation and technical writing skills will help in performing the tasks of collecting and documenting the information requirements, business rules, and usage requirements. Good analytical skills are required for translating requirements and business rules into logical and physical model objects.

Although programming skills are not required, a working knowledge of Structured Query Language (SQL) can be helpful when creating the physical data model. Database administration skills in the selected database platform are required to create a good physical model. Although the modeler need not have these skills, at least one member of the physical modeling team must have a deep understanding of the target environment.

If you have used other data modeling tools, you should find ER*win*'s tools straightforward and intuitive. If ER*win* is your first data modeling tool, you should be able to ramp up quickly, becoming familiar with the most common tools immediately.

Using This Book

Even though ER*win* is probably the best data modeling tool in the marketplace, to use it effectively you need to understand data modeling and collecting the information that defines the model. This book is organized in four parts to help you do just that.

In Part I, "Modeling Concepts," I describe the role of data modeling in the project development cycle and introduce data modeling concepts. You learn about the components of logical and physical models, including some best practices for working with entities, attributes, and relationships.

In Part II, "Introducing ER*win*," you learn about installing ER*win* and setting the logical modeling environment. You also learn how to gather information requirements, metadata, and business rules.

In Part III, "Creating the Logical Model," you learn how to use ER*win* to create a logical model that represents the information requirements and business rules. You also learn how to use ER*win*'s features for organizing a logical model and the steps for delivering the logical model, as well as get an introduction to some of ER*win*'s advanced features for the logical model.

In Part IV, "Creating the Physical Model," you learn how to collect usage requirements and work with a DBA and architect to develop the physical model. You also learn how to create the database objects in the target server. Although ER*win*/ERX generates schemas for most major databases, including Sybase, Oracle, DB2, and Informix, I chose Access to create the examples I used to illustrate the features and functionality of ER*win*. I selected Access because it demonstrates ER*win*'s direct connectivity, which allows it to create a database directly from the data model or reverse engineer an existing database into a model.

NOTE

The terms used in this book are defined within the text. However, if you need more information or further clarification, visit the techweb.com Web site and use the lookup feature to find the definition of most technology-related terms.

This text is a practical, no-nonsense guide that does more than describe modeling constructs. It provides step-by-step instructions for creating good data models. It defines and describes the information that goes into creating a model, as well as supporting documentation. If you want to create good data models using ER*win*, this is the book for you.

Conventions Used in This Book

This book uses different typefaces to differentiate between code and regular English, and also to help you identify important concepts.

Text that you type and text that should appear on your screen is presented in monospace type.

```
It will look like this to mimic the way text looks on your screen.
```

Placeholders for variables and expressions appear in *monospace italic* or *italic* font. You should replace the placeholder with the specific value it represents.

NOTE

A Note presents interesting pieces of information related to the surrounding discussion.

TIP

A Tip offers advice or teaches an easier way to do something.

CAUTION

A Caution advises you about potential problems and helps you steer clear of disaster.

Modeling Concepts

IN THIS PART

Understanding Data Modeling Concepts

Data modeling is the activity of discovering and document-ing information requirements. *Information requirements* describe the data and business rules needed to support a business requirement. A data model can express the com-plex information needs of an entire enterprise or the spe-cific information needs of a single software application. ER*win* is a graphical data modeling tool that allows a mod-eler to use information requirements and business rules to create a logical and physical data model. Like many other tools, ER*win* works best when it is used by someone who understands how to do the job and is using the tool to work smarter.

The sections that follow introduce data modeling concepts and data modeling activities using the Entity Relational (ER) approach by exploring the following topics:

- The role of data modeling
- Producing a data model
- Taking an enterprise view
- Understanding modeling methodology

NOTE

I haven't included every expert's approach to data modeling. In fact, the approach I use is a blend of what I've learned from pioneers of modeling and what I've learned through experience. In most respects I've taken an "ER*win*" approach where possible.

Understanding how to model begins with understanding data modeling concepts, the language of modeling. These first sections explore the concepts from a beginning modeler's perspective. I introduce these concepts in a straightforward manner with no attempt to explain the powerful mathematical background of relational algebra. If you're already familiar with data modeling and data modeling concepts, you might want to flip straight to Chapter 5, "Getting Started with ER*win*."

The Role of Data Modeling

Data modeling tasks provide the most benefit when performed early in the development lifecycle. The model provides information critical to understanding the scope of a project for iterative development phases. Beginning the implementation phase without a clear understanding of the data requirements might cause your project to incur costly overruns or end up on the scrap heap.

An Introduction to Project Development

Many publications discuss project development, and this text does not cover this subject in detail. I included this section to assist modelers in understanding the role of data modeling in project development and to provide an understanding of when modeling should occur.

Most companies follow a methodology that outlines the development lifecycle selected to guide the development process. To some degree, most adhere to the same order of high-level concepts:

1. Problem definition
2. Requirements analysis
3. Conceptual design
4. Detail design
5. Implementation
6. Testing

This development method is generally referred to as the *waterfall method*. As you can see in Figure 1.1, each phase is completed before moving to the next, creating a "waterfall" effect.

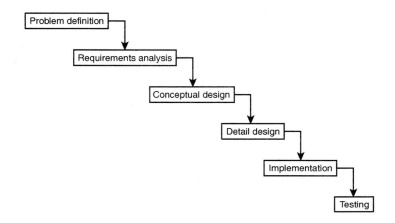

FIGURE 1.1
The waterfall method of project development. Note that the results of each phase cascade into the next.

Many projects are developed using iterations or phases. An iterative development approach decreases risk by breaking the project into discrete manageable phases. Each phase includes analysis, detail design, implementation, and testing. Subsequent phases build upon and leverage the functionality of the preceding phase. However, within each phase, the waterfall method applies.

When to Perform Data Modeling Tasks

Logical modeling should take place as early in project development as possible, often as part of the problem definition activities. Logical data modeling is also a powerful tool for defining and documenting the data requirements, as well as establishing the business rules for how the data should be used. In fact, many industry experts believe that the data model should provide the foundation for project development.

Producing a Data Model

A *data model* is a visual representation of the data structures, data, and business rules for a database. A data model is generally developed as part of a larger development effort.

A data model has two components, a logical model and a physical model. In most cases, a logical model is created first, and then the physical model follows. However, in some cases, a data model is reverse engineered from an existing database. Reverse engineering is discussed later in this book.

As with most engineering projects, you create a data model by following a set of steps.

1. Problem and scope definition
2. Requirements gathering
3. Analysis
4. Logical data model creation
5. Physical data model creation
6. Database creation

Figure 1.2 illustrates how each step provides input for the next.

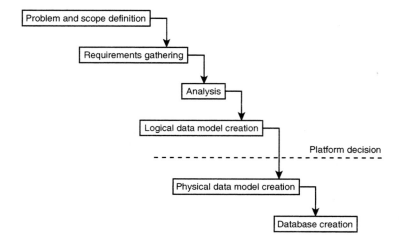

FIGURE 1.2

Logical data model creation can occur prior to selecting a database platform (Oracle, DB2, Sybase, and so on). ERwin can provide support for specific physical properties if the physical data model is produced after the database platform is selected.

Problem and Scope Definition

Begin logical data modeling by defining the problem. This step is sometimes referred to as writing a mission or scoping statement. The problem definition can be a simple paragraph or it can be a complex document that outlines a series of business objectives. The problem definition defines the scope, or boundary, of the data model, much the way a survey defines property boundaries.

Gathering Information Requirements

Most industry experts agree that the most critical task in a development project is an accurate and complete definition of the requirements. In fact, an incomplete or inaccurate understanding of requirements can cause expensive re-work and significant delay.

Gathering information requirements is the act of discovering and documenting the information necessary to identify and define the entities, attributes, and business rules for the logical model. There are two well-recognized methods for gathering requirements: facilitated sessions and interviews. Most development methodologies recommend facilitated sessions. The sections that follow provide high-level guidelines for gathering information requirements using facilitated sessions. A later exercise demonstrates how to use the information gathered to create a data model using ER*win*.

Preparing for Facilitated Sessions

An important factor in conducting successful facilitated sessions is preparation. Preparing for a facilitated session begins with identifying the right list of attendees. Of course, you must address the logistics such as scheduling facilities and equipment. Sharing the problem definition and other information prior to the session can significantly increase productivity. But nothing is as important as having the right people present at the session.

Recommended Attendees

Identifying the right list of attendees is the single most important task in preparing for the session. Participants should have knowledge and experience in the problem domain. It is important to encourage participants to set aside any attachment to a current system or solution. The most successful meetings involve participants who are also stakeholders in the success of the development effort.

A good facilitator is the next critical element. The facilitator ensures that all participants have an opportunity to share their knowledge, experience, and opinion. A session where only a few people speak will probably provide an inadequate set of information requirements.

At least one good scribe should take notes and document the information requirements. Because the logical model will be developed from the information gathered in the session, good documentation is a critical success factor.

A data modeler should be documenting the entities, attributes, and relationships as the information is gathered. The modeler should ask clarifying questions when necessary and validate any assumptions. Although many modelers also facilitate, it is difficult to facilitate and produce a model at the same time.

A representative from upper management should attend to make tie-breaking decisions when consensus cannot be reached among participants. If a management representative is not among the attendees, be sure to document conflicting views for later resolution.

Facilities and Equipment

In these days of videoconferences and teleconferences, scheduling facilities and equipment can be a complex issue. As human beings, we provide significant information through body language and facial expressions. I recommend face-to-face meetings for these sessions whenever possible.

A room with tables and chairs arranged in a horseshoe shape works best for me. The room should be slightly cool, free of distractions, and large enough to accommodate the number of attendees. Provide tablets, pens or pencils, and name cards for each participant. I recommend providing water, soda, and coffee at a minimum. Small, individually wrapped candy can be an important addition.

A dry-erase whiteboard is handy for sharing concepts and information. An electronic whiteboard is even better because you can print copies for the participants. Be sure to get extra markers just in case.

Two flip charts allow the facilitator to use one to record issues and the other to record "parking lot" items that need outside assistance for resolution. All issues and parking lot items should be assigned to one or more attendees for resolution.

Distributing Information Prior to the Session

With email present in almost every company, distributing information about the session has become a simpler task. At a minimum, the attendees for the session should receive the problem definition, an agenda, session rules, and a list of the objectives. A preliminary list of entities and attributes with preliminary definitions and a straw-man model are a plus.

NOTE

A straw-man model provides a starting point for the modeling process. It contains a limited set of entities and attributes. It is produced using the information in the problem definition and any previous work that has been performed in the domain. I like to use entities from the enterprise data model whenever possible.

You can also use the straw-man model as an aid for defining modeling concepts to the session participants.

Encourage attendees to come prepared to participate! Make sure to include a break at least every two hours.

Getting Started

The facilitator begins by introducing the session team and reviewing the purpose of the session in terms of the problem definition. Discuss the agenda to ensure its alignment with the session objectives. Let attendees know the locations of restrooms and telephones.

Session rules help keep the session productive. The following is a list of general rules:

- Start on time.
- Only one person speaks at a time—no free-for-all.
- Let speakers complete their thoughts—no interruptions.
- Everyone participates.
- If consensus can't be reached in a reasonable amount of time, record an issue or a parking lot item.
- Return from breaks on time.
- End on time.

Each attendee should introduce herself and provide a brief explanation of what she brings to, or wants to take away from, the session.

A good facilitator keeps the participants focused on the objectives and ensures consensus when possible. Take breaks on time. I generally ask for a volunteer to give me a signal as break time approaches. At the end of the day, assign all issues and parking lot items to one or more participants and collect a date for completion.

Schedule a follow-up meeting to review the information requirements and preliminary logical model. Thank everyone for participating. Publish meeting minutes within three working days and include an opportunity for participants to provide feedback.

Analysis

You must analyze and research the data requirements and business rules to produce a complete logical model. Analysis tasks should provide accurate and complete definitions for all entities, attributes, and relationships. Metadata, data *about* the data, is collected and documented during the analysis phase.

The analysis can be performed by the modeler or by a business analyst. Either the modeler or the business analyst works with users to document how users intend to use the data. These tasks drive out the corporate business objects needed to support the information requirements. Corporate business objects are also called code, reference, or classification data structures. This is also the opportunity to document code values that will be used. You should carefully document any derived data, data that is created by manipulating or combining one or more other data elements, and the data elements used in the derivation.

The sections that follow take a closer look at the translation and transformation of data, data domains, and default values.

Translation and Transformation of Data

Many times, you must transform or translate data in some way. Mapping data values from the source to the database is an important analysis task. It is important to remember that data should be modeled independently of the source. That is, the way data is provided should not drive the way data is modeled.

In Table 1.1 is an example of using transformation and translation rules to determine that the source code data element actually contains three separate and distinct values. The mapping also defines the business rules for translating the source code into the three distinct attributes it represents.

TABLE 1.1   Translation Rules for Source Code

Source Code	Attribute1 Value	Attribute2 Value	Attribute3 Value
1234567890	123	456	7890
0987654321	098	765	4321
12345	123	450	0000

The business rules illustrated in Table 1.1 include different guidelines for mapping the value of Source Code into its components. The source code value contains Attribute1, Attribute2, and Attribute3. New source code values began being used January 1, 1998, and have 10 digits, but old source code values have five digits. The first three digits of the source code value contain Attribute1. The next three digits contain Attribute2. The last four digits contain the value for Attribute3. For five-digit source code values, you use a zero (0) for the third digit in Attribute2 and fill Attribute3 with zeros.

Data Domains

Data domains should be analyzed and documented. Domains are constraints placed on the value of an attribute. For example, in the United States, a weekday is considered one of the following: Monday, Tuesday, Wednesday, Thursday, or Friday. That list of days is the domain of values for an attribute called Day of Week.

Default Values

Some attributes are assigned default values. A default value for an attribute can be the value that an attribute has most of the time. A default value might provide a value for an attribute to prevent a null value. For example, a default value for Number of Tires might be 4 because most vehicles have four tires. Often, a number field defaults to 0 because null values can cause unexpected results.

> **NOTE**
>
> Nulls and defaults have given modelers cause for concern from the very beginning. Take care to discuss nullity and default values with domain experts. Remember to use caution when reporting against fields that could have been populated using default values, as they can produce unexpected results.

You must define and document all default values for attributes. Default values for attributes should be consistent throughout the enterprise. Validate all default values against the enterprise data model.

Logical Data Model

A logical data model is a visual representation of data structures, data attributes, and business rules. The logical model represents data in a way that can be easily understood by business users. The logical model design should be independent of platform or implementation language requirements or how the data will be used.

The modeler uses the data requirements and the results of analysis to produce the logical data model. The modeler also resolves the logical model to third normal form and validates against the enterprise data model, if available. Later sections provide a description of a complete logical model, resolving a logical model to third normal form, an overview of an enterprise model, and provide some tips on validating a logical model against an enterprise model.

After you compare the logical model and enterprise data model and make any necessary changes, it is important to review the model for accuracy and completeness. The best practice includes a peer review as well as a review with the business partners and development team. Chapter 12, "Reviewing the Logical Data Model," provides details for logical model reviews.

The sections that follow describe a logical data model and a physical data model.

Components of a Logical Data Model

A logical model uses entities, attributes, and relationships to represent the data and business rules. *Entities* represent the objects about which the enterprise has an interest in keeping data. *Attributes* are the data that the enterprise has an interest in preserving. *Relationships* define the associations between entities in terms of business rules.

Entities

Entities represent the things about which the enterprise is interested in keeping data. An entity can be a tangible object such as a person or a book, but it can also be conceptual such as a cost center or business unit. Entities are nouns and are expressed in singular form, CUSTOMER as opposed to CUSTOMERS, for clarity and consistency.

You should describe an entity using factual particulars that make it uniquely identifiable. Each instance of an entity must be separate and clearly identifiable from all other instances of that entity. For example, a data model to store information about customers must have a way of distinguishing one customer from another.

Figure 1.3 provides some examples of entities.

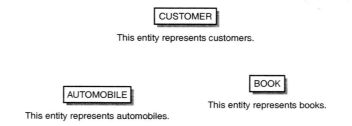

FIGURE 1.3
Here are examples of using ERwin to display entities in their simplest form.

Chapter 2, "Understanding Entities," provides detailed information on entities, entity types, discovering entities, naming and defining, and more.

Attributes

Attributes represent the data the enterprise is interested in keeping about objects. Attributes are nouns that describe the characteristics of entities.

Figure 1.4 uses ER*win* to provide some examples of attributes.

Chapter 3, "Understanding Attributes," provides detailed information on attributes, attribute types, discovering attributes, naming and defining, and more.

Relationships

Relationships represent the associations between the objects about which the enterprise is interested in keeping data. A relationship is expressed as a verb or verb phrase that describes the association. Figure 1.5 provides some examples using ER*win*'s Information Engineering (IE) notation to represent relationships.

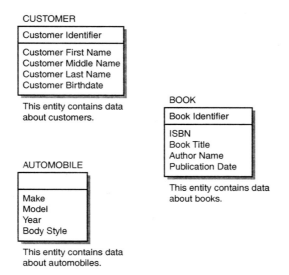

CUSTOMER
Customer Identifier

Customer First Name
Customer Middle Name
Customer Last Name
Customer Birthdate

This entity contains data
about customers.

BOOK
Book Identifier

ISBN
Book Title
Author Name
Publication Date

This entity contains data
about books.

AUTOMOBILE

Make
Model
Year
Body Style

This entity contains data
about automobiles.

FIGURE 1.4

Attributes can include the customer's birth date, the model of a car, and a book's ISBN number.

Understanding Normalization

Normalization is the act of moving attributes to appropriate entities to satisfy the normal forms. Normalization is usually presented as a set of complex statements that make it seem a complicated concept. Actually, normalization is quite straightforward: "One fact in one place," as stated by C.J. Date in his 1999 book *An Introduction to Database Systems. Normalizing data* means you design the data structures in such a way as to remove redundancy and limit unrelated structures.

Five normal forms are widely accepted in the industry. The forms are simply named first normal form, second normal form, third normal form, fourth normal form, and fifth normal form. In practice, many logical models are only resolved to third normal form.

At the end of this chapter a formal Date definition is included for the first five normal forms, including Boyce/Codd normal form (BCNF), which is a more restrictive third normal form.

Clive Finklestein's term Business Normal Forms provides a less formal definition of normal forms, as well as instructions on resolving each form. Although there are some slight differences in the way experts define the normal forms, the end result is the same, a model where every attribute is "dependent on the key, the whole key, and nothing but the key, so help me Codd."

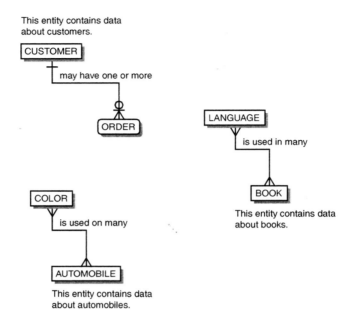

FIGURE 1.5

Relationship examples use ERwin's IE notation that uses a "crow's foot" or "trident" to show the many sides of a relationship.

As a general practice, logical models are normalized to third normal form. Here are some simple rules for normalization:

- Place repeating attributes in a dependent entity.
- Make sure that each fact is represented only once in the model.
- Place attributes that are not dependent on the primary key in a dependent entity.
- Resolve many-to-many relationships.

The examples used to illustrate the normalization process begin with a single non-normalized entity that violates every normal form, and then applies the simple rules to resolve it to third normal form.

Repeating Groups

Repeating groups are attributes for which a single instance of an entity can have more than a single value. For example, a person can have more than one skill. If we have a business need to know the skills and skill level for each, and each person only has two skills, we can create the entity in Figure 1.6. Figure 1.6 shows a person entity with an attribute to contain two skills and a skill level for each.

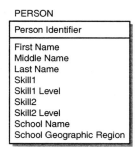

FIGURE 1.6

Shown are examples using Repeating groups.

The problem with repeating groups is that we can't know exactly how many skills a person might have. In the real world, some people have one skill, some people have more than one skill, and some people don't have any skills yet. Figure 1.7 shows the model normalized to first normal form. Notice that I added a Skill Identifier to uniquely identify each Skill.

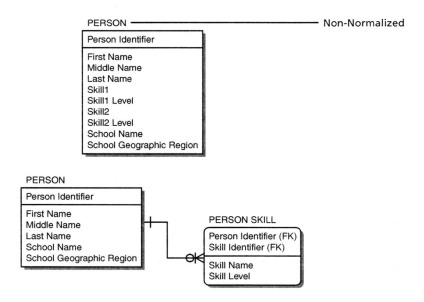

FIGURE 1.7

The model is normalized to first normal form.

One Fact in One Place

When the same attribute is present in more than one entity and it is not a foreign key, the attribute is considered redundant. Logical models should not contain redundant data.

Redundant attributes use more space, and although using space is always a consideration, the real issue is data anomalies. Ensuring that redundant data is kept synchronized requires processing, and you always run the risk of conflicting values.

In the preceding example, the Skill is dependent on the Customer Identifier as well as the Skill Identifier. That means that we cannot have a Skill until we have a Person who has that skill. It also makes it difficult to change the Skill Name. I would have to search for each instance of the Skill Name and change it for every Person who has that Skill.

Figure 1.8 shows the model in second normal form. Note that I added a Skill entity and moved the Skill Name attribute to that entity. Skill Level was left appropriately at the intersection of Person and Skill.

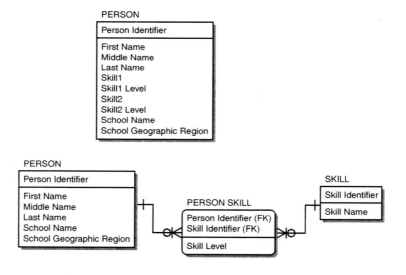

FIGURE 1.8

Second normal form shows the repeating group moved to another entity. This allows the flexibility to add as many Skill instances as needed and change the Skill Name or Skill Description in a single place.

Every Attribute Depends on the Key

Every attribute in an entity should depend on the primary key of that entity. In the previous example, School Name and School Geographic Region are in the Person table, but neither describes a Person. To achieve third normal form, I must move the attributes to an entity where they depend on the key. Figure 1.9 shows the model in third normal form.

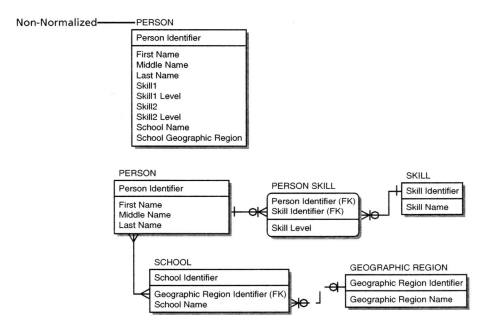

FIGURE 1.9

Third normal form shows the School Name and School Geographical Region moved to a entity where the values are dependent upon the key.

Many-to-Many Relationships

Many-to-many relationships represent a real-world condition. Note in Figure 1.9 that there is a many-to-many relationship between Person and School. The relationship accurately represents the fact that a person can attend many schools, and schools have many persons attending. To achieve fourth normal form, I create an associative entity that resolves the many-to-many relationship by making each instance in the associative entity uniquely relate schools and persons. Figure 1.10 shows the model in fourth normal form.

Formal Definitions of Normal Forms

The following normal form definitions might seem intimidating; just consider them formulas for achieving normalization. Normal forms are based on relational algebra and should be interpreted as mathematical functions. Although this text does not explore normal forms in detail, I encourage modelers to explore the normal forms in depth.

Given a relation R, attribute Y of R is functionally dependent on attribute X of R. In symbols, R.X->R.Y (read "R.X functionally determines R.Y")—if and only if each X-value in R has associated with it precisely one Y-value in R (at any one time). Attributes X and Y may be composite (Date, 1986).

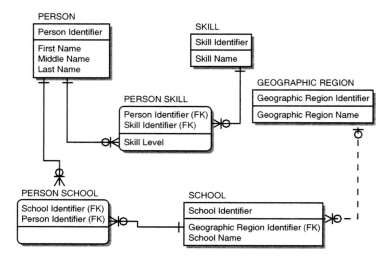

FIGURE 1.10

Fourth normal form shows the many-to-many relationship between Person and School resolved by creating an associative entity that creates unique instances by pairing an instance of Person with an instance of School.

A relation R is in first normal form (1NF) if and only if all underlying domains contain atomic values only (Date, 1986).

A relation R is in second normal form (2NF) if and only if it is in 1NF and every non-key attribute is fully dependent on the primary key (Date, 1986).

A relation R is in third normal form (3NF) if and only if it is in 2NF and every non-key attribute is non-transitively dependent on the primary key (Date, 1986).

A relation R is in Boyce/Codd normal form (BCNF) if and only if every determinant is a candidate key.

NOTE

A brief explanation follows of some of the abbreviated terms used in Date's definition.

MVD is a multi-valued dependency and applies only to entities with three or more attributes. A multi-valued dependency is one in which the value of an attribute depends on only part of the primary key.

FD is functional dependency. A functional dependency is one in which the value of an attribute depends on the value of another attribute that is not part of the primary key.

JD is join dependency. A join dependency is one in which the primary key of a parent entity is migrated to at least third-level children, and it is still capable of being joined again to form the original key.

A relation is in fourth normal form (4NF) if and only if there exists a MVD in R, say A->->B. Then all attributes of R are also functionally dependent on A. In other words, the only dependencies (FDs or MVDs) in R are of the form K->X (that is, a functional dependency from a candidate key K to some other attribute X). Equivalently, R is in 4NF if it is in BCNF and all MVDs in R are in fact FDs (Date, 1986).

For fifth normal form, relation R satisfies the join dependency (JD) *(X,Y,...,Z) if and only if R is equal to the join of its projections on X,Y,...,Z, where X,Y,...,Z are subsets of the set of attributes of R.

There are many other normal forms for complex datatypes and specific situations that are beyond the scope of this text. I encourage every modeling enthusiast to explore the other normal forms.

Business Normal Forms

In his 1992 book, *Strategic Systems Development*, Clive Finklestein takes a different approach to normalization. He defines business normal forms in terms of the resolution to those forms. Many modelers, myself included, find this business approach more intuitive and practical.

First business normal form (1BNF) removes repeating groups to another entity. This entity takes its name, and primary (compound) key attributes, from the original entity and from the repeating group.

Second business normal form (2BNF) removes attributes that are partially dependent on the primary key to another entity. The primary (compound) key of this entity is the primary key of the entity in which it originally resided, together with all additional keys on which the attribute is wholly dependent.

Third business normal form (3BNF) removes attributes that are not dependent at all on the primary key to another entity where they are wholly dependent on the primary key of that entity.

Fourth business normal form (4BNF) removes attributes that are dependent on the value of the primary key or that are optional to a secondary entity where they wholly depend on the value of the primary key or where they must (it is mandatory) exist in that entity.

Fifth business normal form (5BNF) exists as a structure entity if recursive or other associations exist between occurrences of secondary entities or if recursive associations exist between occurrences of their principal entity.

A Complete Logical Data Model

A complete logical model should be in third business normal form and include all entities, attributes, and relationships required to support the data requirements and the business rules associated with the data.

All entities must have names indicative of the contents and a clear, concise, complete definition or description. In Chapter 2, the section "Naming Entities" provides a starter set of conventions for good names and definitions for entities.

Entities must be fully attributed; that is, every fact about each entity is represented by an attribute. Each attribute must have a name that is indicative of the value, a logical datatype, and a clear, concise, complete definition or description. In Chapter 3, the section "Naming Attributes" provides a starter set of guidelines for good names and definitions for attributes.

All relationships must include a verb phrase that describes how entities are related, as well as cardinality and optionality or nullity. In Chapter 4, "Understanding Relationships," I provide some guidelines for writing good verb phrases and determining the business rules for cardinality and optionality or nullity.

> **NOTE**
>
> Relationship *cardinality* refers to the maximum number of instances in a child entity that can relate to a parent entity. Relationship *optionality* or *nullity* refers to the minimum number of instances in a child entity that can be related to a parent entity.

Physical Data Model

Once the logical model is accurate and complete, you are ready to make a platform decision. Platform decisions consider data usage requirements and the architecture strategies of the enterprise. Making platform decisions is a complex subject that is not covered in this text.

In ER*win*, a physical model is a visual representation of the database that is actually implemented. The physical database will contain tables, columns, and relationships. The physical data model is dependent upon the platform selected for implementation and the data usage requirements. A physical model for IMS will look considerably different from one for Sybase. A physical model for dimensional reporting will look considerably different than one for online transaction processing (OLTP).

The data modeler and the database administrator (DBA) use the logical model, usage requirements, and enterprise architectural strategies to develop the physical model. You can denormalize a physical model to improve performance and create views to support usage requirements. Later sections provide details on denormalization and views.

The sections that follow provide an overview of building a physical model, gathering usage requirements, defining the components of a physical model, and reverse engineering. Later chapters cover these topics in detail.

Gathering Usage Requirements

You usually gather usage requirements using interviews or facilitated sessions earlier in the planning process. Usage requirements define and document, as completely as possible, how the users intend to use the data. Oversights or gaps in the physical model could cause costly re-work and project overruns.

Usage requirements include

- Access and performance requirements.
- Volumetrics (estimations of the volume of data that will be retained), which give the database administrator an idea of the physical size of the database.
- An estimation of the number of concurrent users who will need access to the data, which helps you construct the database to provide acceptable performance levels.
- Summaries, roll-ups, and other calculated or derived data, which should be considered candidates for persistent data structures.
- Reporting requirements and standard queries, which help the DBA construct indexes.
- Views (persistent or virtual) that will assist users by performing joins or filtering data.

In addition to the facilitator, scribe, and users, the data modeler, DBA, and data architect should attend the usage requirements session. Discussion should include user requirements for historical data. The length of time that data is retained has a significant impact on the size of the database. Often, older data is kept summarized and the atomic-level data is archived or removed.

Users should bring sample queries and reports to the session. Reports should be well defined and should include the atomic values for any summaries or roll-ups.

Components of a Physical Data Model

The components of a physical data model are tables, columns, and relationships. The entities in the logical model will probably become tables in the physical model. The logical attributes will become columns. The logical relationships will become relational integrity constraints.

Some logical relationships cannot be implemented in the physical database.

Reverse Engineering

When a logical model is not available, it might be necessary to begin by creating a model from an existing database. In ER*win*, this process is called "reverse engineering." Reverse engineering can take several forms. A modeler can examine the data structures in a database and create the tables in a visual modeling tool. You can import the data definitions language (DDL) into a tool that supports reverse engineering, such as ERwin. Robust tools such as ERwin have a feature that allows an ODBC to connect to an existing database and create a model by reading the data structures. Reverse engineering using ERwin is discussed in detail in Chapter 7, "Reverse Engineering and Report Generation in ERwin."

Taking an Enterprise View

When building a logical model, it is important for the modeler to ensure that the new model fits within the enterprise model. Taking an enterprise view means to model data in terms of how it will be used throughout the entire organization. The way an enterprise *uses* data changes more rapidly than the data itself. In each logical data model, data should be represented consistently regardless of the business area it supports. Entities, attributes, and relationships should define the business rules at an enterprise level.

NOTE

Some of my peers call this enterprise view *modeling the real world*. Modeling the real world guides the modeler in looking at information in terms of its own intrinsic relationships.

Taking an enterprise view of appropriately modeled data provides a foundation to support the information needs of any number of processes or applications, allowing the enterprise to better leverage one of its most valuable assets, information.

What Is an Enterprise Data Model?

An enterprise data model (EDM) contains entities, attributes, and relationships that represent the information needs of the entire enterprise. An EDM is usually divided into subject areas that represent groups of entities that relate in support of a specific business need. Some subject areas might cover a specific business function such as contact management. Others might group together entities that define a product or a service.

Every logical data model should fit into an existing subject area of the enterprise data model. If the logical data model does not fit, the model identifies an area that should be added. This comparison ensures that the enterprise model is enhanced or corrected and that all logical modeling efforts are consistent across the enterprise.

The EDM also includes special entities that define the domain of values for key attributes. These entities have no parent and are identified as *independent* entities. Independent entities are often used to enforce relational integrity. These entities are identified by several different names, such as code tables, reference tables, type tables, or classification tables. I prefer the term corporate business object. A *corporate business object* is an entity that contains a set of attribute values that are not dependent upon any other entity. You should use corporate business object entities consistently throughout the enterprise.

Building an Enterprise Data Model by Accretion

It has been my experience that few organizations build an enterprise model from start to finish as a single concerted effort. Instead, most organizations build a fairly complete enterprise model by accretion.

Accretion means to build something a layer at a time, the way an oyster creates a pearl. Each data model created contributes to the creation of an EDM. Building an EDM in this manner requires adding modeling tasks that will add new data structures and subject areas or enhance existing data structures. This allows the enterprise data model to be built by accretion, adding layers of detail and refinement in an iterative process.

Understanding Modeling Methodology

There are several methodologies for visually modeling data. ER*win* supports two, Integration Definition for Information Modeling (IDEF1X) and Information Engineering (IE). IDEF1X is a good methodology, and the notation is widely supported. Personally, I prefer the notation style used in IE and the philosophy taught by Clive Finklestein in his books, so I use IE in this text.

Integration Definition for Information Modeling

Integration Definition for Information Modeling (IDEF1X) is a highly structured data modeling methodology. IDEF1X, an extension of IDEF1, is accepted as a standard by the Federal Information Processing Standards (FIPS). IDEF1X uses an extremely structured set of modeling construct types and produces a data model that requires a physical understanding of the data before such information is available.

The constrictive nature of IDEF1X forces a modeler to assign characteristics to entities that might not fit the real world. For example, IDEF1X requires that all subtype entities be exclusive. The implication is that a person cannot be both a customer and an employee. The real world tells us differently.

I encourage modelers to explore IDEF1X and form their own opinions. The FIPS documents are available on the Web, and there are several good publications on IDEF1X.

Information Engineering

Clive Finklestein is often called the father of Information Engineering, although he and James Martin shared the concept. Information Engineering uses a business-driven approach to information management and uses different notation to represent business rules. IE expands and enhances Peter Chen's ER notation and core concepts.

IE provides a framework for supporting business information requirements by integrating enterprise strategic planning with the information systems being developed. By integrating strategic planning activities with information systems development, information management activities are more closely aligned with the long-term strategic direction of the enterprise. This business-driven approach has led many modelers (myself included) to embrace IE instead of other methodologies, which tend to focus on solutions to short-term development issues.

IE provides a series of steps that can guide an enterprise in the identification of all information the enterprise desires to collect and maintain, and to define the relationships between the objects of information. As a result, information requirements are clearly defined based on management direction, and can be translated directly into information management systems that support the strategic information needs.

It is beyond the scope of this text to explore IE concepts fully. I encourage modelers to explore the writings of James Martin and Clive Finklestein for a deeper understanding of the IE approach to information management.

Summary

Understanding how to use a data modeling tool like ER*win* is only part of the process. You must also understand when to perform data modeling tasks and how to collect the information requirements and business rules that will be represented by the data model. Conducting facilitated sessions provides the best opportunity for collecting information requirements in an environment that includes domain experts, users, and information management specialists.

Producing a good data model requires analysis and research on the information requirements and business rules collected in facilitated sessions and interviews. The resulting data model must also be compared to the enterprise model, if available, to ensure there is no conflict with existing model objects or identify any objects that need to be added.

A data model contains a logical and physical model of the information requirements and the business rules. The logical model should be normalized to third normal form. Third normal form will limit, insert, update, and delete data anomalies and support "one fact in one place." Information requirements and business rules collected must be analyzed and researched. They must also be compared to the enterprise model, if available, to ensure there is no conflict with existing model objects or identity any objects that should be added.

In ER*win*, a data model has both a logical and physical model. ER*win* uses an Entity Relational approach and allows you to create logical modeling and physical modeling objects to represent information requirements and business rules. Logical modeling objects include entities, attributes, and relationships. Physical modeling objects include tables, columns, and relational integrity constraints.

In Chapter 2, I explore identifying entities, defining entity types, selecting entity names and descriptions, and some ways to avoid common modeling mistakes involving entities.

Understanding Entities

Chapter 1, "Understanding Data Modeling Concepts," introduced the essential ideas of data modeling. In this chapter, I explore entities and entity keys in detail. As you recall, entities are the objects or things about which the enterprise is interested in keeping data. In ER*win*, an entity is a graphical representation of a logical grouping of data. Entities can be tangible, real things, or intangible, conceptual things. Entities are not intended to represent single things. Instead, they represent classes containing attributes that represent the items of information for many instances.

In the sections that follow, I explore entities by introducing:

- The Entity Relational Diagram
- Discovering entities
- Defining entity types
- Naming and defining entities
- Common mistakes with entities

Since ER*win* uses an Entity Relational (ER) approach to data modeling, I will begin with a brief introduction of ER concepts. So, let's explore entities—the "containers" that hold the logical model information.

Introducing the Entity Relational Diagram

In this text, I use an Entity Relational Diagram (ERD) to provide the visual representation of entities and the relationships between them using ER*win*. Although there are other methodologies for modeling data, such as Extended Relational Analysis (ERA), Object Oriented (OO), and Object Role Modeling (ORM), the same fundamental ER concepts are present in all.

Entity Relationship (ER) modeling was developed by Peter Chen in the late 1970s. ER uses a rectangular box to represent entities. In Chen's original ER notation, relationships also contained attributes. Allowing relationships to have attributes made it difficult to tell the difference between entities and relationships.

Over time, ER has been refined and extended, but the core concepts still provide the foundation for good data modeling. I explored two refinements of ER in Chapter 1, IDEF1X and IE. In both methodologies, entities are represented by rectangles.

In the sections that follow, I explore entities in detail and provide an introduction to keys, with a particular emphasis on finding the primary key for an entity. I define entity types and discuss guidelines for entity names and descriptions. The final section features a list of common modeling blunders regarding entities and keys.

What Is an Entity?

An *entity* is a physical representation of a logical grouping of data. Entities can be tangible, real things, such as a PERSON or ICE CREAM, or intangible concepts, such as a COST CENTER or MARKET. Entities do not represent single things. Instead, they represent collections of instances that contain the information of interest for all instances or occurrences. For example, a PERSON entity represents instances of things of type Person. Gabriel DeAngelis, R.J. Golcher, Jessica Carter, and Vanessa Westley are examples of specific instances of PERSON. A specific instance of an entity is represented by a row and is identified by a primary key.

An entity has the following characteristics:

- It has a name and description.
- It represents a class, rather than a single instance of a concept.

- It has the ability to uniquely identify each specific instance.
- It contains a logical grouping of attributes representing the information of interest to the enterprise.

Formal Entity Definitions

The following list contains entity definitions from some of the most influential leaders in data modeling. Notice the similarities:

- Chen (1976): "A thing which can be distinctly identified."
- Date (1986): "Any distinguishable object that is to be represented in the database."
- Finklestein (1989): "A data entity represents some 'thing' that is to be stored for later reference. The term entity refers to the logical representation of data."

Discovering Entities

How do you go about the process of discovering entities? Most entities are revealed during facilitated sessions and interviews. The analysis of the information requirements provided by domain experts and users is the best source of information.

The enterprise model is a good source as well. Look for nouns and names of objects; they will probably become logical entities. Take care not to model a single instance as an entity, which often happens when an entity is modeled in terms of a role. Modeling an entity in terms of a role is a common modeling mistake. In Chapter 1, I used the example of CUSTOMER and EMPLOYEE and proposed the idea that both are examples of roles that can be played by PERSON.

Entities are also discovered during normalization, as you saw in the section "Understanding Normalization" in Chapter 1. Resolving the logical model to third normal form will likely give rise to several additional entities.

There are two primary groupings of entities: *independent* and *dependent*. An independent entity does not need information from another entity to identify a unique instance. It is represented in ERwin as a rectangular box with sharp corners. The primary key of an independent entity does not include the primary key of another entity. In Figure 2.1, note that the ICE CREAM and STORE entities have sharp corners.

A dependent entity must have information from another entity to identify a unique instance. It is represented in an ERD as a rectangle with rounded corners. The primary key of a dependent entity contains the primary key of one or more parent entities. In Figure 2.1, note the STORE ICE CREAM entity has rounded corners and is dependent upon the STORE and ICE CREAM entities.

FIGURE 2.1

Note the straight corners of the independent entities, STORE and ICE CREAM and the rounded corners of the dependent entity STORE ICE CREAM.

Defining Entity Types

Within the independent and dependent entities are entity types:

- Core entities—These are sometimes called *primary* or *prime* entities. They represent the important objects about which the enterprise in interested in keeping data.
- Code/reference/classification entities—These entities contain rows that define the set of values, or domain, for an attribute.
- Associative entities—These entities are used to resolve many-to-many relationships.
- Subtype entities—These entities come in two types, exclusive and inclusive.

Core Entity

Core entities are the most important objects about which an enterprise is interested in keeping data. They are often referred to as prime, principal, or primary entities. Because these entities are so important, it is likely that they are used elsewhere in the enterprise. Take the time to look for similar entities because there are many opportunities for the reuse of core entities. Core entities should be modeled consistently throughout the enterprise. Good modelers consider this an essential best practice.

A core entity can be an independent entity or a dependent entity. Figure 2.1 provides examples of core entities for an enterprise that sells ice cream. ICE CREAM represents the base products sold by the enterprise. STORE is an example of a distribution channel, or the vehicle through which a product is sold.

Consider that the enterprise is doing well and has decided to add another STORE. The model requires no change to support the addition of a new instance of STORE. It is simply another row added to the STORE entity. The same applies to ICE CREAM.

Notice the core entities ICE CREAM and STORE. Although the example may seem straightforward, it illustrates a powerful concept regarding the modeling of core entities.

Understanding how to model core entities as scalable and extensible containers of information requires the modeler to think about the entity as an abstract concept and to model the information independently of the way it is used today. In this example, model ICE CREAM completely outside the context of STORE and vice versa. So, if the enterprise decides to sell ICE CREAM using an additional channel, such as the Internet or door-to-door, the new channel can be added without disturbing other entities.

TIP

Correctly modeling core entity information will become increasingly more important as businesses begin to leverage new distribution channels for their information. Consider that the information you are modeling today is likely to be accessed through several different channels in the future. For example, many companies must process Internet requests for information separately because internal systems are not yet capable of interacting with this powerful new channel.

Code Entity

Code entities are always independent entities. They are often referred to as reference, classification, or type entities, depending on the methodology. The unique instances represented by code entities define the domain of values for attributes present in other entities. The relationship between code entities and other entities is explored in Chapter 4. You might be tempted to use a single attribute in a code table. It is a best practice to include at least three attributes in a code entity: an identifier, a name (sometimes called a short name), and a description.

In Figure 2.2, TOPPING is an independent entity; note the sharp corners. TOPPING is also a code or classification entity. The instances (or rows) of TOPPING define the list of toppings available.

Code entities usually contain a limited number of attributes. I have seen instances where these entities contain only a single attribute. I prefer to model code entities with an artificial identifier. Using an artificial identifier, along with a name and description, allows the addition of new kinds of TOPPING to be added as instances (rows) in the entity. Note that TOPPING contains three attributes.

I often refer to code entities as corporate business objects. The name, corporate business objects, indicates that the entities are defined and shared at a corporate level, not by a single application, system, or business unit. These entities are often shared by many databases to allow consistent roll-up reporting or trending analysis.

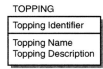

FIGURE 2.2

Code entities allow an enterprise to define a set of values for consistent use throughout the enterprise. The instances of a code entity define a domain of values for use elsewhere in the model.

Associative Entity

Associative entities are entities that contain the primary key from two or more other entities. Associative entities are always dependent entities. They are used to resolve many-to-many relationships between other entities. Many-to-many relationships are those in which many instances of one entity are related to many instances of another. Associative entities allow us to model the *intersection* between the instances of the two entities, thereby allowing each instance in the associative entity to be unique.

NOTE

Many-to-many relationships cannot be implemented in a physical database. ER*win* will automatically create an associative entity to resolve a many-to-many relationship when the model is changed from logical to physical mode.

Figure 2.1 uses an associative entity to resolve a many-to-many relationship between STORE and ICE CREAM. The addition of an associative entity allows the same ICE CREAM to be sold in many instances of STORE, while not requiring every STORE to sell the same ICE CREAM. The associative entity STORE ICE CREAM resolves the fact that an instance of STORE sells many instances of ICE CREAM and an instance of ICE CREAM is sold by many instances of STORE.

Subtype Entity

Subtype entities are always dependent entities. You should use subtype entities when it makes sense to keep different sets of attributes for the instances of an entity. Finklestein refers to subtype entities as secondary entities. Subtype entities almost always have one or more "sibling" entities. The subtype entity siblings are related to a parent entity through a special relationship that is either exclusive or inclusive.

NOTE

Subtype sibling entities that have an *exclusive* relationship to the parent entity indicate that only one sibling has an instance for each instance of the parent entity. Exclusive subtypes represent an "is a" relationship.

Subtype sibling entities that have an *inclusive* relationship to the parent entity indicate that more than one sibling can have an instance for each instance of the parent entity.

Figure 2.3 shows the CONTAINER entity and the subtype entities CONE and CUP. The ice cream store apparently does not sell ice cream in bulk, only single servings. Note that an instance of CONTAINER must be either a CONE or a CUP. A CONTAINER cannot be both a CONE and a CUP. This is an exclusive subtype.

In Figure 2.3, the PERSON entity has two subtypes, EMPLOYEE and CUSTOMER. Note that an exclusive subtype would not allow a single instance of PERSON to contain facts common to both an EMPLOYEE and a CUSTOMER. Of course, this is not true in the real world. An EMPLOYEE can certainly be a CUSTOMER. A VENDOR can also be a CUSTOMER. These are examples of inclusive subtypes.

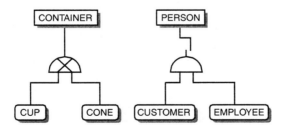

FIGURE 2.3

Two examples of subtype entities, PERSON and CONTAINER. Both use ERwin IE notation to represent exclusive and inclusive subtypes. The (X) in the subtype symbol of CONTAINER indicates exclusive. The absence of the (X) in the subtype symbol indicates inclusive.

Structure Entity

Sometimes, instances of the same entity are related. In his 1992 book *Strategic Systems Development*, Clive Finklestein proposes the use of a structure entity to represent relationships between instances of an entity. Relationships between instances of an entity are called recursive relationships. Recursive relationships are discussed in Chapter 4, "Understanding Relationships." Recursive relationships are a logical concept, a concept sometimes difficult for users to grasp.

Figure 2.4 shows the addition of a structure entity that allows a relationship between instances of EMPLOYEE. The diagram shows that the EMPLOYEE subtype of the PERSON entity has two subtypes, SERVER and MANAGER. The EMPLOYEE STRUCTURE entity represents the relationship between instances of EMPLOYEE.

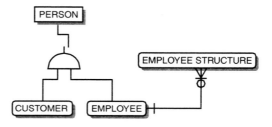

FIGURE 2.4
Structure entity illustrates Clive Finklestein's resolution for recursive relationships.

Defining a Primary Key

To identify a specific instance of an entity, you must define a primary key. A *primary key* is an attribute or set of attributes that uniquely identifies a single instance of an entity. In other words, a primary key can comprise a single attribute or a group of attributes. A primary key that consists of more than a single attribute is called a *composite* or *component key*. In this text, I use the term *composite key*.

Primary keys should be static and non-volatile. By static and non-volatile, I mean that primary keys should not be subject to change. Changing primary keys is difficult to manage, often causing expensive overruns and costly rewrites. In my opinion, the best primary key has no relationship at all with instances of the entity.

NOTE

In the following sections, I add primary keys to the ice cream store database and discuss candidate keys. The concepts of keys are introduced in this section and covered more extensively in Chapter 3, "Understanding Attributes."

Finding a primary key requires examining the data that defines an entity. You discover primary keys for core entities during facilitated sessions and reviews. Domain experts and users are good sources for collecting potential primary keys. Sample data might also provide valuable insight into primary key selection.

Begin the process of finding a primary key by identifying all potential key attributes, called candidate keys. *Candidate keys* may be a single attribute or composed of several attributes. If no candidate keys exist, or are composite keys that are large and unwieldy, consider an artificial unique identifier. Keys that migrate from parent entities are called foreign keys. *Foreign keys* are discussed further in Chapter 4. The following describes the various keys:

- Candidate keys: A candidate key is an attribute or set of attributes that identifies a single instance of an entity. Sometimes, more than one attribute or combination of attributes identifies a single instance of an entity.

- Composite keys: A key that consists of more than a single attribute is called a composite, compound, or component key. For composite keys, each piece of the key must have a value for every instance. No part of the key can have a null value. No part of the key can be optional.

- Artificial primary keys: Sometimes, no attribute or set of attributes defines an instance. In those cases, you use an artificial unique identifier. I am a big proponent of artificial primary keys, which are often simply a numbering of each instance or a code.

- Foreign keys: When the primary key of one entity migrates to another table, it is called a foreign key. Foreign keys are the "links" between entities that represent the relationships between entities. Foreign keys are discussed at length in Chapter 4.

Resolving a model to third normal form will verify that there is no functional dependency and will identify the primary key or composite key. Functional dependency, discussed in Chapter 1, plays a strong role in identifying the primary key and candidate keys.

Naming Entities

The name assigned to an entity should be indicative of the instances of the entity. The name should be understood and accepted across the enterprise. When selecting a name, keep an enterprise view and take care to use a name that reflects how the data is used throughout the entire enterprise, not just a single area. Use names that are meaningful to the user community and domain experts.

I hope you have a set of naming conventions that were developed for use in the enterprise, or an enterprise data model, to guide you. Using naming conventions ensures that names are constructed consistently across the enterprise, regardless of who constructs the name. The following sections provide a starter set of naming conventions and give examples of good and bad names.

Entity Naming Conventions

Naming conventions might not seem important if you work in a small organization with a small set of users. However, in a large organization with many development teams and many users, naming conventions greatly facilitate communication and data sharing. As a best practice, you should develop and maintain naming conventions in a central location and then document and publish them for the whole enterprise.

I include some pointers for beginning a good set of naming conventions, just in case your organization has not yet developed one:

- An entity name should be as descriptive as necessary. Use single-word names only when the name is a widely accepted concept. Consider using noun phrases.

- An entity name should be a singular noun or noun phrase. Use PERSON instead of PERSONS or PEOPLE, or CONTAINER instead of CONTAINERS.

- An entity name should be unique. Using the same entity name to contain different data, or a different entity name to contain the same data, is needlessly confusing to developers and users alike.

- An entity name should be indicative of the data that will be contained for each instance.

- An entity name should not contain special characters (such as !, @, #, $, %, ^, &, *, and so on) or show possession (PERSON'S ICE CREAM).

- An entity name should not include acronyms or abbreviations unless they are part of the accepted naming conventions.

I encourage modelers to use good naming conventions if they are available and to develop them if they do not follow these guidelines.

Examples of Good Entity Names

It is always best to use consistent names across the enterprise. Table 2.1 shows examples of good names as well as some poor names for entities.

TIP

Notice that entity names use all uppercase letters, which is a naming convention that I recommend for entity names.

Table 2.1 Entity Name Examples and Explanations

Good Name	Poor Name	Explanation
MATHEMATICAL FORMULA	FORMULA	FORMULA is vague; adding the word MATHEMATICAL lends considerable clarity.
BOOK	BOOKS	BOOK is singular.
SOFA	SOFA COUCH	SOFA and COUCH have the same meaning. Select one.
ICE CREAM	THE ICE CREAM	THE adds no value or meaning to the term. Avoid the use of articles such as "a", "an," and "the."
PHOTOGRAPH	PICTURE	PHOTOGRAPH is descriptive. PICTURE is somewhat vague.
ESTIMATED TIME OF ARRIVAL	ETA	ETA is an abbreviation or acronym and might not be clear to users.
COMPANY	XYZ COMPANY	XYZ is a specific instance of a company and should be a row in COMPANY.

Describing Entities

Even though a good entity name provides users with an indication of the information to expect, it is not enough. Every entity needs a clear, complete, concise description or definition so it is understood consistently across the enterprise. An entity description should describe an entity and its value to the enterprise.

Although description, definition, and purpose are often used synonymously, I prefer the term *description* because it encourages us to describe entities in terms that users will understand.

Rules for a Good Description

An entity description should describe what the entity is, not how its information is used. You should collect the entity description at the time the entity is identified. Use caution when including usage information, which should be included only for an example or for clarification. The way we use information changes more frequently than the information itself, so usage information is subject to change.

An entity description should be clear, concise, complete, and unambiguous. It should be worded in non-technical terms that are clear to anyone with the slightest understanding of the concept. Make sure the description is worded using business terminology, and be sure to include why the entity is of value to the enterprise.

Examples of Good Descriptions

Table 2.2 is certainly not intended to be comprehensive. Instead, I hope to illustrate a good description and the reasons why the poor descriptions do not meet the guidelines.

TABLE 2.2   Entity Descriptions and Explanations

Good Description	Poor Descriptions	Explanation
PERSON contains information about human beings who interact with the enterprise. The PERSON information assists the enterprise in planning, product development, and promotional activities.	A customer or employee.	A good description includes what an entity is and why it is important to the enterprise.
	Contains name, date of birth, etc. for a person.	Simply restating the attributes of an entity provides no new insight into what an entity is or why it is important to the enterprise.
	Customer and employee information.	Customer and employee are examples of roles for PERSON. Using examples alone does not explain what an entity is or why it is important to the enterprise.
	An entity containing character and numeric data parsed from a POS store using standard compression and packed decimals.	The example is contrived and intended to illustrate that technical definitions and abbreviations are not easily understood by business users.

Common Modeling Mistakes with Entities and Keys

This section of common modeling mistakes is not meant to be comprehensive. I merely want to point out some of the most common mistakes I have seen novice modelers make.

TIP

Sometimes a modeler makes a conscious choice, for very good reasons, to model something a certain way. It is important to understand the consequences of modeling decisions so you have a clear understanding of the implications.

Modeling a Role

What do I mean by modeling a role? In a planning session, users might tell you that they need to store information about employees. It is tempting to create an EMPLOYEE entity. A close examination of the information that the enterprise finds interesting, things such as name, address, and Social Security number, will reveal that the value of the information is not dependent on EMPLOYEE. For a specific instance of EMPLOYEE, the value for NAME does not depend on EMPLOYEE. It is easy to see that your name is still your name, regardless of whether or not you are an EMPLOYEE.

Overloading Entities

Overloaded entities are entities that contain information about more than a single conceptual object. Check for entities where the attributes don't all describe the same concept. Overloaded entities do not have a value for every attribute.

Sometimes, domain experts from different areas in an enterprise use an entity name that is spelled the same and pronounced the same but has a different meaning to different experts. One way to ensure that entities with the same name describe the same object is to verify the description. Make sure that the entity contains data that describes a single concept.

For example, an EQUIPMENT entity might have completely different meanings to the Information Technology department and to the Media and Communication department.

Redundant Entities

Redundant entities are entities that have different names but contain information about similar concepts. The English language has many words that represent the same thing. One way to find these entities is to look for entities that contain similar attributes. Compare the descriptions of each to see whether the entities contain data about similar concepts. Redundant entities are often the result of the tendency to model a role as an entity.

For example, a MANAGER entity and an EMPLOYEE entity might contain similar information because both are roles that an instance of PERSON can play.

Selecting the Wrong Primary Key

Selecting the wrong primary key means you select a primary key that does not withstand the test of time. Common failings of primary keys follow:

- Uniqueness: The primary key fails to be unique for every instance. For example, a modeler might think that the Social Security number is unique for each PERSON. However, Social Security numbers can be reused if the original holder is deceased.
- Required value/no nullity: The primary key fails to have a value for every instance. For example, not every instance of PERSON will have a Social Security number. Resident aliens and young children are two types of people who do not.

Using Bad Entity Names

Unclear, ambiguous, or imprecise names make it difficult for new users or design teams to reuse or enhance an existing model.

Don't use abbreviations or acronyms as part of the name. Abbreviations and acronyms are open to misinterpretation and might even develop different meanings in different business areas.

CAUTION

Don't use proper nouns that indicate a specific instance, such as Wilson Company. This is an indication of a serious modeling problem, not just bad naming.

Don't include a location as part of the name. It has been my experience that you will certainly need another location. A name with a location is an indication that you've modeled a specific instance rather than a class of instances.

Using Bad Entity Descriptions

Don't use the definition from a dictionary alone. A dictionary definition will not contain the business value information important to the enterprise.

Don't simply restate the name of the entity. Don't use the name of the entity in the description.

An unclear, vague, or, even worse, missing definition makes it difficult to reuse or enhance an existing model. Users won't be able to verify that entities contain all the required information.

It also greatly increases the tendency to overload entities and use them to contain information about different objects.

Concepts that seem obvious to all the participants during planning sessions might not remain as obvious as time goes by and a new team is tasked with making enhancements to an existing model.

Summary

Entities represent the objects about which the enterprise is interested in collecting and maintaining information. They are the "containers" to organize and group the facts of importance to the enterprise. The most important entities are usually identified and documented during facilitated sessions and interviews, and as part of the normalization process.

Entities are one of two primary types, independent or dependent. Dependent entities require information from another entity to uniquely identify an instance; independent entities do not. Within the two primary entity types are more refined types with characteristics that support specialized relationships between parent and child entities.

Each entity must have one or more sets of candidate key attributes. Candidate keys uniquely identify a specific instance of the entity. Candidate keys may be composed of a single attribute or a group of attributes. If no candidate keys exist, or are difficult to manage, you may need to create an artificial primary key. Analysis and research play an important role in defining primary keys that will remain unique and robust over time.

Entities need good names and descriptions. Standards and naming conventions provide guidelines for developing names and descriptions with a consistent form. Entity characteristics are defined by the attributes they contain. Attributes within an entity represent the facts that the enterprise is interested in collecting and maintaining about an entity.

In Chapter 3, I discuss discovering attributes and attribute characteristics, defining key and non-key attributes, domains, and optionality, as well as introduce good attribute name and definition conventions.

Understanding Attributes

In Chapter 1, "Understanding Data Modeling Concepts," I introduced data modeling concepts. In Chapter 2, "Understanding Entities," you learned about entities and were introduced to entity keys. In this chapter, I explore attributes and revisit normalization and keys in greater detail.

Attributes represent the items of information that the enterprise is interested in collecting and maintaining. Each attribute represents a fact that serves to identify, characterize, categorize, quantify, or otherwise express, the state of a specific instance of an entity. It is through the value of its attributes that a specific instance of an entity is defined.

In this chapter, you learn about

- Discovering attributes
- Normalizing during attribute analysis
- Naming and describing attributes and attribute-naming conventions

- Determining attribute types and characteristics, such as domains and logical datatypes, and examining keys from the attribute perspective
- Avoiding common mistakes with attributes

In an ER diagram, entities and relationships serve to group and associate attributes. It is the attributes that represent the essence of the model. So, let's explore attributes—the facts that represent the logical model information.

What Is an Attribute?

An *attribute* is a logical representation of a fact, for which the enterprise is interested in storing values. Recall that, in ER*win*, entities are visual representations for logical groupings of attributes. In turn, attributes represent the facts to be collected about an entity in the logical model. An attribute represents a fact that serves to identify, characterize, categorize, quantify, or otherwise express the state of an instance of an entity.

An attribute should represent a single concept. Attributes form logical groups that describe each instance of an entity. A specific instance of an attribute is a *value*. For example, an attribute called First Name defines the domain for a fact about an entity called PERSON. Gabriel, R.J., Will, and Vanessa are examples of specific values for First Name for specific instances of PERSON. A specific value for each attribute for an entity represents a single instance.

An appropriately modeled attribute has the following characteristics:

- The value of the attribute is of interest to the enterprise.
- A single instance of the attribute exists in the logical model.
- The attribute has a logical datatype and domain.
- The value for the attribute is defined as either required or optional.
- The attribute has a name and description.
- A single value is available for every instance of an entity.

NOTE

The example in Figure 3.1 is *not* a good example of modeling; it is a direct representation of the information requirements. In the sections that follow, I will continue to refine this example to demonstrate the process of placing attributes in the appropriate entity.

The enterprise, Betty Wilson's Ice Cream Shop, wants to order more of the most popular flavors and less of the least popular flavors. Betty's offers specials on ice cream and is interested in knowing which ice cream flavors the customers select for banana splits and hot fudge sundaes during the times when the specials are offered. To meet the business need, we will need to collect data on which flavors of ice cream are selected for banana splits and hot fudge sundaes and the date.

Figure 3.1 has two entities, BANANA SPLIT and HOT FUDGE SUNDAE. Each entity contains attributes that represent the components for each dish. Notice that instances of the BANANA SPLIT entity enable the selection of three flavors of ice cream and three toppings, a banana, whipped cream, and a cherry. Instances of HOT FUDGE SUNDAE enable the selection of two flavors of ice cream, hot fudge, whipped cream, and a cherry.

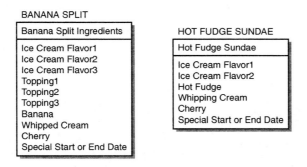

FIGURE 3.1

The entities and attributes that represent (badly) the two primary concepts of HOT FUDGE SUNDAE and BANANA SPLIT.

Discovering Attributes

How do you start the process of discovering attributes? Most attributes are revealed during facilitated sessions and interviews at the time that entities are defined. The analysis of the information requirements provided by domain experts and users is undeniably the best source for identifying attributes.

The enterprise model is also an excellent source for discovering attributes. Compare the entities and attributes in the enterprise model with the entities and attributes in the new logical model. The enterprise model will suggest attributes that have been previously defined for each entity, particularly core entities. If an attribute is not present in the enterprise model entity, analysis will indicate whether it should be added or whether it belongs in another entity.

Aligning Attributes with Information Requirements

Attributes in the logical model should be closely aligned with the information requirements. Each attribute should exist to fulfill one or more information requirements. The model should contain only those attributes necessary to represent the facts of interest to the enterprise, within the scope of the problem domain.

> **TIP**
>
> Attributes that are outside the problem domain and that cannot be tied directly to one or more information requirements should be eliminated. Attributes that do not bring enough value to the enterprise to justify the expense of sourcing and maintaining them should also be eliminated.

Each fact of interest to the enterprise should be accurately and completely represented in the logical model. The information requirements are the measure of whether the necessary attributes have been identified. I find it useful to document the association between the attributes and the information requirements.

Analyzing Attributes

You should analyze each attribute to determine its relationship to every other attribute in the model. Performed properly, analysis will ensure that each attribute exists only once in the model and is placed in an entity according to third normal form.

It is particularly important to analyze each primary key, and each part of a composite primary key, to verify that a value exists for each instance of an entity. You must also ensure that the primary key identifies one and only one instance of an entity.

Analysis should also ascertain whether the enterprise is interested in collecting and maintaining any details about the attribute itself. If an attribute is so important that other attributes are required to hold details about it, you should consider creating a new entity.

You must analyze every attribute in the logical model to ensure that it exists only once in the model and that only a single value exists for each instance of the entity. You must place the attribute in the appropriate entity using the rules of normalization and define its characteristics.

There Should Be Only One

An attribute should exist only once in the logical model. "One fact in one place," (Date, 1986). To ensure that a single attribute represents each fact, examine any attributes that have similar names or similar descriptions. You must also determine whether attributes are actually instances, or specific values that have been mistakenly modeled as different attributes.

Attributes with similar names and descriptions can actually represent a single concept and should be represented by a single attribute. In our language, the same word can represent several different concepts. To make matters worse, English also has different words that represent the same concept.

An attribute with "indicator" or "flag" as part of its name probably represents a specific value within the domain of an attribute. A *specific value* is an instance of an attribute. Modeling an instance of an attribute is a common modeling mistake. For example, Black Hair Indicator contains a Yes value if Black Hair is present, and a No value if Black Hair is not present. A better choice is to model an attribute called Color of Hair that can have a specific value of Black.

An attribute should represent a single business concept. It should not contain multiple values for an instance of an entity. Figure 3.1 shows two entities, BANANA SPLIT and HOT FUDGE SUNDAE. Both entities contain a multi-valued attribute, called Special Start or End Date. The name indicates that the value for the attribute can be either a Special Start Date or a Special End Date, and we have no way of knowing which! This attribute must be separated into two attributes, each of which represents a single fact.

NOTE

Although separating the single attribute into two distinct facts resolves the issue of an attribute representing multiple values, there is still a problem: The values of Special Start Date and Special End Date are not dependent on the identifier of BANANA SPLIT or HOT FUDGE SUNDAE. This is a normalization issue and will be addressed in the next section.

Allowing an attribute to contain multiple values can create "hidden" attributes that are tightly bound. The previous example is fairly obvious. Not all multi-valued attributes can be resolved so easily. It might surprise you to know that attributes that contain a block of text, such as a comment or note, are likely to bury rich attribute values within the text.

Normalization: Placing Attributes in the Right Entity

The attributes determine the number of entities that will exist when the logical model is resolved to third normal form. The process of normalization is an analysis of the way the attributes in an entity relate to one another, and the way they relate to the primary key. Resolving the logical model to third normal form often gives rise to new entities.

Normalization, if performed properly, ensures that the model will be scalable and extensible by placing attributes in the appropriate entity.

CAUTION

Take care when adding new attributes to entities in a normalized model. The new attribute must be dependent on the value of the key, the whole key, and nothing but the key. Consider the case of an existing composite primary key: Adding a new attribute whose value is dependent on the value of only part of the composite key violates second normal form.

Other benefits of normalization follow:

- Eliminates or minimizes redundancy. Redundant data can be represented by differently named attributes that represent the same concept, or by repeating groups. Representing every fact one time in one place minimizes redundancy.

- Eliminates or minimizes insert, delete, and update anomalies. Non-normalized data structures allow the same fact to exist in more than one place and with incomplete or partial dependency on the primary key. Insert, delete, and update anomalies are data discrepancies that can cause unexpected or inaccurate data retrieval when these conditions exist.

- Eliminates or minimizes the use of null values for attributes. Repeating groups of attributes often contain nulls for many instances because they represent a fact for which some entities might have more that a single value and others might not. Entities that contain instances with null values can cause data structures to be sparsely populated.

Each attribute matches the appropriate entity when the model is resolved to third normal form. As you resolve the model to third normal form, you often discover new attributes and entities.

Functional Dependency

Functional dependency refers to the relationship of attributes to other attributes in the model. Every attribute in an entity must be functionally dependent on the primary key of that entity (and not functionally dependent on any other attribute in the model). If this is not the case, the attribute should be moved to a new entity where it will be.

NOTE	

Given a relation *R*, attribute *Y* of R is functionally dependent on attribute *X* of R. In symbols, R.X->R.Y (read "R.X functionally determines R.Y") if and only if each X-value in R has associated with it precisely one Y-value in R (at any one time). Attributes X and Y might be composite (Date, 1986).

To identify any attributes that are functionally dependent, first group attributes into sets that have a common theme. Closely examine the themes for similarities. Examine the attributes in the themes to determine whether any attribute is functionally dependent on an attribute within the theme. If an attribute, or group of attributes, is not dependent upon the value of the primary key of an entity, it should be moved to another entity.

Attributes that appear to share common themes might be redundant. Redundant attributes can be combined into a single entity or can share a higher level of abstraction as a subtype of a parent entity. Figure 3.1 shows at least two common themes, Ice Cream Flavor and Toppings. These attributes are good candidates for removal to other entities. Consider the functional dependency issue. The value for Ice Cream Flavor does not depend on the value of the primary key, Banana Split Ingredients. The same statement applies to Hot Fudge Sundae.

Figure 3.2 shows a solution that removes Ice Cream Flavor and Topping to entities in which the value is dependent upon the primary key. This solution resolves some obvious redundancy issues.

First Normal Form

Resolution to first normal form means to move any repeating attributes to another entity. Repeating attributes are usually fairly easy to identify because they are often numbered, such as Topping1 and Topping2, or Flavor1 and Flavor2.

Create a dependent entity that has a set of attributes to represent the repeating attributes. The primary key of the dependent entity has a composite primary key that includes the primary key of the parent entity and at least one additional attribute to guarantee uniqueness.

In Figure 3.2, I moved the repeating groups for Ice Cream Flavor and Topping to dependent entities. Note the creation of a FLAVOR entity.

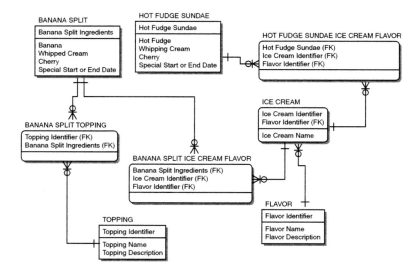

FIGURE 3.2

Resolved redundant attributes.

Second Normal Form

Resolution to second normal form means to eliminate redundant attributes. *Redundant attributes* can be any of the following:

- Different attributes that represent the same concept
- Attributes in different entities that share a common theme
- Attributes which do not have a value for every instance of an entity

---

TIP

Closely examine entities with similar attributes. These entities can be related or can even represent the same concept. If so, they should be combined.

Attributes that represent the same concept should be resolved to a single attribute. Redundant attributes might not have values for every instance of an entity and therefore do not depend on the value of the primary key for existence. Move these attributes to an entity where a value exists for every instance of the entity.

Create an entity with attributes to represent the redundant attributes. The new entity has a primary key that identifies a single instance. The primary key becomes a foreign key in the original entity. Foreign keys are discussed in Chapter 4, "Understanding Relationships."

Figure 3.2 shows the resolution of the some of the redundant attributes for BANANA SPLIT and HOT FUDGE SUNDAE. Consider the redundancy between the two core entities. The entities share common themes, ice cream and toppings. This indicates that the core entities might share a higher level of abstraction.

Figure 3.3 shows the creation of a super-type called SUNDAE, of which BANANA SPLIT and HOT FUDGE SUNDAE are instances. I added a discriminator attribute, Sundae Type, to the parent entity, SUNDAE, to identify whether a SUNDAE is an instance of BANANA SPLIT or HOT FUDGE SUNDAE. An instance of SUNDAE can be either a BANANA SPLIT or HOT FUDGE SUNDAE but not both.

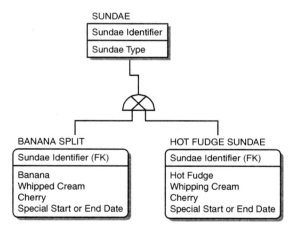

FIGURE 3.3
Redundancy of core entities is resolved by moving the common attributes to a SUNDAE super-type entity. Note that the primary key, Sundae Identifier, migrates to the BANANA SPLIT and HOT FUDGE entities.

Third Normal Form

Resolution to third normal form means to eliminate any attributes that are dependent upon values of other attributes in addition to the primary key. This is sometimes referred to as *transitive dependency*.

Create a new entity and move the attributes that are not dependent on the primary key of the original entity to the new entity. Identify a primary key for the new entity that guarantees uniqueness.

In Figure 3.3, the attributes Whipping Cream and Cherry are not dependent on the value of the primary key of BANANA SPLIT or HOT FUDGE SUNDAE. In fact, you should consider whether Whipping Cream and Cherry might be instances of TOPPING.

NOTE

The BANANA SPLIT entity contains an attribute called *Whipped Cream* and HOT FUDGE SUNDAE entity contains an attribute called *Whipping Cream*. Comparing the descriptions for the attributes shows that they clearly define the same concept. Whipping Cream was selected as the logical name to represent the concept and moved to the super-type SUNDAE entity.

In Figure 3.4, notice the addition of a Sundae Date attribute to provide an understanding of when that instance of SUNDAE was prepared. I removed Special Start and End Date from BANANA SPLIT and HOT FUDGE SUNDAE. A new entity, SPECIAL, now carries the two dates and an Ice Cream Flavor attribute to indicate which ice cream flavor is on special.

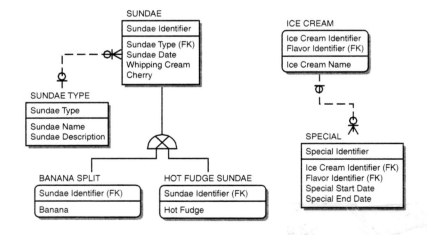

FIGURE 3.4

Every attribute is dependent on the value of the primary key, the whole key, and nothing but the key.

Defining Attribute Characteristics

Attributes fall into one of two groups. An attribute is either a key or non-key. Figure 3.5 shows the key attributes for the SUNDAE logical model. Note that, in ERwin, the primary key attributes are *above* the line inside the entity and other attributes are *below* the line.

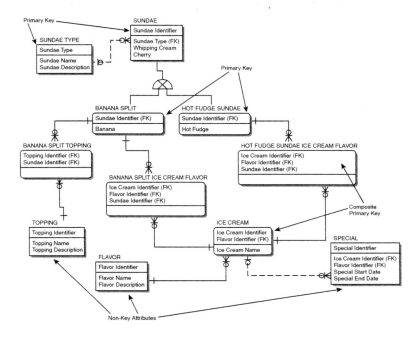

FIGURE 3.5
All attributes that are not part of the primary key are displayed below the line within the entity. This can include candidate keys, foreign keys, and alternate keys, as well as simple attributes.

Key Attributes

Key attributes are those attributes whose value determines the values of other attributes. The value of key attributes is not determined by the value of any other attribute. A key can consist of a single attribute, or it can be a composite key that has more than one attribute. These attributes can be primary keys, composite primary keys, candidate keys, foreign keys, or alternate keys.

Primary Key Attributes

Whether the primary key is a single attribute, or a group of attributes, the value of the primary key determines the value of every other attribute.

A good primary key will exhibit the following characteristics:

- The value guarantees uniqueness for every instance.
- The value has no intrinsic meaning.
- The domain of values will remain consistent over time.
- A value exists for every instance.

Artificial Primary Keys

Artificial primary keys are attributes that are created for the single purpose of identifying a specific instance of an entity. In some cases, no attribute or group of attributes uniquely identifies a single instance of an entity. In other cases, the composite primary key is large and awkward to use. An artificial primary key is also referred to as a *pseudo key* or *system-generated key*. It is also called an *artificial unique identifier*, which is indicative of its purpose.

Artificial primary keys are often created by simply consecutively numbering each instance of an entity. These artificial keys have the added benefit of carrying no meaning in association with the instances defined, other than to guarantee uniqueness. In fact, artificial primary keys created in this fashion are guaranteed to have the characteristics of good primary keys. (I believe I mentioned previously my affinity for artificial primary keys.)

Note that most of the primary keys in Figure 3.5 are artificial primary keys. For the most part, the primary key is merely a unique number for each instance.

Candidate Key Attributes

A *candidate key* is an attribute or group of attributes that identifies a specific instance of an entity. Candidate keys represent the mechanism for identifying the potential primary keys for identifying a specific instance within an entity.

Candidate keys that are not selected as the primary key are also called alternate keys. An *alternate key* is an attribute or group of attributes that can be used to create an index.

Foreign Key Attributes

A *foreign key* is an attribute or group of attributes that forms the primary key in another entity. Foreign keys can be a key attribute or a non-key attribute in a related entity. Notice the term *related entity*. Foreign keys represent relationships between entities; they are discussed in greater detail in Chapter 4.

Migrating Primary Key Attributes

Foreign key attributes are primary key attributes of another entity that have migrated through a relationship between the entities. Foreign keys are either identifying or non-identifying. *Identifying foreign keys* become part of the primary key in the migration. *Non-identifying foreign keys* become non-key attributes.

Non-Key Attributes

Non-key attributes are those attributes whose values depend upon the values of primary key or composite primary key attributes. These non-key attributes should depend only on the value of the key, the whole key, and nothing but the key.

In his book *Strategic Systems Development*, Clive Finklestein defines several types of non-key attributes:

- Selection attribute—An attribute used to identify a single instance of an entity when a key is not unique. Can also be called a *secondary key*.
- Group attribute—An attribute within which a group of more detailed attributes resides.
- Repeating group attributes—Attributes that represent several occurrences of the same attribute within an entity.
- Derived attribute—An attribute whose value is determined by the value of other attributes.
- Fundamental data attribute—An attribute that is not a selection attribute, group attribute, repeating attribute, or derived attribute.

Selection attributes, group attributes, and repeating group attributes should not be present if the logical model has been resolved to third normal form. Selection attributes should become part of the primary key if they are required to identify a single instance of an entity. Group attributes are multi-valued attributes. In my opinion, group attributes are best represented in the logical model as a code or classification entity. As discussed earlier, repeating groups should be moved to a child entity.

In third normal form, non-key attributes should be simple (fundamental) attributes or derived attributes.

Simple Attributes

Simple attributes are attributes that have been decomposed to their finest level of granularity; that is, they are completely dependent on the primary key for values and have a value for every instance of an entity. They are not selection criteria and cannot be used to group instances. They represent simple atomic facts that are of interest to the enterprise.

Derived Attributes

A *derived attribute* is an attribute whose value is derived or calculated by using the value of one or more other attributes. There has been considerable discussion as to whether derived attributes should be represented in the logical model. Some experts say that, because the values for derived attributes are dependent upon the derivation attribute values, derived attributes should not be represented in the logical model.

The logical model is intended to be a complete and accurate representation of the information requirements. You can make the decision to physically create derived attributes in the physical model in accordance with usage requirements.

Although I can see the point of not including derived attributes, I am convinced that the logical model is the best place to name and describe all attributes. Therefore, I am inclined to include derived attributes in the logical model. However, I caution modelers not to use a derived attribute as a primary key or as part of a composite primary key. Also, remember to include derivation rules as part of the attribute description.

Defining Attribute Domains

Attribute domains define the list of permitted values that an attribute can take for a specific instance of an entity. A domain consists of at least a general datatype domain and can also include a user-defined domain. You must define a domain for every attribute in a complete logical model.

It has been said that an attribute must have a domain of at least two values. An attribute that always has only a single permitted value has probably been modeled incorrectly. In Figure 3.5 there are two such attributes, Banana and Hot Fudge.

In the BANANA SPLIT entity, there is a Banana attribute. The business rules state that every instance of BANANA SPLIT contains a banana. Since there can be only one value for the Banana attribute, an attribute is probably not necessary. Instead the description of BANANA SPLIT should indicate that a banana is included for every instance. The same is true for the Hot Fudge attribute in the HOT FUDGE SUNDAE entity.

Table 3.1 indicates the logical datatype domains for the SPECIAL entity in the SUNDAE logical model.

TABLE 3.1 Examples of Logical Datatypes

Attribute Name	Logical Datatype
Special Identifier	Number
Ice Cream Identifier	Number
Flavor Identifier	Number
Special Start Date	Date
Special End Date	Date

Datatype and Extended Datatype Domains

Datatype domains define the manner in which a value for an attribute is represented. A datatype domain is required for every attribute in a complete logical model. The following list provides some examples of logical datatypes in ER*win*:

- Datetime
- Number
- String

Many newer database platforms also support more extended datatypes. However, it is important to remember that these complex datatypes are, to some extent, platform dependent. In any case, if users request an attribute, it should be included in the logical model, regardless of the datatype. Some commonly supported extended datatypes are

- Image
- Sound
- Video

User-Defined Domains

User-defined domains are specific domains that further refine the set of values for an attribute. These domains are often specific to an organization and should be defined and used consistently across the enterprise. For example, an attribute with a datatype domain of Number might also have a user-defined domain that limits the range of values to numbers between 1 and 100. Consistency enables the enterprise to make a change in a single entity and extend the domain for every attribute that uses it.

Defining Attribute Optionality

A value for an attribute can be required or optional. If a value is required, or mandatory, a value must be present when an instance is created. If a value is optional, then you can create an instance without a value.

In his book *Information Engineering: Strategic Systems Development*, Clive Finklestein defines the optionality characteristic of an attribute in a series of "edit rules":

- Add now; cannot modify later.
- Add now; modify later.
- Add later; modify later.
- Add later; cannot modify later.

Pay careful attention to attributes that are optional. If an attribute or set of attributes has values available only for specific instances of an entity, consider moving those attributes to an entity where a value is available for every instance of an entity.

Table 3.2 indicates the optionality for the attributes in the SPECIAL entity. Consider the fact that to create an instance of SPECIAL, a value is required for every attribute except Special End Date.

TABLE 3.2   Examples of Optionality

Attribute Name	Optionality
Special Identifier	Required
Ice Cream Identifier	Required
Flavor Identifier	Required
Special Start Date	Required
Special End Date	Optional

Table 3.2 represents a business rule that says an instance of SPECIAL requires the following information:

- An instance identifier (Special Identifier)
- An identifier for the flavor on SPECIAL (Ice Cream Identifier and Flavor Identifier)
- A date for the start of the SPECIAL (Special Start Date)

An end date for each instance of Special is not required. The business rule is that an instance of SPECIAL must start, but it never has to end!

An attribute whose value is required cannot have a null value. Some experts believe that a value should be required for every instance of an entity. Of course, this implies that a value for every attribute in an instance of an entity is collected or known prior to the creation of the instance.

An attribute whose value is optional can have a null value. Some experts say attributes should not exist in an entity where a value is not available for every instance. One of the reasons is the difficulty of interpreting a null value. Does a null value mean that the value for that instance is unknown or that it simply was not collected?

NOTE

Among modelers, a discussion of the merits and drawbacks of required and optional values can be very lively. Some modelers believe strongly that no attribute should ever contain a null value and argue that the domain should contain values such as *unknown* or *not collected*. Others believe that requiring a value and using domains to represent nulls also requires the use of default values, which causes the value to be suspect.

I prefer to allow nulls and let the application code or query tool manage the handling of nulls. In my opinion, this is the most accurate and flexible solution, as it allows nulls to be interpreted in different ways to meet different business needs.

Naming Attributes

Every attribute should have a name that is clear, concise, and unambiguous. The name of an attribute should not conflict with its description. The name should be indicative of the values that will be collected for instances of the attribute. The attribute name should be understood and accepted across the enterprise.

TIP

When selecting an attribute name, keep an enterprise view and take care to use a name that reflects what the attribute is, rather than how it will be used. Use names that are meaningful to the user community and domain experts.

I hope you have a set of attribute-naming conventions that were developed for your enterprise, or an enterprise data model, to guide you. Using attribute-naming conventions ensures that attribute names are constructed consistently across the enterprise, regardless of who constructs the name.

Attribute-naming conventions are important whether you work in a small organization or a large organization. However, in a large organization with many development teams and many users, naming conventions facilitate communication and understanding data elements. As a best practice, you should develop and maintain attribute-naming conventions in a central location and then document and publish them for the enterprise.

I have included some pointers for beginning a good set of attribute-naming conventions, in case your organization has not yet developed one:

- An attribute name should be as descriptive as necessary. Consider using noun phrases of the form *object/modifier/class word*.
- An attribute name should include the entity name if possible. Use Person First Name rather than First Name.
- An attribute name should be indicative of the values for specific instances of the attribute. Using the same attribute name for different data, or a different attribute name for the same data, is needlessly confusing to developers and users alike.
- An attribute name should use business language as opposed to technical language.
- An attribute name should not contain special characters (such as !, @, #, $, %, ^, &, *, and so on) or show possession (Person's First Name).
- An attribute name should not include acronyms or abbreviations unless they are part of the accepted naming conventions.

I encourage modelers to use good attribute-naming conventions if they are available and to develop them if they are not.

Object/Modifier/Class Word Attribute Names

The *object/modifier/class word* attribute-naming convention is a widely accepted industry guideline. This guideline encourages the use of a three-part attribute name. The *object* portion is sometimes called the subject or prime word. I generally use the entity name in the object part.

The *modifier* can be a single term or a group of terms. Although there is no standard list of modifiers, I encourage modelers to create brief, meaningful modifiers. Using modifiers helps you create descriptive attribute names. If the name becomes unacceptably burdensome for the user or extensive enterprise usage requires it, you can make compromises to the three-part attribute name approach.

The root part of the attribute name is the *class word*, which classifies the type of information being represented by the attribute. Some commonly used class words are

Identifier

Code

Date

Number

Amount

Quantity

Rate

Examples of Attribute Names

It is always best to use consistent attribute names across the enterprise. Table 3.3 shows examples of good names as well as some poor names for attributes. Notice that each attribute name word is separated with a space, begins with an uppercase letter, and uses lowercase letters for the remainder.

TABLE 3.3   Attribute Names and Explanations

Good Name	Poor Name	Explanation
Person First Name	Name	Name is a class word and needs an object word, Person, and a modifier word, First.
Ice Cream Sales Quantity	The Quantity of Sales	Quantity is a class word and should be in last position. "The" and "of" add no meaning.

Good Name	Poor Name	Explanation
Item Cost Amount	Cost of Item	"of" adds no meaning. The class word "Amount" lets users know what to expect.
Product Identifier	Product Identifiers	"Identifiers" is plural. Attribute names should be singular nouns.
Point of Sale Location Code	POS Code	"POS" is an abbreviation. The use of the "Code" class word needed a modifier word.
Person Birth Date	Birthday	Birthday does not contain the Date class word. Including the object and modifier adds clarification.

Describing Attributes

An *attribute description* is a brief narrative of what the attribute *is*, not how the attribute is used. The description should not contradict the attribute name and should not be a restatement. Include the class word and object along with a sentence that concisely defines the data. If the attribute is derived or calculated, include the derivation rules or formula for calculation. The following rules cover describing attributes:

- An attribute description should be clear, concise, and unambiguous.
- An attribute description should be consistent with the attribute name.
- An attribute description should not rely on the description of another attribute.
- An attribute description should be worded using business language as opposed to technical language.
- An attribute name should describe what an attribute is, not how it is used.
- An attribute description should spell out any acronyms or abbreviations used in the attribute name.

I encourage modelers to provide good descriptions for every attribute. Good attribute descriptions make it easy for anyone to use the model. Those who follow a good modeler learn a deep appreciation for well-modeled information requirements. See the comparisons in Table 3.4.

TABLE 3.4 Attribute Names, Descriptions, and Explanations

Attribute Name	Good Description	Poor Description	Explanation
Person First Name	The first name of a Person that enables the enterprise to address a Person using a familiar term.	A 40-character field.	Does not use business terms; uses technical terms.
Ice Cream Sales Quantity	The quantity of a specific ice cream sold during a specific sales event.	The Quantity of Sales.	Adds no new information, simply restates the attribute name in vague language.
Item Cost Amount	The cost amount for a specific item at a specific point in time. Represents the purchase cost plus any shipping costs.	A six-digit decimal with precision of two.	Much too technical. Offers little or nothing of meaning to users of the data element.
Product Identifier	An artificial unique identification number for a specific product.	Product Identifiers.	Simply restates the attribute name.
Point of Sale Location Code	A unique code that identifies the geographical location of a point of sale.	POS code.	Uses an acronym that might not be understood by users and fails to use a critical modifier in the description.
Person Birth Date	The date on which a person was born.	Birthday for a person.	Does not include the class word "date" as part of the description.

Common Mistakes with Attributes

This section about common attribute modeling mistakes is not meant to be comprehensive. I merely want to point out some of the most common mistakes I have seen novice modelers make.

Sometimes, a modeler makes a conscious choice, for very good reasons, to model something a certain way. It is important to understand the consequences of modeling decisions so you have a clear understanding of the implications.

Modeling a Value

What do I mean by modeling a value? In a planning session, users might tell you they need lists of attributes that indicate the age range for an instance of PERSON. There are at least three problems with this scenario.

1. The way the enterprise defines an age range has the potential to change over time.
2. The value of a specific person's age range will absolutely change over time.
3. All the attributes represent values for an attribute Person Age. Of course, Person Age will change over time, so the best solution is to model the simple attribute of Person Birth Date.

TIP

If purchased or inferred data, such as age range, is all that is available, then it should certainly be modeled. If both age range and birth date are available, I would model both a range and a birth date and derive the age range for instances that have a value for birth date. Frequency of derivation and whether or not the derived age range has physical persistence would depend on the usage requirements.

Modeling Multi-Valued Attributes

Multi-valued attributes are attributes that contain more than a single value for a concept. Check for attribute descriptions that indicate several values for the same concept.

Sometimes domain experts from different areas in an enterprise use an attribute name that is spelled the same and pronounced the same, but has a different meaning to different experts. One way to ensure that attributes with the same name describe the same object is to verify the description. Make sure that the attribute values describe a single concept.

For example, you can create artificial codes by concatenating one or more codes to relate data that was not previously related. Text blocks can hide many rich attributes and values in blocks of text.

Failing to resolve multi-valued attributes can cause some important business rules to remain undefined and undocumented.

Modeling Redundant Attributes

Redundant attributes are attributes that have different names but contain information about similar concepts. The English language has many words that represent the same thing. One way to identify redundant attributes is to look for entities that contain similar attributes. Compare the descriptions of each attribute to see whether the entities contain data about similar concepts. Redundant attributes are often the result of a tendency to model a value as an attribute.

For example, a MANAGER entity and an EMPLOYEE entity can contain Manager First Name and an Employee First Name. Because both MANAGER and EMPLOYEE are roles that an instance of PERSON can play, you should move the attribute to the PERSON entity and call it Person First Name.

Using Bad Attribute Names

Unclear, ambiguous, or imprecise attribute names make it difficult for new users or design teams to reuse or enhance an existing model.

Don't use abbreviations or acronyms as part of the attribute name. Abbreviations and acronyms are open to misinterpretation and can even develop different meanings in different business areas.

Don't use proper nouns that indicate a value for specific instances. An attribute name with a proper noun is an indication of a serious modeling problem, not just bad naming.

Don't include the location of the attribute as part of the name. If a value exists for one location, it will almost certainly be defined for another location. An attribute name with a location is an indication that you have modeled a specific instance rather than a class.

Using Bad Attribute Descriptions

Don't use an attribute definition from a dictionary alone. A dictionary definition does not contain the business value that makes the attribute important to the enterprise.

Don't simply restate the name of the attribute. Don't use the name of the attribute in the description.

Unclear, vague, or, even worse, no attribute definitions make it difficult to reuse or enhance an existing model. Users won't be able to verify that the model contains all the required information. It also greatly increases the tendency to model specific values as attributes or multi-valued attributes.

Concepts that seem obvious to all participants during planning sessions might not remain as obvious as time goes by and a new team is tasked with making enhancements to an existing model.

Summary

Attributes represent the facts that the enterprise is interested in collecting and maintaining. They are the essence of the model and are generally discovered during facilitated sessions. Modeling attributes accurately and completely requires good analysis to ensure that attributes are closely aligned with information requirements. An attribute should exist only once in a model and should represent a single business concept. Normalization rules should be used to place an attribute in the appropriate entity.

Attributes are either key or non-key. A key can be a single attribute or group of attributes. Primary keys are selected from among the candidate keys that identify a unique instance of an entity. Primary key attributes migrate from a parent entity to become foreign key attributes in a child entity. The value of all non-key attributes should be functionally dependent upon the value of the primary key.

Domains define the range of values for an attribute. Logical domains can be as simple as a datatype, such as number, or string. They can also be complex user-defined datatypes that are tailored to meet the specific needs of the enterprise. Newer DBMSs also support extended datatypes, like image and sound.

Attribute values are either required or optional. If a value is required, the attribute is not allowed to have a null value. Attributes should have a name and description. Naming standards of object/modifier/class word form are recommended as the basis of attribute-naming guidelines. Every attribute should include a good description that uses business terminology to define what the attribute is, rather than how it is used.

Entities and relationships serve to group and relate attributes. In Chapter 4, I discuss the role of relationships in the modeling process and the relationship properties and types. I include some tips for avoiding common mistakes when modeling relationships.

Understanding Relationships

In the previous chapters, I introduced data modeling concepts, entities, and attributes for discovering and defining the information requirements of the business area being modeled. You might recall that logical models are represented in an ERD by entities, attributes, and relationships. In this chapter, I focus on relationships in greater detail.

In the sections that follow, I cover the following topics:

- Relationships as part of the modeling process
- Relationship properties, such as degree and direction
- Primary relationship types (identifying and non-identifying), cardinality, and optionality
- Common mistakes in identifying relationships

In an ER diagram, entities represent containers for attributes, attributes represent the facts of interest, and relationships allow you to use relational algebra to relate groups of attributes according to business rules. Let's explore relationships—the heart of a relational data model.

What Is a Relationship?

A *relationship* is the association or "link" between two entities. A relationship is represented in the model by a line connecting two entities and a verb phrase that describes how two entities relate to one another. Verb phrases are the mechanism for describing the business rules that define the relationship. Good relationship verb phrases describe the relationship using business language, rather than technical terms. Figure 4.1 shows a relationship line between two entities.

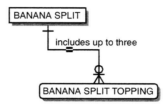

FIGURE 4.1

Relationships are represented in an ER diagram as a line between two entities, or between an entity and itself. The relationship type and properties represent business rules. An instance of BANANA SPLIT may have zero, one, two, or three instances of BANANA SPLIT TOPPING. An instance of BANANA SPLIT TOPPING can belong to one and only one instance of BANANA SPLIT.

Relationships are used in both the logical and physical model and are represented in both as one or more migrating foreign key attributes. Relationships are bi-directional and represent a significant association between two entities or between an entity and itself.

A relationship is defined by the following properties:

- Degree
- Direction
- Type
- Cardinality
- Optionality

NOTE

It is important to note that not all modeling methodologies use these terms to describe relationships, although most use similar concepts.

Discovering Relationships

How do you begin the process of discovering the relationships between entities? Most relationships are revealed during facilitated sessions and interviews. The analysis of the information requirements and business rules provided by domain experts and users is the best source of relationship information. During the facilitated sessions, after two or more entities are identified and defined with attributes, the session participants should determine whether a relationship exists between the entities.

The enterprise model is also a good source. Examine the relationships between entities within the subject area that is being modeled. Take care to explore the foreign keys that define the relationships between code entities and other entities. These relationships might reveal entities that should be added to your model or levels of abstraction that could add extensibility.

You also discover relationships during normalization; as new entities emerge, so do the relationships between them. Resolving many-to-many relationships in the logical model will likely give rise to several additional entities and relationships.

NOTE

Rarely is there a relationship between each entity and every other entity in an application. If a data model has only a few entities, then there might be relationships between them all. However, in a larger application, there might not always be relationships between all of the entities.

Reading a Relationship

By defining appropriate verb phrases, you can read relationships from right to left using the form *entity-verb form describing relationship-entity*. Using the ice cream store example, you could define a relationship of

   Customers Buy Sundaes

or

   Stores Sell Ice Cream Flavors

Reading relationships using sentence structure in this *entity-relationship-entity* form (sometimes referred to as a *relationship entity pair*) is a useful mechanism for representing relationships to business partners. Relationship entity pairs are bi-directional. That is, the entities are related in both directions. Therefore, *Customers Buy Sundaes* is the same as *Sundaes Are Bought by Customers*.

Reading relationships in this manner provides validation that the design of the logical model is correct. Although relationships do not describe all the business rules completely, they allow business partners reviewing the model to get a sense of the connections between the entities. I consider it a best practice to ensure that each verb phrase in the model produces valid statements. Reading the model with business partners is one of the primary methods of validating that the model correctly captures the business rules.

Relationship Degree

The *degree* of a relationship represents the number of entities associated with the relationship. Generally, relationships are considered to have a unary or binary degree. *Unary*, or *recursive*, relationships represent those cases where an instance of an entity is related to another instance of the same entity. *Binary* relationships represent those cases where one entity is related to another entity. Binary relationships represent the most common real-world relationship. In fact, most modelers consider a unary or recursive relationship to be a binary recursive relationship relating an instance of an entity to another instance. For example, "Some employees are managed by other employees" represents a relationship between instances of EMPLOYEE.

NOTE

Some methodologies recognize *n*-ary relationships (with *n* representing the degree of the relationship). N-ary relationships are those involving more than two entity types. For example, Customer Buys a Sundae from a Store is a ternary (third-degree) relationship that involves three entities. However, most methodologies recognize only binary relationships and resolve all *n*-ary relationships to binary ones.

Relationship Direction

The direction of a relationship indicates the originating entity of a binary relationship. The entity from which a relationship originates is called the *parent entity*. The entity where the relationship terminates is called a *child entity*.

The direction of a relationship is determined by the relationship between the entities. In a relationship between an independent and dependent entity, the direction is *from* the independent entity *to* a dependent entity. If both entities are independent, the direction is arbitrary. If the relationship is one-to-many, the entity occurring once is the parent. The direction of many-to-many relationships is arbitrary.

Defining Relationship Types

In ER*win*, a relationship between two entities, or between an entity and itself, is one of the following types:

- Identifying relationship
- Non-identifying relationship
- Subtype relationship
- Many-to-many relationship
- Recursive relationship

Each relationship type defines the behavior of the foreign key attributes that migrate from the parent primary key to the child entity. In the sections that follow, I describe the characteristics of each relationship type.

Identifying Relationships

An *identifying relationship* is a relationship between two entities in which an instance of the child entity is identified through the values of the attributes of the parent entity. This means an instance of the child entity is dependent on the parent entity for identity and cannot exist without an instance of the parent. In an identifying relationship, a single instance of the parent entity is related to multiple instances of the child. The primary key attributes of the parent entity migrate to become primary key attributes of the child entity. Figure 4.2 shows an identifying relationship between FLAVOR and ICE CREAM. Note that the primary key attributes of the parent entity, FLAVOR, migrated to become the primary key of the child entity, ICE CREAM.

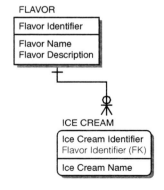

FIGURE 4.2

Identifying the relationship between ICE CREAM and FLAVOR. An instance of ICE CREAM cannot exist until there is a parent instance in FLAVOR. Note the solid line between the two entities.

Non-Identifying Relationships

A *non-identifying relationship* is a relationship between two entities in which an instance of the child entity is not identified through its association with a parent entity. This means the child entity is not dependent on the parent entity for identity and can exist without an instance of the parent. In a non-identifying relationship, one instance of the parent entity is related to multiple instances of the child. The primary key attributes of the parent entity migrate to become non-key attributes in the child entity. Figure 4.3 shows a non-identifying relationship between SUNDAE and SUNDAE TYPE. Note that the primary key of the parent entity, SUNDAE TYPE, migrates as a non-key attribute in the child entity, SUNDAE.

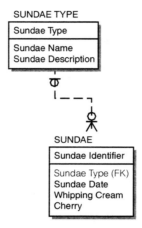

FIGURE 4.3

A non-identifying relationship between SUNDAE TYPE and SUNDAE. Note that ERwin represents a non-identifying relationship as a dashed line.

Subtype Relationships

Subtype relationships are relationships between a parent entity and one or more child entities. You should use subtype relationships when it makes sense to identify those relationships where an instance of a parent entity defines different sets of attributes in child entities.

Clive Finklestein refers to subtype entities as secondary entities. Subtype entities almost always have one or more sibling entities. The subtype entity siblings are related to a parent entity through a subtype relationship that is either exclusive or inclusive.

Exclusive Subtype

Exclusive subtype relationships indicate that only one child entity is defined by an instance of the parent entity. In other words, an instance in the parent entity does not have related instances in more than a single child entity. Exclusive subtypes represent an "is a" relationship. Figure 4.4 shows an exclusive subtype relationship between the super-type parent entity, SUNDAE, and two subtype child entities, BANANA SPLIT and HOT FUDGE SUNDAE.

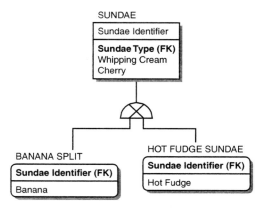

FIGURE 4.4

An exclusive subtype relationship between the super-type parent entity, SUNDAE, and two subtype child entities, BANANA SPLIT and HOT FUDGE SUNDAE. Note the (X) in the subtype symbol indicates that this is an exclusive subtype using ERwin's IE notation. The business rule represented states that an instance of SUNDAE is either a BANANA SPLIT or HOT FUDGE SUNDAE; it can never be both.

Inclusive Subtype

Inclusive subtype relationships indicate that more than one child entity can be defined by an instance of the parent entity. In other words, an instance in the parent entity has related instances in more than a single child entity. Figure 4.5 shows an inclusive subtype relationship between a super-type parent entity, PERSON, and two subtype child entities, CUSTOMER and EMPLOYEE.

Many-to-Many Relationships

Many-to-many relationships are relationships where a single instance of one entity relates to more than one instance of a second entity, and a single instance in the second entity also relates to more than one instance in the first. These relationships are also referred to as non-specific relationships. Many-to-many relationships are used in the preliminary stage of logical model development. They are usually resolved using an associative entity containing the keys of the parent entities. The associative entity allows an instance of each parent to be represented as a unique pair in the child. Figure 4.6 shows a many-to-many relationship between the HOT FUDGE SUNDAE and ICE CREAM entities.

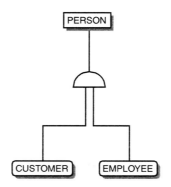

FIGURE 4.5

An inclusive subtype relationship between the super-type parent entity, PERSON, and two subtype entities, CUSTOMER and EMPLOYEE. Note the absence of the (X) in the subtype symbol indicates that this is an inclusive subtype using ERwin's IE notation. The business rule represented states that an instance of PERSON can be both a CUSTOMER and EMPLOYEE.

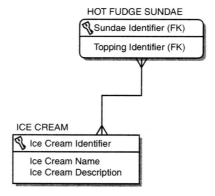

FIGURE 4.6

Many-to-many relationship between HOT FUDGE SUNDAE and ICE CREAM. Using IE notation, ERwin represents many-to-many relationships with a solid line with a "crow's foot" at both end points.

Recursive Relationships

A *recursive relationship* is a non-identifying relationship between two entities that indicates that an instance of the entity can be related to another instance of the same entity. In a recursive relationship, the parent entity and the child entity are the same entity. Figure 4.7 shows two implementation examples of a recursive relationship in the EMPLOYEE entity, one without a rolename and one with a rolename. Note that ER*win* "unifies" the foreign key and primary key attributes when a rolename is not used. Using a rolename places a foreign key as a non-key attribute.

Because recursive relationships can be confusing to users and novice modelers, it is a good practice to use rolenames for the migrating attributes. I discuss using rolenames and ERwin's interesting unification feature in Chapter 10, "Building Logical Relationships."

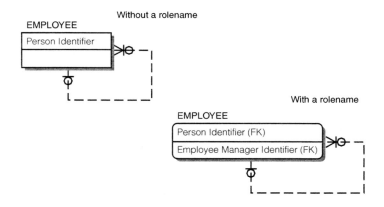

FIGURE 4.7

Recursive relationship implementation examples with a rolename and without a rolename in PERSON. Note that without a rolename, ERwin combines the foreign key attribute and the primary key attribute.

Relationship Cardinality

Relationship cardinality specifies the maximum number of instances of one entity that can be related to the instances of another entity. Cardinality is defined for both sides of a relationship, the originating entity and the terminating entity. *Cardinality* defines the maximum number of entity instances that can participate in a relationship, whereas *optionality* defines the minimum number of instances. You'll read more about optionality in the next section.

Cardinality is often expressed as simply *one* or *many*. One and many can be expressed in three distinct combinations:

- One-to-one (1:1)—One and only one instance of an entity is related to one and only one instance of another entity.

- One-to-many (1:N)—One and only one instance of the parent entity is related to many instances of a child entity.
- Many-to-many (M:N)—Many instances of one entity are related to many instances of another entity (also called a *non-specific relationship*).

One-to-One

One-to-one relationships are those in which one and only one instance of an entity is related to one and only one instance of another entity.

These relationships are sometimes the result of normalization to remove attributes that do not have a value for every instance of an entity. Take care to examine the attributes of the parent entity that participates in the relationship to identify a discriminator attribute whose value determines whether an instance exists in the dependent entity. If a discriminator exists, consider using a subtype relationship, rather than a one-to-one relationship.

TIP

One-to-one relationships are truly rare. In most cases, you should collapse attributes into a single entity. You should also examine the relationship to ensure that a one-to-many relationship has not been incorrectly modeled as a one-to-one.

Figure 4.8 shows a one-to-one relationship between PERSON and PERSON ADDRESS.

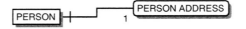

FIGURE 4.8

A one-to-one relationship example between the PERSON entity and the PERSON ADDRESS entity. The business rule represented states that an instance of PERSON can have exactly one address. Like many one-to-one relationships, this is actually incorrectly modeled one-to-many.

One-to-Many

One-to-many relationships are those in which one and only one instance of an entity is related to many instances of another entity. The entity on the one-instance end is the parent, or *originating*, entity, and the entity on the many-instance end is the child, or *terminating*, entity.

4

UNDERSTANDING
RELATIONSHIPS

> **NOTE**
>
> Most modelers agree that a logical model should contain only one-to-many relationships.

These relationships often result through normalization to remove repeating attribute groups to a dependent entity. Figure 4.9 shows the PERSON and PERSON ADDRESS relationship correctly modeled as a one-to-many relationship.

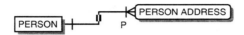

FIGURE 4.9
A one-to-many relationship example between the PERSON entity and the PERSON ADDRESS entity. The business rule represented states that an instance of PERSON can have more than one address. This one-to-many relationship corrects the previously modeled (although incorrect) one-to-many.

Many-to-Many

A many-to-many relationship indicates a situation in which a single instance of one entity relates to one or more instances of a second entity, and, a single instance in the second entity also relates to one or more instances in the first. These relationships are also called non-specific relationships.

Many-to-many relationships should only exist in the preliminary stage of logical model development. Because many-to-many relationships often hide important business rules or constraints, they should be fully resolved as part of the modeling process. Resolution of many-to-many relationships requires the creation of an associative entity that contains the keys of both parent entities and allows a single instance of each parent to be unique pairs within the child.

> **CAUTION**
>
> Many-to-many relationships are logical relationships and cannot be represented in the physical model in ER*win*. ER*win* automatically creates an associative entity to resolve many-to-many relationships when the model is changed from logical to physical mode.

Figure 4.10 shows PERSON and PERSON ADDRESS modeled as a many-to-many relationship.

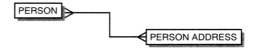

FIGURE 4.10

A many-to-many relationship example using the PERSON and PERSON ADDRESS entities. This relationship allows an instance of PERSON to have more than one address and allows an instance of PERSON ADDRESS to have more than one PERSON living there.

Relationship Optionality

In contrast to cardinality, the optionality of a relationship specifies whether an entity instance must participate in a relationship. Optionality is sometimes referred to as *modality* or *existence*. Whereas cardinality indicates the maximum number of entity instances that can participate in a relationship, optionality specifies the minimum number of instances that must participate in a relationship. The optionality value is zero if an instance is optional or not required, and one if an entity occurrence is required or mandatory.

When deciding the optionality of a relationship, consider whether an instance of one entity must always exist for another entity to be included in a relationship; if so, it is mandatory. For example, "Every employee must be assigned a single manager" is an example of a mandatory relationship. If the instance of the entity is not required, it is optional. For example, the statement, "Some employees may be assigned a single manager" is optional.

In a mandatory, non-identifying relationship, the attributes that are migrated into the non-key area of the child entity are required in the child entity. This means that the foreign key values cannot be null. Figure 4.11 shows a mandatory relationship.

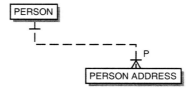

FIGURE 4.11

A mandatory relationship using the PERSON and PERSON ADDRESS entities. The business rule represented states that an instance of PERSON must have at least one address. Note that ERwin's IE notation at the terminal point of the relationship does not include a zero (circle) symbol at the base of the crow's foot, the many symbol.

In an optional, non-identifying relationship, the attributes that are migrated into the non-key area of the child entity are not required in the child entity. This means that null values are allowed in the foreign key. Figure 4.12 shows an optional relationship between PERSON and PERSON ADDRESS.

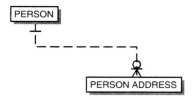

FIGURE 4.12

An optional relationship using the PERSON and PERSON ADDRESS entities. The business rule represented states that an instance of PERSON does not need an address. Note that ERwin's IE notation at the terminal point of the relationship includes a zero (circle) symbol at the base of the crow's foot, the many symbol.

Common Mistakes with Relationships

This section about common relationship modeling mistakes is not meant to be comprehensive. I merely point out some of the mistakes I made as a novice modeler.

Relationships are the heart of the relational model. Modeling one relationship incorrectly can violate the integrity of the entire model. ER*win* will not allow you to create the most obvious mistakes with relationships.

Unnecessary Relationships

Assigning a verb phrase name, direction, degree, type, cardinality, and optionality to a relationship should confirm the validity of that relationship. If you cannot provide all of these properties for a relationship, then perhaps there is no relationship after all.

One-to-One Relationships

Take care to closely examine the attributes of each entity in a one-to-one relationship. Analyze the attributes of the parent entity that participates in the relationship to determine whether a discriminator attribute exists. A discriminator attribute is one whose value determines whether an instance exists in the dependent entity. If a discriminator exists, consider using a subtype relationship rather than a one-to-one relationship. In my experience, true one-to-one relationships are rare and even more rarely implemented.

Many-to-Many Relationships

In a many-to-many relationship, multiple instances of one entity are related to one instance of another, and vice versa. Many-to-many relationships cannot be translated into physical database tables and relationships. This is a restriction of the database systems, not of the application. You must resolve all many-to-many relationships before you can construct the physical data model and develop the database. I encourage modelers to resolve many-to-many relationships during facilitated sessions. The session participants can usually define an appropriate entity to provide the resolution.

To resolve a many-to-many relationship means to convert it into two one-to-many, many-to-one relationships. A new entity is created between the two original entities, and this new entity is referred to as an *associative entity* or *intersection entity*. Adding this entity allows for every possible matched instance between the other two entities. Sometimes, the associative entity defines a range or point in time.

Mandatory or Optional

When determining the optionality of a relationship and considering whether an instance of one entity should be required for the existence of an instance in another, it is important to ensure that the required instance is always available.

It might be tempting to provide default values for mandatory foreign key values. However, there is often little to be gained by populating required information with contrived values. If the information is so important to the enterprise that it is mandatory, what is gained by populating it with a default value? If there is a chance that it will not be available for every instance, it is best to make it optional.

Summary

Relationships represent the associations or links between entities. They are the core of a relational data model. A relationship is visually depicted in an ER diagram as a line connecting two entities. A verb phrase describes the relationship, allowing you to "read" a relationship using the form *entity-verb phrase-entity*. Relationships are discovered during facilitated sessions or normalization analysis, and by comparing a model to the enterprise data model (if available).

Relationships are defined in terms of degree, direction, type, cardinality, and optionality. Degree defines the number of entities that participate in a relationship. Unary, binary, and *n*-ary describe relationship degrees. Unary is a relationship between instances of the same entity. Binary is a relationship between two entities. An *n*-ary relationship is a relationship between *n* entities, where n represents a number larger than two. Binary relationships are most commonly used. Relationship direction is from the originating, or parent, entity to the terminating, or child, entity.

Relationship type defines the behavior of migrating foreign keys. In ER*win*, relationship type is expressed as one of the following:

- Identifying
- Non-identifying
- Subtype
- Many-to-many
- Recursive

An identifying relationship is one in which the primary key of the parent entity is required to identify an instance of the child entity. In a non-identifying relationship, the primary key of the parent entity becomes one or more non-key attributes in the child entity. A subtype relationship, one in which a parent has two or more child entities, may be exclusive or inclusive. An exclusive subtype indicates that an instance of the parent may have corresponding instances in only a single child entity. An inclusive subtype indicates that an instance of the parent may have corresponding instances in more that one child entity.

Many-to-many relationships are those in which an instance of an entity is related to many instances of another entity, and vice versa. These are logical relationships that cannot be represented in the physical model and must be resolved by placing an associative entity between the two entities. The associative entity contains the primary key of each original entity allowing the instances of the associative entity to be unique. Recursive relationships are those in which an instance of an entity is related to another instance of the same entity.

Cardinality describes the maximum number of instances of entity that can participate in a relationship. Optionality defines the minimum number. Cardinality is expressed in terms of *one* or *many*. Optionality is expressed in terms of zero or one.

Understanding entities, attributes, and the relationships between them is essential to using ER*win* effectively. In Chapter 5, "Getting Started with ER*win*," I discuss installing ER*win* and setting the modeling environment, and introduce some of ER*win*'s powerful display options.

Introducing ER*win*

PART
II

IN THIS PART

Getting Started with ER*win*

The remainder of this book discusses modeling using Platinum ER*win*. It does not cover every aspect of the tool. The online documentation does a good job of describing the mechanics of how to use the tool. Instead, this text provides insight into building a good model using Platinum ER*win* to document the process.

Platinum ER*win* is a visual data modeling tool that supports logical and physical data modeling. Originally developed by LogicWorks, ER*win* is owned by Computer Associates, which offers a suite of complementary tools that work well with ER*win*. Check out the Computer Associates Web site, `http://www.cai.com`, for a complete list of the suite of tools that complement ER*win*. ModelMart, for example, is an environment for storing and managing data models, and it is one of the most powerful tools in the suite.

NOTE

ModelMart is a data model management environment that provides security and controlled access to ER*win* data models. Models are stored on a central server so that all modelers work with the most current models. ModelMart is platform and network independent and can be hosted by a Sybase server, Microsoft SQL Server, or Oracle RDBMs. Although describing ModelMart is outside the scope of this book, I encourage modelers to explore its features and consider its use for data model management.

This chapter addresses the following topics:

- Learning ER*win* features and functionality
- Installing ER*win*
- Opening and closing ER*win*
- Setting the modeling environment
- Choosing display options
- Saving a model

ER*win* Features and Functionality

ER*win* automates the design process, allowing modelers to quickly create complete, accurate data models. ER*win* supports the creation of a dictionary of reusable entities and attributes, enabling the enterprise to use consistent names and definitions in all database design and development activities. Database views are maintained as integrated model components, allowing changes in the base tables to be automatically reflected in the view definition. Automatic key migration guarantees the referential integrity of your database.

ER*win* also supports the design of large complex models by dividing them into smaller, more manageable subject areas that allow individual modelers to focus on specific subject area development. Stored displays allow multiple views of the same subject area, which facilitates communication with different user communities and development teams.

You can edit, view, and print ER*win* data models in a variety of ways. RPTwin, which comes bundled with ER*win*, is an easy-to-use report writer and browser. RPTwin contains a set of predefined common reports as well as custom reporting options that allow modelers to define the appearance and contents of data model reports.

Now that you have an understanding of some of the features and functionality in the tool, it's time to install ER*win* and get an overview of the modeling tools that ER*win* comprises.

System Requirements for Installing ER*win*

Before installing ER*win*, it is important to make sure you meet the minimum system requirements for hard drive space, RAM, and operating system. The version used for this text is Platinum ER*win* 3.5.2.

ER*win* 3.5.2 requires a 32-bit operating system. You must have Windows 95, Windows 98, or Windows NT 4.0 to use this version. I use Windows 95, version 4.00, 950B. The minimum memory required is 16MB RAM. However, 32MB RAM is recommended for large models. I have 64MB.

If you are not sure how much RAM you have or which version of Windows you are using, perform the following steps:

1. Click the Start button on the taskbar at the bottom of your screen.
2. Select Settings, Control Panel.
3. Click the computer labeled System.

The System Properties dialog lists the Windows version and the amount of RAM on your machine. Figure 5.1 shows an example.

FIGURE 5.1

System properties has several tab displays that contain information about your operating system and hardware configuration. The System section at the top of the General tab tells you the version and build of Windows installed on your machine. The last line on the tab indicates how much RAM is available on your machine.

Although the ERwin documentation indicates you need 40MB of hard drive space, a complete installation, including RPTwin, used 46MB on my machine.

Installing ER*win*

ERwin installation is fairly straightforward. If you have installed software before, you should have no problem installing ERwin. If you purchased a CD-ROM package, simply insert the CD-ROM. If you downloaded the software from the Computer Associates Web site, just double-click on the file. The installation for each medium is the same; follow the onscreen instructions.

If you are comfortable with software installation, you might want to skip to the section "Setting the Modeling Environment" later in this chapter.

The Platinum ERwin splash screen is displayed after the installation wizard has done its work. Figure 5.2 shows the splash screen. If you are using a different version, the splash screen might look different.

FIGURE 5.2
The Platinum ERwin splash screen.

User Information and Serial Number

After carefully reading the warning on the Welcome screen and pressing the Next button, you are prompted to enter your name, company name, and the serial number assigned to you. Enter this information.

ER*win* Installation Directory

The next screen lists the files that will be installed on your computer and displays the default installation directory. The following list outlines the functionality of the installation directory dialog:

- Pressing the Browse button allows you to select a different installation directory. If the directory you enter does not exist, it is created for you.
- Pressing the Disk Space button provides details about your available hard drive space, if you have more than one drive.
- Pressing the Back button returns you to the previous screen.
- Pressing the Cancel button stops the installation of ER*win*.

If you have no preference about the directory, simply press the Next button to continue.

RPTwin Destination Directory

The next screen displays the default installation directory for RPTwin, with three buttons:

- Pressing the Browse button allows you to select a different installation directory. If the directory you enter does not exist, it is created for you.
- Pressing the Back button returns you to the previous screen.
- Pressing the Cancel button stops the installation of ER*win*.

If you have no preference, simply press the Next button to continue.

Installation Directory Confirmation

The next screen displays the installation directory and program folder that will contain ER*win*; the screen has two buttons:

- Pressing the Back button returns you to the previous screen.
- Pressing the Cancel button stops the installation of ER*win*.

Make sure the directory and program folder are what you want because this is your last chance to make changes. If the directory and program folder are okay, simply press the Next button to start installing the files. Figure 5.3 shows the directory in which ER*win* will be installed and the program folder through which you will launch it.

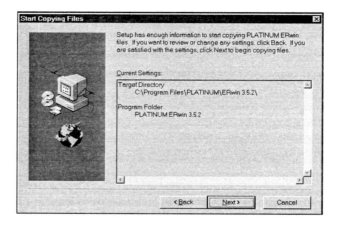

FIGURE 5.3

The Start Copying Files screen shows the destination directory in which ERwin will be installed and the program folder that will contain the icons for launching ERwin and RPTwin. This is your last opportunity to change the location.

Completing the Installation

A series of splash screens lists the suite of tools available for enterprise modeling and a meter that measures the installation progress.

When the installation is complete, you see the Platinum ER*win* program folder, shown in Figure 5.4. Click the Finish button to end installation, and you are ready to begin using ER*win*!

TIP

If you have problems with the installation, contact technical support at 800-833-7528 or 609-514-2020. Alternatively, you can visit the Web site at http://www.cai.com/erwin. The knowledge base on the Web site contains a lot of good information. Be sure to add /erwin to the URL; otherwise it is difficult to locate.

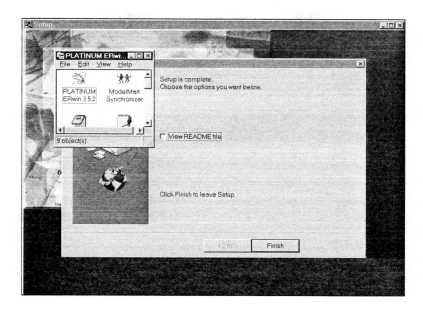

FIGURE 5.4

The Installation Complete screen lets you know that installation is complete. The Program Folder is opened and shows the icons for launching the ERwin applications and help files.

Opening and Closing ER*win*

To open ER*win*, perform the following steps:

1. Click the Start button on the taskbar at the bottom of your screen.

2. Select Programs, Platinum ER*win* 3.5.2 (or the name you entered for your folder), and select Platinum ER*win* 3.5.2 from the list.

I use ER*win* so often that I created a shortcut on my desktop. Here's one way to create a shortcut:

1. Right-click the Start button on the taskbar.

2. Select Open.

3. Double-click the Programs folder. Figure 5.5 shows the Start menu with the Programs folder inside.

FIGURE 5.5

The Start menu with the Programs folder.

4. Find the Platinum ERwin folder (you might need to scroll around) and double-click to open it. Figure 5.6 shows the Platinum ERwin folder opened.

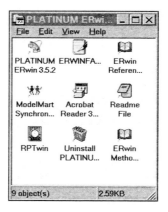

FIGURE 5.6

Platinum ERwin folder opened.

5. Drag the Platinum ERwin icon and drop it on your desktop. Here's how to do it. Using the right mouse button, click and hold the Platinum ERwin 3.5.2 icon; continue to hold the right mouse button while you drag the icon outside of the window. Release the right mouse button when the icon is outside the window and over the desktop. When you release the button, you should see something that looks like Figure 5.7. Select Create Shortcut(s) Here. Figure 5.7 shows the icon dropped on the desktop and the right-click task menu.

You just created a shortcut to ERwin. Double-click the shortcut to open ERwin. Figure 5.8 shows the Platinum ERwin shortcut on the desktop.

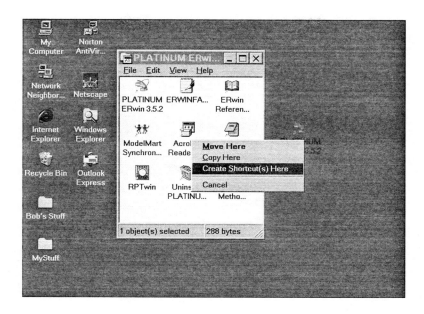

FIGURE 5.7

Selecting Create Shortcut(s) Here produces a shortcut to ERwin on your desktop.

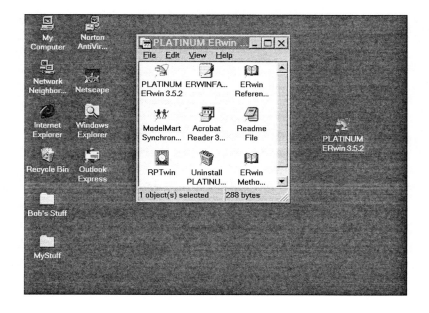

FIGURE 5.8

A Platinum ERwin shortcut is on the desktop along with all my other shortcuts. You can also create folders on your desktop to organize them for quick access. Just drag and drop an icon onto a folder to add it to the folder.

To close ERwin, click the Close button in the upper-right corner. If you have any diagrams open, ERwin asks whether you want to save them before closing.

Figure 5.9 shows ERwin closing with the Close Diagram window.

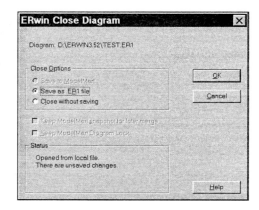

FIGURE 5.9

ERwin Close Diagram dialog provides information on the status of the model—"There are unsaved changes." ERwin recognizes even simple actions, like slightly moving an entity, as a change.

Setting the Modeling Environment

The availability of items on the ERwin menu varies, depending on whether ERwin is in logical or physical model mode. Some menu items are not available in logical mode, and some are not available unless a diagram is loaded. I discuss the ERwin menu in Chapter 6, "Introducing ERwin's Menus and Tools." Here, I explore only the Option menu items.

ERwin has several options you can set that allow you to model in accordance to enterprise modeling standards or to set the environment to your own personal preferences.

In this section, I explore the Option menu items and stored diagram display options. You can specify these options to set the modeling environment for a new model. You can also save your options as a template and reuse the template for setting the options for new models.

Option Menu

From the ERwin menu bar, select Option. Figure 5.10 shows the menu items available. The functionality of each menu item is described in the sections that follow.

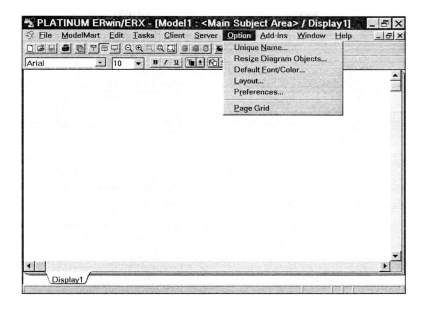

FIGURE 5.10
The Option menu allows you to set some important modeling preferences.

Unique Name

From the Option menu, selecting Unique Name allows you to tell ER*win* how to handle duplicate attribute names. In most instances, it is not advisable to store the same fact in more than one place. You face extra work to keep values in sync as well as the potential for data anomalies. It's important to make sure that the business need for maintaining the same fact in multiple locations is worth the effort.

NOTE

Data anomalies refer to the difficulties in keeping redundant data synchronized during inserts, updates, and deletes when data structures are not normalized.

This is not to say that you should never have attributes with the same name. For example, if every entity in a data model includes an extract date, it is appropriate for every entity to use the same name for the extract date.

Figure 5.11 shows the Unique Name Option dialog, which presents four options:

- Allow—Select to accept the duplicate name without changing it. This is the initial ER*win* default setting.

- Rename—Select to accept the duplicate name but append a forward slash (/) and number after the name. The forward slash provides a visual cue that the name is already in use in the diagram. The number indicates the number of times the name has been used.

- Ask—Select to have ER*win* warn you that a duplicate name exists. You can type a different name or accept the duplicate. Take care—the new name is not checked for uniqueness.

- Disallow—Select to prohibit the use of duplicate names. If you enter a duplicate name, a message box is displayed, stating that the non-unique name is disallowed.

TIP

The Rename or Disallow options are the recommended settings. Selecting either of these options does not allow attributes to have the same name unless they are foreign key attributes.

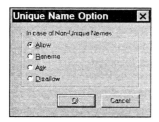

FIGURE 5.11

The Unique Name Option dialog allows you to tell ERwin how to handle duplicate names for attributes.

Resize Diagram Objects

From the Option menu, selecting Resize Diagram Objects allows you to tell ER*win* to make all your entities a specific size or let them resize themselves as needed.

I prefer to let ER*win* auto-size my entities as needed. Selecting the Automatic option for width and height tells ER*win* to increase the size of each entity to accommodate the number of attributes and the attribute with the longest name. Test the feature to see what you think. Figure 5.12 shows the Resize Diagram Objects dialog.

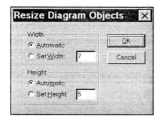

FIGURE 5.12

The Resize Diagram Objects dialog allows you to tell ERwin the width of all entities. You may specify a shorter height, but ERwin will refuse to make entities taller than necessary to display the number of attributes.

Default Font/Color

Default Font/Color lets you change everything about the appearance of every object on your diagram. Some might find this dialog a little intimidating—so many options to choose from. Figure 5.13 shows the All Default Font/Color Editor dialog. The most important things to note follow:

- Default font/color is a property of the object. These global settings are used everywhere the object is used. You cannot assign an entity a different fill color in a stored display or subject area.

- Take care to make a selection in the Apply Settings to options in the lower-left corner. The default is for New Objects Only. Changes to font/color settings are not applied to existing objects unless you select Current Object Pool or All Objects. Always save your work before changing font/color options. I've seen this dialog act up and refuse to change color after changing my mind about entity fill color several times.

- The window inside the dialog that shows a miniature display of the model can be resized and moved around. You can scroll and change settings on several entities without closing the dialog. No visual cue lets you know when you select an entity; simply click the entity. You can zoom out on the model before opening the dialog to reduce the amount of scrolling—a nice feature. I use it a lot.

- The tabs across the top scrollbar allow you to change the display properties of the diagram and every object in the diagram. There is a tab for every possible object that can appear in a diagram. Some of the most used options are not visible when the dialog opens. Figure 5.13 shows the mouse pointer at the scroll control for the object tabs.

- Experiment with the color settings for Entity Fill and Foreign Key. You have to scroll right to find these tabs. Remember to print a test page when you use color. Sometimes, colors are interpreted differently between devices. You can get unexpected results. Take care when using a colored font with a color-filled entity. Some color combinations are difficult to read.

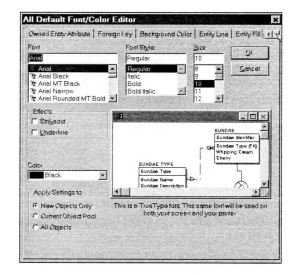

FIGURE 5.13

The All Default Font/Color Editor dialog.

Layout

Selecting the Layout option causes new objects to align according to the grid. I do not use this option often. Figure 5.14 shows the Layout dialog.

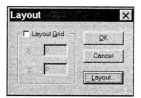

FIGURE 5.14

The Layout dialog box.

Pressing the Layout button asks ER*win* to lay out your diagram for you. Note that you *cannot* undo the choice. I have seen some unexpected arrangements by allowing ER*win* to lay out my diagram. I encourage you to save your diagram before selecting this option, just in case you don't like the results. The rather strong warning about this irreversible selection is shown in Figure 5.15.

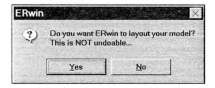

FIGURE 5.15
The ERwin layout warning dialog box.

Preferences

Selecting Preferences shows the dialog in Figure 5.16. The three tabs of options are Editing Option, Methodology, and Display Options.

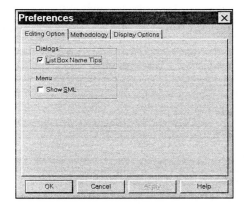

FIGURE 5.16
The Preferences dialog box.

Editing Option

The two editing options are List Box Name Tips and Show SML.

- List Box Name Tips—Selecting this option displays the entire name in a list box, even if the name is wider than the list window. I recommend selecting this option.
- Show SML—Selecting this option adds the Structured Modeling Language (SML) options to the menu. SML options allow you to export SML files. To export a diagram as an SML file, first select SML Report from the Option menu. Open an SML file by selecting File, Open and changing the file type to SML. The SML options do not appear unless Show SML is selected. I do not use this option.

Methodology

ER*win* supports two notation methodologies for logical modeling—IDEF1X and IE—and three for physical modeling—Integration Definition for Information Modeling (IDEF1X), Information Engineering (IE), and dimensional modeling (DM). The default when creating a new diagram is IDEF1X for both logical and physical notation. Although there are considerable differences in the philosophies of these methodologies, in ER*win*, the difference is primarily one of notation.

The methodology selected determines the tools that are available in the toolbox. Entities and relationship tools appear slightly different in the toolbox depending on the methodology selected and whether the model is in logical or physical design mode. Change from IDEF1X to IE, click the Apply button, click the OK button, and note the change in the toolbox.

ER*win* allows the use of different methodology notations for logical and physical models. In this text, I use IE notation for both logical and physical models and include a brief introduction to DM. I prefer IE notation. It seems easier for users to interpret. Figure 5.17 shows the Methodology tab.

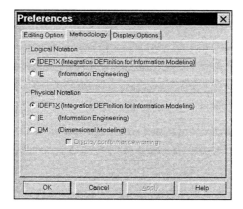

FIGURE 5.17
The Methodology options.

In ER*win*, IDEF1X is the default methodology for new diagrams.

Figure 5.18 shows the logical toolbox for IDEF1X.

FIGURE 5.18
The IDEF1X logical toolbox.

Figure 5.19 shows the physical toolbox for IDEF1X.

FIGURE 5.19
IDEF1X physical toolbox.

Standard IE notation is altered somewhat to leverage some of ER*win*'s features. For example, a solid line can be used to represent identifying relationships and a dotted line used for non-identifying relationships. This does not follow IE notation conventions.

Figure 5.20 shows the logical toolbox for IE methodology.

FIGURE 5.20
The IE logical toolbox.

Figure 5.21 shows the physical toolbox for IE methodology.

FIGURE 5.21
The IE physical toolbox.

DM is a physical modeloption only. Selecting DM notation for your physical model takes advantage of ER*win*'s data warehouse support features. This option enforces star schema diagramming standards. If you use the DIMENS template for your model, DM notation is selected for the physical model.

After choosing DM notation, selecting the Display conformance warnings check box displays warning messages if the dimensional model fails to conform to dimensional modeling rules. ER*win* automatically verifies the relationship and dimensional modeling role for star schema design rules.

Figure 5.22 shows the toolbox for DM methodology.

FIGURE 5.22
The DM toolbox.

Display Options

Display options control how some objects are displayed in the diagram. Figure 5.23 shows the Display Options tab.

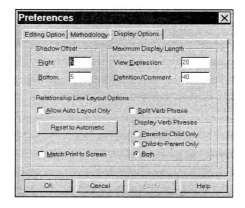

FIGURE 5.23
The Display options.

The following list explains the purpose of each control:

- Shadow Offset—Enter the width for entity and table shadows. Right indicates the shadow to the right of the object. Bottom indicates the shadow beneath the object. The default for each is 5 pixels; I prefer this setting.

- Maximum Display Length—Enter the number of characters to be displayed. This controls the display length of a view column expression (default is 20 characters) and the entity definition and comment text (default is 30 characters).

- Relationship Line Layout Options—Select the layout for relationship lines. I prefer ER*win* to lay out relationship lines and to split relationship verb phrases.

- Display Verb Phrases—Specify the parts of the relationship verb phrase to display. I generally choose to display both.

Page Grid

Selecting Page Grid displays the print grid lines on the diagram to indicate how much of the diagram prints on each page. You can change the page boundary lines by dragging the page lines with the mouse. I seldom use this feature, but I have colleagues who use it frequently.

Diagram Display Options

Diagram display options allow you to organize and present the model in one or more stored displays. Right-click the diagram to set the display options for the current stored display. Be sure to click an empty area; clicking a diagram object opens that object's edit box. Figure 5.24 shows the diagram display options menu. To view all the stored display tabs, from the Window menu option, select Stored Display Tabs.

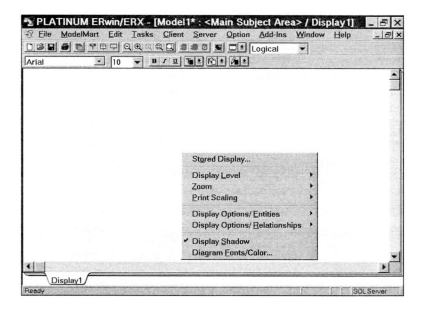

FIGURE 5.24
Diagram display options.

Stored Display

Selecting Stored Display opens the Stored Display Editor dialog box (shown in Figure 5.25) that allows you to set the display options and display level for the current subject area.

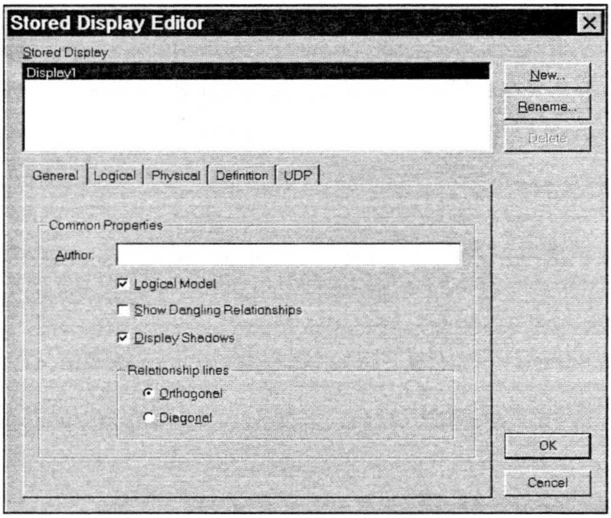

FIGURE 5.25

Stored Display Editor.

You can show multiple displays for a subject area. Figure 5.25 shows the Stored Display dialog with the following options:

- The General tab options let you enter information that applies to all objects in the stored display, both logical and physical:
    - Display1 is the default name. Click the Rename button to rename, or click New to create a new stored display. I encourage modelers to develop and follow standard conventions for naming and defining stored displays.
    - Selecting the Logical Model option indicates that you only want to use the stored display in the logical model.
    - Show Dangling Relationships displays relationship lines on the diagram when the related object is not in the view. Sometimes, letting the dangling relationships show helps users understand the model. Seeing the line gives them a "connecting point."
    - From the Relationship Lines options, select Orthogonal to keep relationship lines as straight lines. Select Diagonal to allow to slanted lines. I prefer Orthogonal.

- The Logical tab options allow you to specify the display level, entity options, and relationship options for the logical view of that stored display. I prefer to display at the attribute level most of the time.

- The Physical tab options let you specify the display level, entity options, and relationship options for the physical view of the stored display. Again, I prefer to display at the attribute level most of the time.

- The Definition tab options allow you to enter a definition for the stored display. I encourage you to add a definition of the reason for the stored display and what is featured within.

- The UDP tab is where you add User Defined Properties to the stored display. User Defined Properties can be anything that assists in managing an ER*win* object. The most common UDP is a "list." Follow naming conventions. Remember that UDPs are not created in the physical database. More on UDPs appears later in Chapter 14, "Advanced Features for the Logical Model."

Display Level

ER*win* has five different display levels to view the logical information about a data model. The different levels display different information about the entities in the diagram. To access the menu, right-click an empty spot in the diagram. You can also select the display level using the icons on the toolbar. Place the mouse pointer over an icon to see a bubble that explains its purpose. Select each and look at the difference in the display. I prefer to display at the attribute level most of the time. Figure 5.26 shows the options available for display level.

Display Options/Entities

Figure 5.27 shows the options list for entity display. Each option displays a different set of information. For large models, I display the main subject area at the entity level and subject areas at the attribute level.

Display Options/Relationships

You must select one of these options to display relationship lines on the diagram. Figure 5.28 shows the list of options available for displaying relationship lines.

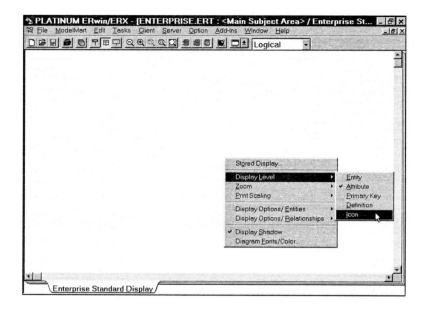

FIGURE 5.26

The Display Level options.

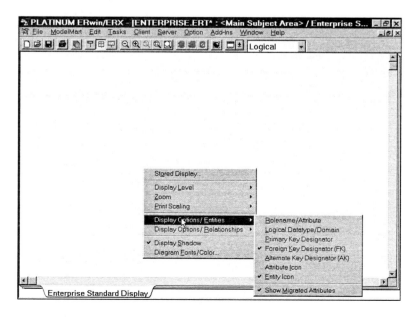

FIGURE 5.27

The Display Options/Entities.

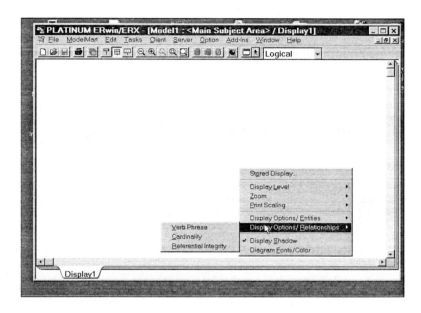

FIGURE 5.28
The Display Options/Relationships.

Best Practice: Using Color for Meaning

Color can add a richness and meaning to the model. I encourage modelers to use color when it improves communication and adds clarity. However, keep in mind that busy, multicolored models can be difficult to read.

The following is a starter list of ideas for using color to enhance models:

- Keep the background for the diagram set to white. This helps entity fill colors and attribute font colors stand out.
- Set the font for migrating foreign keys to red. This makes migrating keys easy to identify.
- Use an entity fill color such as yellow to designate entities that are reused from other models.
- Use a common entity fill color to group entities together.
- Avoid using a color that does not impart meaning.

Experiment and find the uses of color that work well for you, your clients, and your development partners. I encourage you to develop standards and guidelines for using color to convey consistent meaning because it can speed the process and improve communication.

5

GETTING STARTED
WITH ERWIN

The following is a starter list of general guidelines for good data models:

- Keep a white background and use Arial 12-point font.
- Create stored displays for Business and Technical. I created a template to store all my settings.
- Write good names and definitions for all data modeling objects, even if you're the only one who sees it.
- Put entity names in ALL CAPS. Attribute names should use the *object/modifier/class word* standard with lowercase letters.
- Display relationship lines' verb phrases.
- Use the default position and depth for the shadow.
- Set the migrated foreign keys font to red.

Saving a Model

ER*win* can save data model information in several different file types, as shown in Figure 5.29.

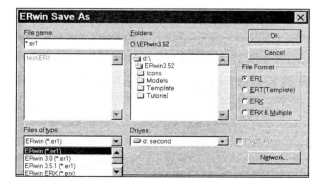

FIGURE 5.29

Save the model.

The Files of type list box in the lower-left corner of the ERwin Save As dialog box provides a list of the file types that can be saved in ER*win*:

- ER1—ER1 is the standard ER*win* diagram file format. Each time an ER1 file is saved, the earlier version is saved as a BK1 file.
- Earlier Version of ER*win*—You can also save the diagram as an earlier ER*win* version. ER*win* version 3.5.2 saves as a 3.0 version or 3.5.1.

- Template—ERT is an ER*win* diagram file saved as a template. This feature is a real time-saver. Open a template and save it as an ER1 to reuse modeling environment settings or even data structures. I discuss templates later in Chapter 6.
- ERX—ERX is a text-based version of the ER*win* diagram file format. ERX files can be opened by other applications, such as word processors. Note that ERX files created with an earlier version of ER*win* should be opened and saved as an ER1 diagram. ERX files saved in older versions of ER*win* might not open in newer versions.

Selecting the ERX save option enables the Expand button. Figure 5.30 shows the options available after you click the Expand button. I explore these options in Chapter 6.

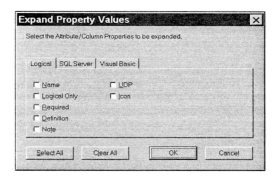

FIGURE 5.30
Expand button options.

- ERX/Multiple—ERX & Multiple is an ER*win* diagram saved in multiple ERX text files, rather than in one large file. Text files are separated into diagram data sections. Separating the ERX file makes editing the file simpler.

Summary

Installing ER*win* is fairly straightforward, provided you have the appropriate system requirements. ER*win* contains several dialogs that allow you to set preferences to customize the modeling environment.

ER*win* offers many rich, powerful features for creating data models. Although each feature will be covered with as much detail as required, only the display options and preferences are explored to any great depth.

ER*win* provides options that allow you to control the appearance of every model object. ER*win* enables you to control the width and height of entities, with the provision that the height cannot be greater than that required to display all the attributes. You can control the font and font size, as well as the color for any text, including attribute and entity display names. You also can control the default color of the lines used to draw the entity boxes and the color that fills the inside of the entity. Take care to use color in ways that make your model easy to read and understand.

In Chapter 6, I explore some of the functionality available in the ER*win* menus. I explain how to open, close and save a model, and introduce some ER*win* editors. The diagram display options and tips for using them effectively also are explained.

Introducing ERwin's Menus and Tools

In the previous chapters, I covered basic modeling concepts and the role of modeling in the development process, installing ERwin, and using options for setting the modeling environment, as well as the options for controlling the appearance of diagram objects. In this chapter, I introduce ERwin's menu options and the tools for creating diagram objects.

In ERwin, a diagram contains a logical and physical model. The logical and physical models share a collection of objects, and may also contain objects that are specific to each. ERwin provides several tools for creating and managing diagram objects. In the sections that follow, I provide a brief introduction to ERwin's work environment and cover the following topics:

- Creating new diagrams in ERwin
- Using templates and file types to create diagrams
- Finding and using ERwin's object editors
- Creating diagram objects using ERwin's toolbox

ER*win* has an editor for every object included in an ER diagram. Each editor can create new objects, as well as set the properties for an existing object. You can create the most commonly used diagram objects using the tools in ER*win*'s toolbox, and then set the object's properties using the appropriate editor. The following sections introduce ER*win*'s menu and tools. This chapter is intended to familiarize you with the functionality and options available, as well as the location of the tools used to create and edit diagram objects. In chapters 9, "Developing the Logical Data Model," and 10, "Building Logical Relationships," we will use ER*win*'s menu options and tools to build a logical model.

Using the ER*win* Menus

The ER*win* menu options vary depending upon the methodology selected (IE, IDEF1X, or DM) and whether the model is in logical or physical mode. This section provides an overview of ER*win*'s menu items focusing on the most commonly used Edit menu items, the model object editors. The use of diagram logical object editors is covered in greater detail in Chapter 9, and the physical object editors are covered in Chapter 16, "Building the Physical Model in ER*win*."

File Menu Options

The ER*win* File menu follows Windows standards for content, with the addition of some options specific to modeling that allow ER*win* to interact with other development tools. Figure 6.1 shows the File menu items. Er*win* has a "smart" Save function that knows when to make itself available. The Save item is available only when the current diagram changes.

Creating a New Diagram

When you launch ER*win*, a blank diagram is automatically created using ER*win*'s default options. As I discussed in Chapter 5, "Getting Started with Er*win*," you can use the set diagram properties.

Selecting New on the File menu, clicking the New button on the ER*win* Toolbar, and selecting Reverse Engineer on the Tasks menu all allow you to select a template from the list in the ER*win* Template Selection dialog.

Using ER*win* Templates

In ER*win*, templates can store diagram objects, or display settings and preferences. You can save any model as a template to preserve its settings and contents for reuse in creating other data models. Templates provide powerful support for maintaining a consistent look and feel across all data models, since you can use them to create new diagrams.

Introducing ERwin's Menus and Tools

CHAPTER 6

117

6

INTRODUCING
ERwin's MENUS
AND TOOLS

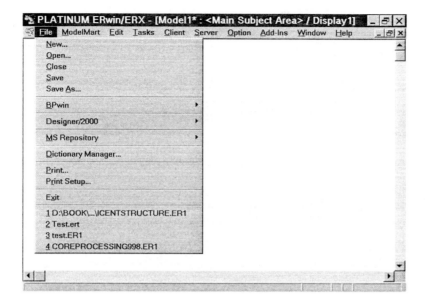

FIGURE 6.1

ERwin's File menu provides some standard Windows functions, with the addition of options that allows ERwin to interact with other tools.

Creating a new diagram from a template gives you a head start in adding objects, settings, and preferences. All the diagram objects (entities, attributes, relationships, and so on), preferences, and display settings in the template are automatically applied to the new diagram. Figure 6.2 shows the ERwin Template Selection dialog.

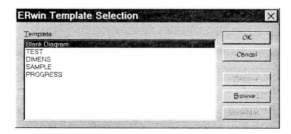

FIGURE 6.2

ERwin template selections that come bundled with the tool provide a good starter set that you can tailor to meet the special needs of the enterprise.

NOTE

The list of templates shown in Figure 6.2 is delivered with ERwin. They provide good examples of what can be included in the templates you create. You can modify and enhance these templates to support the particular needs of your enterprise.

You can save any ERwin diagram as a template, by selecting the Save As option and selecting ERwin Template (*.ert). Use the template to create new diagrams.

Selecting Blank Diagram creates a new diagram using the following ERwin default settings:

- Start in logical model mode.
- Allow non-unique names.
- Resize diagram objects automatically.
- Use the IDEFX1 methodology for logical and physical models.
- Show the main subject area and Display1 stored display.

Selecting DIMENS creates a new diagram with the following settings:

- Start in physical model mode.
- The client is PowerBuilder.
- The server is Oracle.
- Allow non-unique names.
- Resize diagram objects automatically.
- Use the DM methodology for the physical model with display conformance warnings.
- Use the IDEF1X methodology for the logical model.
- Show the main subject area and two stored displays, tables, and columns.

Selecting PROGRESS creates the new diagram with the following settings:

- Start in physical model mode.
- The client is PowerBuilder with validation rules and defaults.
- The server is Progress with predefined triggers, a stored procedure template, and scripts for preprocessing and post-processing.
- Rename non-unique names.
- Resize diagram objects automatically.
- Use the IDEF1X methodology for both logical and physical models.
- Show the main subject area and two stored displays, tables, and columns.

Introducing ERwin's Menus and Tools

CHAPTER 6

119

6

INTRODUCING
ERwin's MENUS
AND TOOLS

Using File Types to Create and Save Diagrams

Using the File menu options Open, Save and Save As, ERwin allows you to open and save data model information in several different file types. When you open certain file types, ERwin automatically reverse engineers the file and creates a data model.

The file types you can open and use to create a diagram in ERwin are shown in the list box in the lower-left corner of the Open File dialog. They are

- ERwin (*.er1)—The standard ERwin diagram file format. Each time an ER1 file is saved, the earlier version is saved as a BK1 file.

- ERwin (*.ert)—An ERwin diagram file saved as a template. This feature is a real time-saver. Open a template and save it as an ER1 to reuse modeling environment settings or even data structures.

- SQL DDL (*.sql, *.ers)—A Data Definition Language schema script text file. ERwin reads the DDL and automatically reverse engineers the database to create a data model diagram. Note that *.ers is an ERwin physical database schema script text file.

- Access Database (*.mdb)—A Microsoft Access database. ERwin automatically reverse engineers the database and creates a data model diagram. Note that you might need to enter admin as the user, even if you do not specify a user and password for the MDB.

- DBF (*.dbf)—A dBASE database file. ERwin automatically reverse engineers the database and creates a data model diagram.

- Progress 4GL (*.df)—A Progress data definition text file. ERwin automatically reverse engineers the database defined in the text file and creates a data model diagram.

- Import from BPwin (*.bpx)—A text file created using Platinum's BPwin business process modeling tool. This file contains entity, attribute, and activity names from a BPwin model. ERwin reads the text file to import the BPwin model.

- SML Script (*.mps, *.sml)—A Structured Modeling Language text file that defines an ER diagram. SML defines models in much the same way that DDL (Data Definition Language) defines physical data structures. SML allows models to be imported by tools that support SML format.

ERwin also allows you to save data model information as a previous version of ERwin, an ERwin template, or as an ERX file. An ERX file is a text file that contains the diagram objects. These files can be imported into several other tools, including BPwin, ERwin's process modeling tool.

The Files of Type list box in the lower-left corner of the Save As dialog provides the list of the file types that you can save in ERwin. Note that ERwin has a "smart" Save function that automatically presents Save As for new diagrams.

> ### TIP
>
> Use standard naming conventions when naming and saving ER*win* models. I recommend names of the form *object/modifier/development stage—object* is the primary business name, *modifier* is the business intent, and *development stage* is design, development, or implementation. This naming convention supports a phased development approach.

To close the current diagram, select Close item on the File menu or click the close button in the upper-right corner of the diagram display window.

Notice the following options:

- Save as .ER1 file—Click this selection to save the diagram as an ER1 file before closing. If the diagram is a new one that you have not saved before, you see the Save As dialog.
- Close without saving—Click this selection to close the diagram without saving it.
- Status—Provides a message indicating whether the diagram has unsaved changes.

Introducing Object Editors

Er*win*'s Edit menu contains options for opening the editors for the diagram objects. Some menu options vary or become unavailable when you switch between the logical and physical models. Figure 6.3 shows the items that are available for both logical and physical models.

The first two menu items let you toggle between logical model and physical model edit mode. Click your selection, and a check appears as a visual cue to the left of the active mode.

The Domain Dictionary Editor allows you to define new domains with logical and physical properties for reuse as independent attributes and independent columns. This editor also lets you modify the properties of user-defined domains. You can also modify all the properties of the five standard domains in ER*win*, with the exception of domain name and domain parent. I discuss creating domains with the Domain Dictionary Editor in Chapter 14, "Advanced Features for the Logical Model."

Using the UDP Editor allows you to define custom properties and attach them to ER*win* model objects. User-defined properties (UDPs) let you add details that are more descriptive and tailored to meet your needs. One of the most commonly used UDPs is List, which allows you to provide a pick list of values.

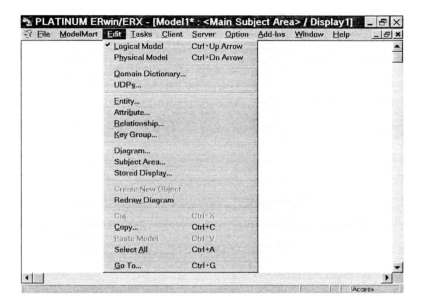

FIGURE 6.3
The Edit menu provides access to the editors you use to set properties for diagram objects, as well as Windows edit functions.

A user-defined property can be any useful or important information about an ERwin object. A UDP can be attached to an object using its editor but cannot be shared across logical and physical models. All of the ERwin object editors have a UDP tab that allows you to set values for UDPs attached to the object, or to open the UDP editor to create a new value. All the tabs function the same way.

When creating a UDP, perform the following steps:

1. Name the UDP. Click the plus signs in the next open name field. If you do not enter a name, ERwin assigns a default name of UDP. Each successive UDP is named UDP#, wherein # is the next available consecutive number. I encourage the use of good conventions for naming and defining UDPs. As with all modeling objects, writing good names and definitions is a best practice.

2. Select the datatype. Click in the Type field to get a list of UDP datatypes. Note that you can select Command as a datatype and attach an executable as the default. The object to which the UDP is attached displays a button with the UDP name that, when pressed, launches the default application. You'll read more about this in Chapter 14.

3. Add default values. Default values are optional for some datatypes. However, the List data type requires a list of default values. Separate the list items with commas. The default item in a list is preceded by a tilde (~). Default values can be an invitation to erroneous data or a real time-saver. Take care that your defaults add value.

4. Add a definition. Do it, do it, do it. I cannot place too much emphasis on including definitions with all modeling objects. The value of UDPs will likely be lost if you do not write good names and definitions.

It is important to note that UDPs do not translate into physical database objects. That is, they are not created in the database. UDPs are tools that allow you to more easily manage a data model. In Chapter 14, I present examples of creating and using UDPs.

Like most menu items in ER*win*, the object editor items differ according to whether the diagram is in logical or physical mode. If you are viewing the logical model, the items are Entity, Attribute, Relationship, and Key Group. In physical mode, the items are Table, Column, Relationship, Index, and View. Diagram, Subject Area, and Stored Display are available for both logical and physical models.

NOTE

In addition to selecting the editor from the Edit menu, you can right-click a diagram object to get the shortcut menu for that object, or double-click an object to open the editor last used.

Each ER*win* object has its own editor. All the editors function in much the same way. All allow you to enter a name, definition, note, and UDP, in addition to the properties specific to that model object. The editors are introduced here and explored in detail in Chapter 9.

Some ER*win* editors span the logical and physical models. Properties set using these editors are reflected in both logical and physical modes:

- Diagram—The Diagram Editor allows you to enter a name, author name, definition, target server, and version, and then attach UDPs. I encourage modelers to provide detailed information about the diagram and consider doing so a best practice.

- Subject Area—The Subject Area Editor allows you to enter a name, author name, and definition; specify the objects that will be members; and attach UDPs. Provide detailed information about subject areas and consider doing so a best practice. Note that every diagram has a <Main Subject Area> that contains all the objects for the diagram. You cannot rename or delete this subject area.

- Stored Display—The Stored Display Editor allows you to enter a name, author name, and definition; specify the logical and physical objects that will be members; and attach UDPs. Provide detailed information about stored displays and consider doing so a best practice. Note that every diagram contains a default stored display called Display1. Rename this stored display with a more meaningful name, even if the model has only a single stored display.

Introducing the Logical Object Editors

ERwin's logical object editors allow you to create, edit, delete, and add properties to the logical model objects. The logical model objects are

- Entity—The Entity Editor allows you to enter the name and definition, attach an icon, attach a UDP, and add sample values or queries as notes.
- Attribute—The Attribute Editor allows you to enter the name, definition, and domain; attach a note; attach a UDP; and designate the primary keys and key groups.
- Relationship—The Relationship Editor allows you to enter the verb phrase, cardinality, definition, role name, relational integrity (RI) actions, and UDP.
- Key Group—The Key Group Editor allows you to specify the members of the key group, designate the key type, add a definition and note, and attach UDPs.

Introducing the Physical Object Editors

ERwin's physical object editors allow you to create, edit, delete, and add properties to the physical model objects. The physical model objects are

- Table—The Entity Editor allows you to enter the name, comment, owner, and volumetrics; attach a UDP and validation rules; and then add preprocessing and post-processing script templates. Note that the list box with column names appears to have no functionality. You can highlight the column names, but you cannot perform any actions.
- Column—The Column Editor allows you to enter the name, comment, platform server datatype, nullity, and domain; attach a UDP; and designate the index members.
- Relationship—The Relationship Editor allows you to enter the foreign key constraint name, cardinality, type, nullity, comment, and relational integrity (RI) actions, and to attach UDPs.
- Index—The Index Editor allows you to specify the members of the index group, specify the platform specific properties of the index, designate the key type, add a comment, and attach UDPs.

- View—The View Editor allows you to specify the columns of the view (on the Select tab) and the tables that supply the columns (on the From tab). You can also constrain the rows in the view (on the Where tab), view the SQL that will populate the view, add a comment and script templates, and attach UDPs. To populate the column availability in the Select tab, you must first select tables to include using the From tab.

Additional Editing Features

ERwin uses many Windows standard features to allow you to perform edit functions using familiar Windows terms with the following functionality:

- The Redraw Diagram option refreshes the diagram.
- Cut is only available if an entity or relationship is selected. If an object is selected, the type of the selected object (entity or relationship) is added to the menu item. Select an entity by clicking, and select one of the following:
    - Remove from Subject Area—Selecting this option removes the object from the subject area, but it still remains present in the model.
    - Delete from Model—Selecting this option removes the object from the model. You can select Copy to Clipboard for pasting it later.
- To Copy an object, select an entity by clicking, and choose one of the following:
    - Model—Selecting this option copies only the object selected to the ERwin clipboard. You can paste the object into another diagram.
    - Picture—Selecting this option copies the entire model as a metafile or bitmap.
- Selecting Paste Model pastes the objects from the ERwin clipboard to the current diagram or a new diagram.
- Choosing Select All selects every object in the current diagram. This is a handy option.
- In the list of the Go To Entity dialog, shown in Figure 6.4, selecting the entity name finds and selects that entity in the current diagram. This feature saves you from having to search for an entity in a large model. Show Table Names is a toggle that shows the physical table names or the logical entity names.

TIP

You can also use the standard Ctrl+C, Ctrl+X, and Ctrl+V hotkeys to copy, cut, and paste model objects to ERwin's clipboard.

Introducing ER*win*'s Menus and Tools

CHAPTER 6

125

6

INTRODUCING
ER*WIN*'S MENUS
AND TOOLS

FIGURE 6.4
ERwin's Go To Entity dialog allows you to select an entity from a list of all the entities in the model and make it the current entity. This feature can help locate a specific entity in a large model.

Other Menu Options

I provide an overview of the remaining ER*win* menu items in this section and cover them in detail in later sections. I discuss logical modeling tasks in Chapter 7, "Reverse Engineeering and Report Generation in ER*win*," and physical modeling tasks in Chapter 19, "Delivering the Physical Data Model." I discuss the client and server options in Chapter 16.

Logical Tasks

The logical tasks addressed in detail in Chapter 7 are

- Reverse Engineer—ER*win* can interpret the information in your database or script file and automatically create logical and physical models. You can edit or enhance the resulting diagram as needed. You can reverse engineer all or part of an existing database. The quality of a reverse-engineered logical model varies depending on the amount of logical information carried in the physical schema.

- Generate Reports—ER*win* has a robust set of reporting capabilities. You can report on any object class in a diagram. ER*win* includes a set of standard reports, and you can create custom reports as well. You can explore reporting in Chapter 13, "Delivering the Logical Data Model."

Physical Tasks

The physical tasks addressed in detail in Chapter 19 are

- Forward Engineer/Schema Generation—ER*win* can create the physical data structures from the physical model, including tables, columns, triggers, stored procedures, and platform-specific database objects. You can connect ER*win* to the target server and create the data structures directly in the database. Or you can generate a DDL script that is run as a separate step on the server to create the data structures.

- Reverse Engineer—As described in the preceding section, ER*win* can interpret the information in your database or script file and automatically create logical and physical models.

- Update Model—ER*win* can update an existing model by connecting to a target database, reading a DDL script, or reading an ER1 or ERX file. ER*win* makes any changes necessary for synchronization. You then have the option to selectively undo the changes made. You can also document the changes by printing a report of the differences. Note that the existing *model* is changed, not the database or the ER1 or ERX file to which the comparison is being made.

- Alter Database—ER*win* can alter a database by connecting to a target database and making the changes directly, generating a DDL script, or reading an ER1 or ERX file. You also have the option to document the changes by printing a report of the differences. Note that you must use an existing database, DDL script file, or ER*win* data model with which to compare.

- Complete Compare—ER*win* can make bi-directional changes to a model and alter a database. ER*win* reports the differences and gives you the option to change the model or to alter the database by connecting to a target database and making the changes directly, generating a DDL script, or reading an ER1 or ERX file. You also have the option to document the changes by printing a report of the differences. Note that you must compare the changes to an existing database, DDL script file, or ER*win* data model.

- Generate Reports—ER*win* has a robust set of reporting capabilities. You can report on any object class in a diagram. ER*win* includes a set of standard reports, and you can create custom reports as well. You can further explore reporting in Chapter 13.

The Client and Server Menu Options

The Client menu option is only available when a model is open and in the physical mode. Selecting the Target Client item allows you to specify the client (application) development environment. The items in the menu vary, depending upon the target client selected. You can select PowerBuilder, Visual Basic, or None as the client development platform. Selecting PowerBuilder also allows you to select the version of PowerBuilder and the library (PBL file) to store the data windows ER*win* generates.

Introducing ERwin's Menus and Tools

CHAPTER 6

127

6

INTRODUCING
ERwin's MENUS
AND TOOLS

I further explain the Target Client feature in Chapter 16. In the modeling activities in this text, I use the None option.

The Server menu option is only available when a model is open and in the physical mode. The menu items vary, depending upon the target server selected.

Selecting the Target Server item allows you to specify the database (RDBMs) platform. You can select the target server anytime; it need not be selected before you build a logical model. However, if you select the target server before working on the physical model, ERwin provides DBMS-specific datatypes and name-length warnings. I consider this a best practice.

The Add-In menu option allows you to launch other applications from within the ERwin work environment. An add-in is a secondary software application that you can use with a primary software application. An add-in application is one developed by a third party to perform specific tasks that cannot be performed by the primary software application. A full discussion of add-ins is beyond the scope of this book.

Workplace Display Options

The Window menu options allow you to show or hide some of the tool components available for an ERwin diagram window. The following list describes the items on the Window menu:

- Stored Display Tabs—Shows or hides the stored display tabs.
- Toolbar—Shows or hides the ERwin toolbar.
- Font & Color Toolbar—Shows or hides the ERwin Font and Color toolbar.
- Status Bar—Shows or hides the status bar.
- Independent Attribute/Column Browser—Shows or hides the Independent Attribute Browser dialog when the diagram is in logical mode, or the Independent Column Browser when the diagram is in physical mode. Since the model is in logical mode, Figure 6.5 shows the Independent Attribute Browser.
- ERwin Toolbox—Shows or hides the ERwin toolbox.
- Cascade—Arranges diagrams such that the windows overlap one another.
- Tile Horizontal—Arranges several diagrams such that the client areas are parallel to one another.
- Tile Vertical—Arranges diagrams such that the client areas appear stacked up and down.

Figure 6.5 shows the menu items available in the Window menu.

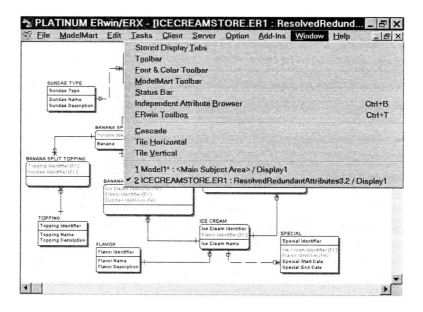

FIGURE 6.5

Using the ERwin Window menu options allows you to select the toolbars, toolboxes, and display options for the model-ing environment.

Introducing the ER*win* Toolbox

In Chapter 5, I discussed how the mode and methodology selection affects the appearance of the tools available in the ER*win* Toolbox. This section reviews the toolbox, providing an overview of what each tool does. The ER*win* toolbox contains the tools that perform common tasks such as creating an entity, a table, or a relationship. Details of using each tool are covered in Chapters 9 and 16.

NOTE

If the toolbox is not visible in the diagram window, examine the Window options to be sure that ERwin Toolbox is checked.

The appearance of the tools in the toolbox changes when you switch methodologies from IDEF1X to IE notation. Some of tools change depending on whether the edit mode is logical or physical. The following tools are available in the toolbox regardless of the methodology selected or whether the model is in logical or physical mode:

- Pointer—Use the pointer to select a diagram object. Simply click the object to select it.
- Multiple Select—Hold down the Shift key and click each object you want to select more than a single diagram object. Or use the pointer to draw a selection box around a group of entities, as shown in Figure 6.6. A diagram object must lie completely within the selection box to be selected.
- Using the Hand—The hand can move entities if you click the diagram object (entity and relationship) and drag the object to a new position. The hand also moves and copies attributes. To move an attribute from one entity to another, select the attribute by clicking it. Then, holding down the left mouse button, drag the attribute to the new entity and drop it. Note that a line in the entity indicates the position where the new attribute will be placed. To copy an attribute from one entity to another, select the attribute by clicking it. Then, holding down the Control key and the left mouse button, drag the attribute to the new entity and drop it. Note that a line in the entity indicates the position where the copy of the attribute will be placed.

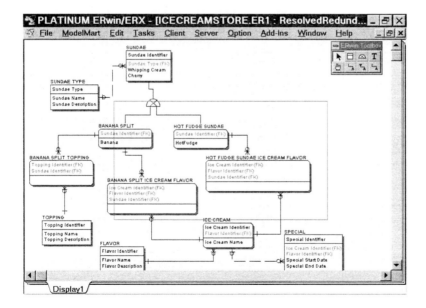

FIGURE 6.6

You can select multiple diagram objects by using the pointer to draw a box around a group of objects, or by holding down the Shift key and clicking your choices. Only HOT FUDGE SUNDAE and HOT FUDGE SUNDAE ICE CREAM FLAVOR are selected here because they are the only ones completely within the selection box.

ER*win* toolbox tools appear slightly different depending on the methodology and the edit mode. The toolbox for IE and IDEF1X uses slightly different notation, but in ER*win*, each tool creates a similar diagram object, with the exception of subtype relationships. Subtype relationships have a slightly different meaning in the two methodologies. The following section explains the concepts represented in each. Figure 6.7 shows the logical toolbox using IE methodology. Figure 6.8 shows the logical toolbox for IDEF1X.

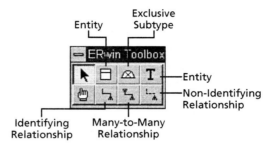

FIGURE 6.7

IE toolbox contains the tools for creating logical model objects using ERwin's representation of the IE notation.

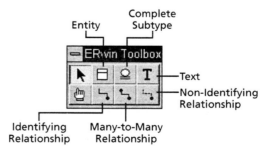

FIGURE 6.8

IDEF1X toolbox contains the tools for creating logical model objects using ERwin's representation the IDEF1X notation.

The Textbox Tool is the same regardless of the methodology selected. Adding text blocks to an ER*win* diagram can improve clarity and help clients identify diagram objects. Text blocks can include any text, such as the author name, diagram version numbers, notes, titles, and captions.

To create a text block, click the Textbox Tool in the ER*win* toolbox and click the diagram. The new text block is created and ready to accept text.

NOTE	

Within the text block, you can press the Enter key to create line breaks. You can use any keyboard character but the tab.

To edit an existing text block, right-click the text block to use the Text Block Editor. Read more about text blocks in Chapter 11, "Organizing and Enhancing the Logical Data Model."

Using the Entity/Table Tool

The Independent Entity/Table Tool creates dependent and independent entities in the logical model, and tables in the physical model. An entity is independent or dependent depending on the type of relationships it has with other entities. An entity is always independent when it is first created. Independent entities appear as rectangles with sharp corners.

ERwin decides whether an entity is dependent based on the relationship type at the time the relationship is created. A dependent entity appears as a rectangle with rounded corners. As long as the entity tool is selected, clicking on the diagram creates an entity.

NOTE	

When the entity tool is selected, the cursor is represented by cross hairs with a tiny entity icon.

Using Relationship Tools

Use the Identifying Relationship Tool to create a relationship between two entities in the logical model, or two tables in the physical model. An identifying relationship is a relationship between two entities or tables in which the attribute values of a child are defined by the value of the primary key of a parent. In other words, the child is dependent on the parent for its identity, and an instance, or row, of the child cannot exist without an instance of the parent. An instance, or row, in the parent is related to multiple instances, or rows, in the child.

To create an identifying relationship, click the Identifying Relationship Tool in the ERwin toolbox, click the parent, and then click the child. To edit the relationship, right-click the relationship line to use the Relationship Editor. You'll read more about relationships in Chapter 10.

Use the Many-to-Many Relationship Tool to create a relationship between two entities in the logical model. Many-to-many relationships do not exist in the physical model. A many-to-many relationship is a relationship between two entities in which multiple instances of the first entity can be related to multiple instances of the second entity, and vice versa. To create a many-to-many relationship, click the Many-To-Many Relationship tool in the ERwin toolbox, click one entity, and then click another entity. The order is not important, as there is no parent to child relationship in a many-to-many relationship. To edit the relationship, right-click the relationship line and use the Relationship Editor.

Use the Non-Identifying Relationship Tool to create a relationship between two entities in the logical model, and two tables in the physical model. A non-identifying relationship is a relationship between two entities/tables in which the primary key of one entity/table migrates as a non-key attribute in another entity/table. The value of the migrated attribute is dependent on the value of the primary key of the entity/table to which it migrated. To create a non-identifying relationship, click the Non-Identifying Relationship Tool in the ERwin toolbox, click the parent entity/table, and then click the child entity/table. To edit the relationship, right-click on the relationship line and open the Relationship Editor.

Using the Subtype Relationship Tool

In ERwin, in much the same way that all entities are created independent, all subtype relationships begin as an exclusive subtype relationship. To create a subtype relationship, select the Subtype Relationship Tool, click the parent entity, and then click the child entity. For subsequent child entities, select the Subtype Relationship Tool (if it is not already selected), click the subtype relationship symbol, and then click the child entity.

The Exclusive Subtype Tool is in the ERwin IE logical toolbox. Note that you must use the subtype relationship editor to change the subtype Type to inclusive. You'll find more on creating subtype relationships in Chapter 9.

The Complete Subtype Tool is in the ERwin IDEF1X logical toolbox. The process is similar to subtype relationships in IE; you also use the subtype relationship editor to change the subtype Type from complete to incomplete. Although subtype notation is represented in a similar manner for IE and IDEF1X, there is a significant difference in the definition of complete/incomplete and exclusive/inclusive. I provide details of the differences in Chapter 10.

Physical Toolbox

The ERwin physical toolbox provides the same tools to create diagram objects as the logical toolbox, with the exception of the View and View Relationship tools. The notation is slightly different for IE, IDEF1X, and DM methodologies, but the diagram objects created are the same. Note that subtype relationships are not supported in the physical view. Figure 6.9 shows the physical toolbox using IE methodology. Figure 6.10 shows the physical toolbox using IDEF1X methodology.

Introducing ERwin's Menus and Tools

CHAPTER 6

133

6

INTRODUCING
ERwin's MENUS
AND TOOLS

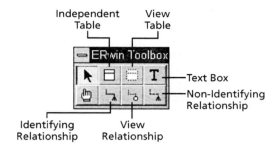

FIGURE 6.9

IE physical toolbox contains the tools for creating physical model objects using ERwin's representation of IE notation.

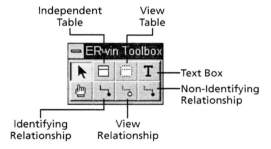

FIGURE 6.10

IDEF1X physical toolbox contains the tools for creating physical model objects using ERwin's representation of IDEF1X notation.

A *view* is an SQL query that is permanently stored in the database under an assigned name. The result of the view query is a virtual table that exists only while it is being used. A view looks like a physical table with a set of named columns and rows of data, but a view is not permanently stored in the database like a table. Instead, the rows and columns of data in the view are the results returned by the query that defines the view.

To create a view, click the View Table Tool and click the diagram. To add attributes, use the View Relationship Tool or right-click the View diagram object to use the View Editor. Use the View Relationship Tool to create a relationship between a parent entity and a view. To add attributes to the view, click the View Relationship Tool in the ERwin Toolbox. You can also right-click the view diagram object to use the View Editor.

DM Physical Toolbox

The toolbox for DM physical is available if DM is selected for the physical modeling methodology on the Option, Methodology tab. Figure 6.11 shows the toolbox using DM methodology.

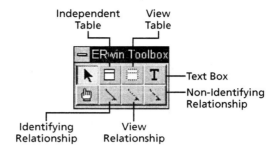

FIGURE 6.11

DM physical toolbox contains tools that support dimensional modeling. Dimensional modeling is often used in the decision support environment.

Summary

In ER*win*, a diagram contains logical and physical models. The logical and physical models share a collection of objects, and there also are objects that are specific to each. ER*win* supports two methodologies for logical modeling, Information Engineering (IE) and Integration Definition for Information Modeling (IDEF1X), and three methodologies for physical modeling, IE, IDEF1X, and Dimensional (DM). ER*win*'s work environment provides menu options and tools that allow you to create and manage the properties for diagram objects. The menus and tools in ER*win* have different options depending on whether the diagram is in logical or physical mode, and which methodology is selected.

When you launch ER*win*, a blank diagram is automatically created using a set of default options. You can immediately begin creating diagram objects in the blank diagram, reverse engineer a model by opening one of a set of file types supported, or use a template. One way to reverse engineer a model is to use the Open option on the File menu and select one of the file types listed. ER*win* will automatically create a model from the file selected. Another option for creating a new diagram is to use a template that contains a set of options, preferences, and model objects. To create a new model diagram using a template, select the New option on the File menu and select a template from the ones delivered with ER*win*. You can modify the templates delivered with ER*win*, or save any existing ER*win* model as a template. Templates can be used to give all your models a consistent look and feel.

Logical object editors allow you to manage the properties of logical model objects, such as entities and attributes. Physical object editors allow you to manage the properties of physical objects, such as tables and columns. In addition to managing properties, each editor also enables you to create new objects. You can open an editor by selecting one of the options on the Edit menu, right-clicking an object and accessing the shortcut menu, or double-clicking an object to open the most recently accessed editor for that object.

The ERwin Toolbox tools allow you to quickly create the most commonly used model objects. The Pointer Tool allows you to select one or more diagram objects. The Hand Tool allows you to copy or move attributes or columns between entities and tables. The Text Box Tool allows you to add one or more containers of text to the diagram. Text boxes can add clarity and under- standing to a model diagram. The appearance and availability of the other tools in the ERwin Toolbox vary, depending on whether the diagram is in logical or physical mode, and which methodology is selected. In logical mode, you can add entities and identifying, non-identify- ing, many-to-many, or subtype relationships. The appearance and meaning of the subtype rela- tionship symbol depends on which methodology is selected, IE or IDEF1X. In physical mode, you can add tables and identifying and non-identifying relationships, as well as views and view relationships.

ERwin's workplace menu also includes a Tasks option that contains a set of activities, only two of which are available when the diagram is in logical mode. In Chapter 7, I introduce these two topics, Reverse Engineering and Generate Reports. Reverse engineering allows you to cre- ate a model using an existing database, or certain file types. Generate Reports allows you to report on the objects and properties within an ERwin diagram.

Reverse Engineering and Report Generation in ER*win*

In the previous chapters, I introduced basic modeling concepts and the role of modeling in the development process, installing ER*win*, and using options for setting the modeling environment, including the options for controlling the appearance of diagram objects. In the Chapter 6, "Introducing ER*win*'s Menus and Tools," I provided an overview of ER*win*'s menu options, object editors, and tools for creating diagram objects in the logical and physical models. In this chapter, I cover two of ER*win*'s most powerful features, Reverse Engineer and Generate Reports.

In the sections that follow, I explore the following topics:

- Reverse Engineering
- Using the Report Browser

When the diagram is in logical model mode, the Tasks menu contains two available tasks, Reverse Engineer and Generate Reports. The Reverse Engineer menu option allows you to create a model using an existing database or database schema file. The Generate Reports option allows you to produce reports on the diagram objects and their properties.

Understanding Reverse Engineering

In ER*win*, *reverse engineering* allows you create a model diagram of an existing database. Most enterprises today are using databases to support business critical functions that have little or no design documentation. Many did not use a graphical data modeling tool to document the design decisions or follow a set of defined standards and guidelines, as these tools are fairly new. Perhaps the database was delivered as part of an off-the-shelf, purchased application, or the database for a developed application was not recorded using a graphical data modeling tool. Reverse engineering allows you to create a model that can be used to provide a foundation for planned enhancements, or simply to enhance understanding of the underlying data structures that support a software application.

ER*win* can reverse engineer a model using information in your database or script file and automatically create logical and physical model diagrams. You can then use ER*win*'s tools to edit or enhance the resulting diagrams as needed.

Physical database objects that are reverse-engineered include

- Tables
- Columns
- Datatype and length
- Triggers
- Stored procedures
- Validation rules
- Comments

Some database platforms support reverse engineering better than others do. The quality of a reverse-engineered logical model depends on the amount of logical information carried in the physical schema.

Note

It is important to remember that a reverse-engineered model is a physical model. The logical model needs work. Logical names are abbreviated physical names, and physical comments for tables and columns are often limited or absent.

ER*win* allows you to reverse engineer a diagram using the following methods:

- Connecting to a database
- Reading a script file
- Opening a file

ER*win* automatically selects the target server when you reverse engineer using one of these options. Of course, you have the option of changing the target server after the diagram is generated. Other than the selection of the method, the reverse-engineering process is the same whether you use a database connection or a script, or open a file.

ER*win* supports direct connection for some database platforms such as Access, Sybase, and Oracle. For others, such as Progress, DB2, and Informix, an ODBC data source is required. The process for creating an ODBC data source is explained in Chapter 19, "Delivering the Physical Data Model."

7

REVERSE
ENGINEERING
AND REPORTS

NOTE

An initial ODBC connection to DB2 might take a considerable amount of time because DB2 performs a one-time binding operation. Subsequent connections take much less time.

Also note that you might need to enter a password to connect to an Access database, even if a password was not specified. In such a case, use admin as the password.

Reverse engineering using a script requires you to enter the name of the script. Note that the file type is set to look for files of type *.sql or *.ers.

ER*win* automatically reverse engineers certain file types when you open them. To reverse engineer a diagram by opening a file type, select the Open option from the File menu and select a file type from the drop-down list of file types supported by ER*win*.

You may also reverse engineer a model by selecting the New option from the File menu or Reverse Engineer from the Tasks menu and performing the following steps:

1. Select a template.
2. Select a target server.
3. Set the reverse-engineering options.

Selecting a Template

In ER*win*, templates can store diagram objects, display settings, and preferences. You can save any model as a template to preserve its settings and contents for reuse in creating other data models. Templates provide powerful support for maintaining a consistent look and feel across all data models. After you save a template, you can use it as the basis for creating new diagrams.

ER*win* includes four templates that you can use "as is" or customize to meet your standards:

- A blank diagram
- PROGRESS
- DIMENS
- SAMPLE

None of the templates supplied contains entities or attributes. Each contains display settings and preferences for some options. All except the blank diagram contain examples that illustrate ER*win*'s support for producing the physical database for specific database platforms.

If you're not sure how to start, use the blank diagram. It is important to note that the blank diagram uses the last selected options for some preferences. Figure 7.1 shows the ERwin Template Selection dialog.

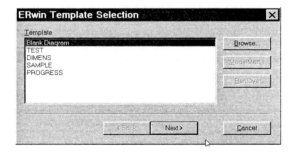

FIGURE 7.1

ERwin delivers a set of template selections. These templates can be modified or enhanced to support the particular needs of your enterprise.

Selecting the Target Server

Selecting the target server allows you to specify the database (RDBMS) platform. The target server selected determines the reverse-engineering options available.

The Select Target Server dialog, shown in Figure 7.2, offers the following options:

- Target SQL DBMS—Selecting one of the database platforms in this section allows you to use an SQL script in addition to a database connection to create a data model. Select the target server by clicking the option button next to the target server name.

- Target Desktop DBMS—Selecting one of the database platforms in this section allows you to connect to an existing database to create a data model. Select the target server by clicking the option button next to the target server name.

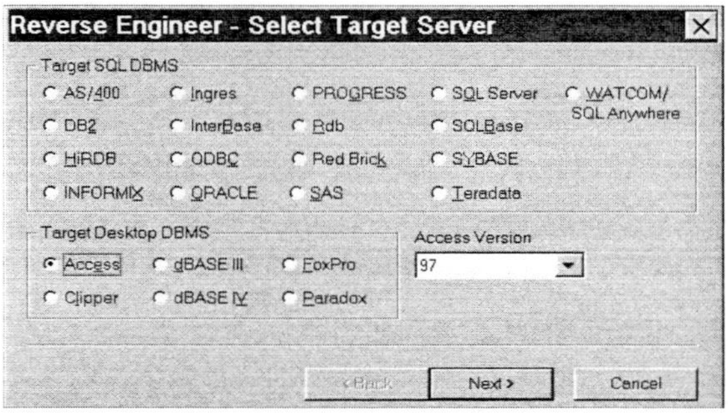

FIGURE 7.2
Selecting a target server allows ERwin to tailor the physical options using the properties of the selected data-base, including datatypes, nullity options, indexes, triggers, and stored procedures using the appropriate syntax.

Setting Reverse-Engineering Options

ER*win* allows you to select the database objects to be reverse engineered, as well as choosing the option of reverse engineering by connecting to an existing database or by reading a script file using the dialog shown in Figure 7.3. Note that the script option is only available if an SQL DBMS target server is selected. Selecting Script File requires you to enter the name of the script file. Click the Browse button to browse for the script file.

The section labeled Items to Reverse Engineer allows you to specify which database objects and properties will be brought into the data model. You can save a set of selections as a new option set, update an existing option set, or delete an option set.

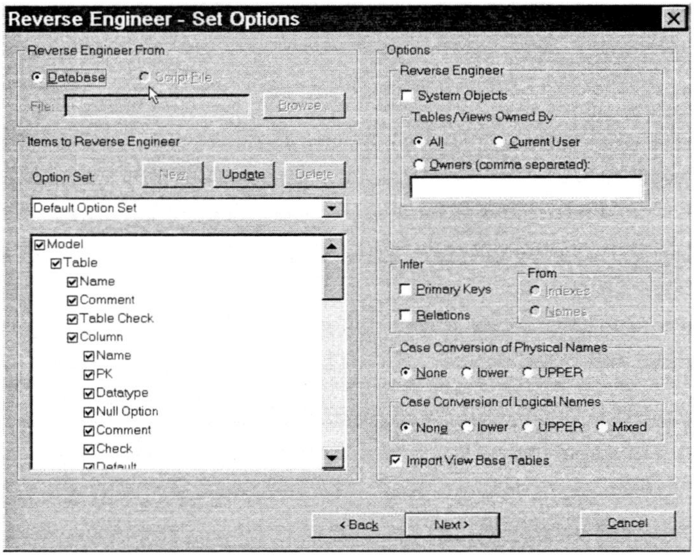

FIGURE 7.3

ERwin's Reverse Engineer/Set Options dialog allows you to reverse engineer all or part of an existing database. Although ERwin's documentation indicates that you can save the items to reverse engineer as an option set, I have not been able to do so.

TIP

To enable the New button, type in a new option set name in the drop-down edit box. Clicking the drop-down arrow displays a tiny up/down scroll for selecting a different option set.

Take care when using the Back button to return to the previous step. Option sets cannot be saved. Returning to the previous dialog will remove any newly created option sets.

Option sets are only available during the current session and cannot be saved for future use.

You can define one or more option sets to be used in the current session, or simply select each item. The options listed are those supported by ER*win*'s Complete Compare feature. The database objects available for selection vary, depending upon the target server selected.

ER*win* allows you the option of including the system database objects during reverse engineering. System objects are specific to the RDBMS selected, representing objectsthat define the database environment and that are not generally accessible to users. Click the Systems Objects check box to include them (see Figure 7.3). I do not often reverse engineer systems objects, preferring to leave them in the domain of the database administrators.

You may also elect to reverse engineer only tables and views that have a specific owner. You can select All, select only those owned by the Current User identified by the User Name field in the Database Connection dialog, or provide a list of owners separated by commas.

ER*win* provides an option that will allow it to infer primary keys and relations using indexes or names. Some database platforms support the declaration of primary keys and foreign keys. In that case, you need not select this option because ER*win* will define the keys using the declarations. I recommend reverse engineering without inferring primary keys or relations. Look at the model that is generated to determine if you need to use the infer option. You may get unexpected results if the RDBMS uses declarations and you instruct ER*win* to infer primary keys and relations from indexes.

ER*win* allows you to change the physical and logical name case or use the case of the database or script. Most naming conventions use mixed case for logical names and all uppercase for physical name abbreviations. ER*win* will replace underscores in physical names with spaces in logical names.

You can specify whether or not ER*win* should import view and base tables. Base tables are the tables that contain the columns in the view. ER*win* automatically creates the relationships between base and view tables.

Reverse Engineering Status and Discrepancies

After you set the reverse engineer options and click the Next button, ER*win* displays the Reverse Engineer Status dialog, shown in Figure 7.4. The dialog lets you monitor the progress as the model is reverse engineered.

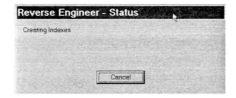

FIGURE 7.4

ERwin's Reverse Engineer Status dialog allows you to monitor the reverse-engineering process. You can press the Cancel button to stop the process at any time.

7

REVERSE ENGINEERING AND REPORTS

Upon completion, ER*win* displays any discrepancies encountered in the reverse-engineering process to let you correct them in the model. Figure 7.5 shows an example of reverse-engineering discrepancies.

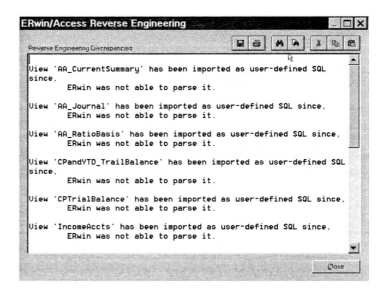

FIGURE 7.5

ERwin's Reverse Engineer Discrepancies dialog provides standard editing controls so you can save, print, search, cut, and paste the contents of the dialog.

NOTE

Reverse engineering rarely produces a precise model diagram. ER*win* reports how it handled any discrepancies.

ER*win*'s Report Browser

This section introduces ER*win*'s report-generation capability and provides an overview of its major functionality. I explore the details of producing reports in Chapter 13, "Delivering the Logical Data Model."

The ER*win* Report Browser tool allows you to generate and browse reports on ER*win* diagrams. You can also create new reports and report type folders. The Report Browser window is shown in Figure 7.6.

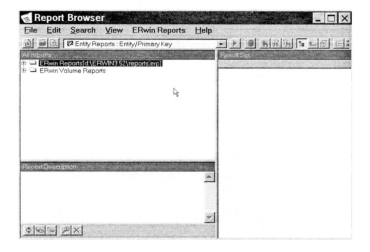

FIGURE 7.6
ERwin's Report Browser allows you to create, edit, and run reports on diagram objects and their properties.

The window features a menu, toolbar, and three panels:

- The upper-left panel contains a tree view of the predefined report types for ER*win* diagrams. The report type folders contain a set of predefined reports that support the most common reporting needs for ER*win* diagram objects. Note that the report types are based upon the details ER*win* captures for each diagram object. Each report has a set of options that you can include or exclude as needed. Some reports include preset filtering and sorting options. After you create a report, ER*win* adds a report icon to the folder.
- The lower-left panel displays the definition for the report type selected, if one is available.
- The right panel contains the result set generated by running a report.

Menu items allow you to create a new ER*win* report and create a new report type folder. As in most ER*win* menus, the items available vary, depending upon the selection in the Report Type panel.

Running a Report

ER*win* provides two major groups of reports:

- ER*win* reports—These reports provide details on the logical and physical model objects such as entities, attributes, tables, and columns. A special set of reports called *model validation reports* helps you ensure that the model contains all necessary information. More on this feature appears in Chapter 13.

- ER*win* volume reports—These reports provide estimates of the space required for the physical database objects. ER*win* provides default estimates for some physical objects such as indexes and primary keys. Good estimates require that you enter volumetric information for each entity. Read more about volumetric information in Chapter 16, "Building the Physical Model in ER*win*."

Figure 7.7 shows examples of the predefined reports available for entity diagram objects.

FIGURE 7.7
You can modify and enhance ERwin's predefined reports.

To generate a report, simply double-click the report icon or the editable report icon. You can also select the report in the report type window and select the Execute Report item from the File menu. The Report Browser shows the result set generated by the report in the Result Set pane on the right side of the window. When a report is generated, ER*win* adds a result set icon to the tree control under the report icon. Figure 7.8 shows an example of a result set icon and the Result Set panel after a report has been generated.

ER*win* does not save the result set generated by a report. You can save the format and options to reproduce a result set, but the result set itself is only available during the session in which it was created.

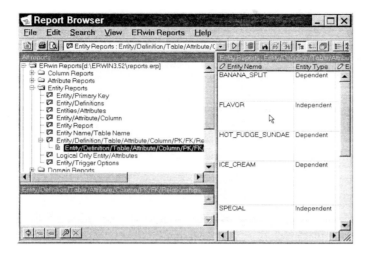

FIGURE 7.8
A report result set.

Result Set Functions

After generating a report, you can perform several functions on the result set. The result set functions include the following:

- Edit the report format.
- Print the result set.
- Export the result set.
- Preview the result set.
- Rename the result set.

Figure 7.9 shows the shortcut menu available by right-clicking the result set.

You can change the formatting of the result set displayed in the browser as follows:

- Rename the column headings.
- Change the column display order.
- Make the columns visible or hidden, bold or grayed.
- Display the rows according to a sort order.

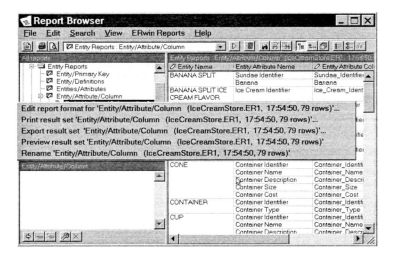

FIGURE 7.9

The result set shortcut menu provides options for customizing a result set.

To edit the format of a report, select the result set icon you want to edit, and then choose Edit, Report Format. You can also use the shortcut menu by right-clicking the result set and selecting Edit, Report Format.

The Column Options tab allows you to perform the following:

- Rename column headings by selecting the column and clicking the Heading button. (Figure 7.11 shows the Column Heading dialog in which you can enter a column name.)

- Select the order in which columns are displayed by selecting the column and clicking the Move Up or Move Down buttons.

- Select whether the column values are to be displayed in bold or grayed typeface or whether the value is to be displayed as a pop-up from a right-click on the row. Select the display option from the drop-down list, and then choose the columns that will use that display option. Note that a column can be associated with more than one display option. For example, a column can be both bold and grayed.

Figure 7.10 shows the Report Format dialog Column Options tab, and Figure 7.11 shows the Column Heading dialog for renaming column headings.

The Sort tab, shown in Figure 7.12, allows you to select the order in which the rows of the result set are displayed. Select the column name and whether you want to sort in ascending or descending order. I generally sort by entity name in ascending order.

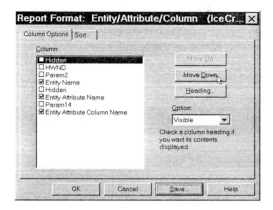

FIGURE 7.10
You can modify the appearance of the result set on the Report Format Column Options tab.

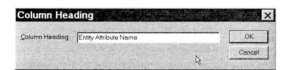

FIGURE 7.11
Rename a column heading by clicking the Heading button to launch the Column Heading dialog.

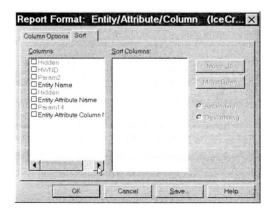

FIGURE 7.12
Use the Report Format Sort tab to group the result set rows.

You can save the changes to a report format as a named report view. The report view is displayed below the report in the tree control and can be generated just like a predefined report. You can do the work of developing a report presentation only once and then reuse it. A single report can have many views. You can switch between views without regenerating the result set. Figure 7.13 shows the Save View dialog.

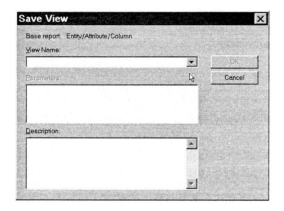

FIGURE 7.13

Use the Report Format Save View option to save a report using the options you selected.

Printing a Result Set

You print a result set by selecting it and choosing File, Print. The Print Result Set options appear in Figure 7.14.

Some of the options you can select from include:

- Print range—Choose all or select specific pages or a range of pages.
- Print what—Choose to print all or only selected parts of a result set.
- Copies—Print multiple copies and decide whether to collate.
- Presentation—Select from several presentation forms. To decide which works best for you, select one and click the Print Preview button to view the report.

Exporting a Result Set

You can export a result set generated by the Report Browser to a comma-separated values (CSV) or Hypertext Markup Language (HTML) file. You can also export a result set to RPTwin, the reporting tool shipped with ER*win*, or to an application that supports Dynamic Data Exchange (DDE), such as Microsoft Word.

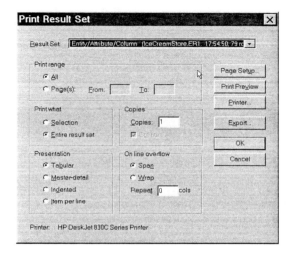

FIGURE 7.14
You can choose to print all or part of a result set.

To export a result set, select the result set and then choose File, Export or click the Export button in the Print Result Set dialog. Then follow these steps:

1. Select the export format from the options in the drop-down list. Options include

    CSV, which exports the result set as comma-separated values. CSV files can be imported by most spreadsheet applications, such as Microsoft Excel.

    HTML, which exports the result set in HTML format. You can open HTML files using a Web browser or import them into other applications that support HTML, such as Microsoft Word or Excel.

    DDE, which exports the result set to another application that supports Dynamic Data Exchange (DDE), such as Microsoft Word.

    RPTwin, which exports the result set to RPTwin, the reporting tool that comes with ER*win*.

2. Select the presentation format. The export presentation formats are the same as the print presentation formats.

3. Click the Export button to complete the process.

Figure 7.15 shows the Export from Report Browser dialog.

7

REVERSE ENGINEERING AND REPORTS

FIGURE 7.15
Choose a format for your result set in the Export from Report Browser dialog.

Creating a New ER*win* Report

Create a new ER*win* report by selecting File, New or choosing the New Report or Folder icon from the toolbar and selecting the New Report object. The ERwin Report Editor dialog, shown in Figure 7.16, appears.

The dialog allows you to set the following options:

1. Name the new report. As always, follow naming conventions.
2. Select whether the new report is a logical or physical object report.
3. You must choose a Category from the report type drop-down list to select options. Note that the category items vary depending on whether a logical or physical report is selected.
4. Select the options for the new report.
5. Enter a definition for the new report. This is a best practice.
6. You can attach a note to the new report if you want.

Searching the Report

The Report Browser has a search feature that allows you to find specific information within a result set. The search criteria can include strings, numbers, or dates for the column or columns so that the result set contains only those rows that satisfy the search criteria. You can also find a change of value in a column or hide rows that do not match the search criteria. Figure 7.17 shows the Find in Result Set dialog.

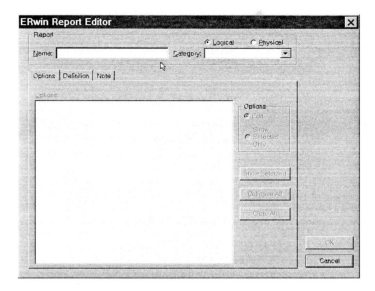

FIGURE 7.16

Define new reports in the ERwin Report Editor.

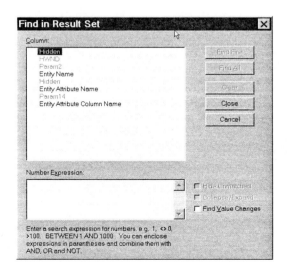

FIGURE 7.17

Use the Find in Result Set option to search a report for a specific diagram object or property. Since you cannot search ERwin to find a specific attribute, this is a handy feature for locating attributes or columns.

Summary

The Tasks menu in ER*win* has two options available when the diagram is in logical mode, Reverse Engineer and Generate Reports. Reverse Engineering allows you to create a new diagram from an existing database and Generate Reports allows you to report on the diagram objects and their properties.

ERwin's Reverse Engineering feature provides three methods for creating a new model diagram. You can create a diagram by connecting directly to some RDBMSs, reading a database schema script file, or using the Open option in the File menu for certain file types. You have the option of reverse engineering all or part of database by selecting which items to reverse engineer, as well as setting options to include system objects, filter objects by owner, and whether ER*win* should infer primary keys and relationships using indexes or names.

ER*win*'s Generate Reports facility allows you to report on the logical and physical objects in a diagram. ER*win* provides several predefined reports that can be run to produce a result set. Result sets are only available during the session in which the report is run. You can easily customize the format of a result set. You can also use the Report Editor to create new reports that you attach to one of ER*win*'s report categories. In addition to printing a result set, ER*win* allows you to export a result set in different formats, such as comma-separated values (CSV) or Hypertext Mark-up Language (HTML). You can also use Dynamic Data Exchange (DDE) to send a result set to applications that support DDE, such as Microsoft Word or Excel. ER*win* does not provide a diagram feature that allows you to search for a specific attribute or column, but you can run a report and use the reporting Search feature to locate specific attributes and columns, as well as other properties.

Understanding the location and functionality of ER*win*'s workplace menus and tools is only part of using ER*win* to create accurate and complete data models. You must also collect the information requirements and business rules. In Chapter 8, "Discovery: Gathering Information Requirements, Metadata, and Business Rules," I explore gathering information requirements and business rules, and how they translate into diagram objects.

Discovery: Gathering Information Requirements, Metadata, and Business Rules

Chapter 1, "Understanding Data Modeling Concepts," introduced the project development lifecycle and identified the stages in the lifecycle in which data modeling provides the most value. Although some methodologies propose that problem definition, requirements gathering, and analysis should occur prior to beginning data modeling tasks, in fact, data modeling is one of the best mechanisms for defining the problem (scope), as well as documenting the information requirements and business rules.

It's true that each task provides information that drives and constrains the next task. In this chapter, I discuss the following topics:

- Understanding requirements gathering
- Gathering information requirements
- Documenting the metadata
- Documenting the business rules

Understanding Requirements Gathering

Recall that a data model has two modes, logical and physical. Logical modeling is part of the requirements definition process and should occur as early in the development lifecycle as possible. Physical modeling should begin when the logical model is complete and the database management system is selected.

In most cases, problem definition occurs prior to beginning the requirements gathering process. Because in the real world projects must compete for resources and funding, many projects include a business assessment to justify the business need. Most people consider it a best practice to define the problem or business need before beginning the requirements gathering activity.

Entire books discuss problem definition and requirements gathering alone. It is beyond the scope of this text to explore these two areas to the degree their importance deserves. Consider this section a guideline encouraging modelers to model from the user perspective of the business need. No matter how technically elegant a solution might be, if it doesn't satisfy the business need and meet user expectations, you cannot consider it successful.

In the sections that follow, you learn more about the fictional company, Betty's Ice Cream Shop. You will use the techniques introduced in Chapter 1 to define the problem and gather the information requirements.

Defining the Problem

The problem definition provides the domain or scope for information requirements gathering and often involves a business need. The business need should be well defined and clearly understood by the session participants. It can be a simple paragraph or a complex document that outlines a series of business objectives. The purpose of a problem definition is to define the scope, or boundary, of the data model, much the way a survey defines property boundaries.

Begin the session by writing the problem definition and placing it in view of session participants. Keeping the problem definition visible helps the group stay focused on the goal. Asking participants what information, or data, is needed to accomplish the goal provides the information requirements.

CAUTION

I caution modelers against attempting to gather requirements for a problem that is not clearly defined. It is difficult to complete a task that has no clear boundaries.

For the example, I use the following problem definition:

> Ms. Betty Wilson, the owner of Betty's Ice Cream Shop, is interested in knowing which flavors of ice cream her customers select for banana split and hot fudge sundaes. She also wants to know which toppings are preferred on banana split sundaes. Ms. Wilson runs specials on ice cream flavors from time to time. She wants to know whether the specials are working.

Finding the Right Participants

Having the right attendees at the meeting is the single most important factor in a successful session. Participants should include a representative set of users, as well as experts with knowledge and experience in the problem domain. It is an added bonus when the session participants are also stakeholders in the success of the development effort.

Provide advance notice of the meeting time and location. Publish the problem definition and any supporting documentation. Include an agenda and a preliminary list of meeting attendees. Encourage attendees to assign alternate representatives and suggest additional attendees if appropriate.

An upper-management attendee who is empowered to make decisions on behalf of the enterprise can significantly increase the productivity of the session. Often you simply need to make a business decision and move on to the next issue.

In the example, Ms. Wilson participates in the requirements session with the store manager and an ice cream server. The store manager and the server are daily users. Ms. Wilson makes enterprise decisions and decisions regarding scope. The store manager and Ms. Wilson also act as domain experts.

Gathering Information Requirements in Facilitated Sessions

Gathering information requirements means discovering and documenting the information necessary to identify and define the entities, attributes, relationships, and business rules for the logical model. Most industry experts agree that defining the requirements completely and accurately is the single most critical task in a development project. In fact, an incomplete or inaccurate understanding of requirements can cause expensive re-work and significant delay.

The sections that follow provide guidelines for gathering information requirements in a facilitated session, including some recommendations on what should happen before, during, and after the session.

The goal of the facilitated session is to accurately and completely define and document the information requirements necessary to produce a logical model that meets the business need. The focus should be on *what* information is required, not *how* the information is collected, created, or stored.

Before the Session

Prior to the session, distribute any supporting materials that will assist attendees in preparing for the session. Be sure to distribute the material early enough to give participants sufficient time for review. Giving participants time to prepare should help make the session more productive.

At a minimum, the attendees for the session should receive the following:

- Problem definition of the business need
- Agenda
- List of objectives
- List of proposed attendees
- List of potential entities and attributes
- Guidelines for a productive session (session rules)
- Straw-man model (if appropriate)

Make sure the agenda addresses the session objectives and allows enough time to appropriately explore each. Remember to include a break at least every two hours. Encourage attendees to come prepared to participate.

During the Session

The sections that follow describe some good facilitation practices. I provide guidelines for introducing modeling concepts to session participants and driving out requirements to an appropriate level of granularity. Finally, I introduce two methods for refining requirements, functional decomposition and using sample data.

During the session, the facilitator is responsible for guiding the participants in accomplishing the session objectives and keeping the users focused on the issues at hand. It is also important for the facilitator to ensure that all participants have a chance to contribute and do not begin designing a solution before the information requirements are clearly understood.

To keep participants focused on the session objectives, the facilitator should closely monitor the interactions of participants. Encourage participants to move on when it appears that consensus has been reached or, even more important, when it becomes obvious that consensus cannot be reached in an appropriate length of time. Record unresolved objectives or issues as parking lot items for resolution outside of the session.

The facilitator should take note of any participants who are not contributing. Less assertive participants are sometimes reluctant to contribute. Lively, impassioned participants tend to dominate sessions and might be prone to interrupt or even discourage views that do not align with theirs. It is essential that the facilitator cultivate an environment where all participants feel encouraged to contribute. An important part of facilitation is providing an opportunity to hear input from all participants. A session that is driven by a small set of participants might not provide a complete set of information requirements.

TIP

It is essential that the session remain focused on defining *what* information is required to meet the business need and not become distracted by *how* the information is collected, created, or stored. Participants are often tempted to prematurely begin designing the solution. The facilitator should discourage participants from pursuing solutions prior to understanding all the information requirements.

Introducing Modeling Concepts

The facilitator or data modeler must provide an introduction to basic modeling concepts. The language of modeling helps session participants define the information requirements in terms of entities, attributes, and relationships. Using modeling concepts helps participants focus on the information using concepts that are independent of the processes that use the information or the platform that provides storage. In fact, thinking in the abstract—thinking of logical groupings of attributes as a single entity—is a natural way to conceptualize. It has been my experience that session participants readily embrace modeling concepts and are eager to understand the modeling process.

Introduce data modeling concepts using examples within the domain familiar to the session participants. For example, most business activities include information about customers. Using entities that are familiar helps participants recognize that CUSTOMER represents an entity with attributes and relationships.

Remember that the participants are providing the information requirements. The facilitator and the data modeler are simply providing the expertise to help users define and document.

Driving Out Information Requirements

Driving out the information requirements means defining the entities, attributes, and relationships to the degree of detail necessary to produce a logical model. It is the responsibility of the facilitator to guide session participants as they refine information requirements to the appropriate level of granularity.

It probably will not be possible to define every entity and attribute during the facilitated sessions, even if the scope of the project is fairly small. However, you should define major entities, primary keys, significant attributes, and relationships. Remember to collect the definitions for entities and attributes from the session participants.

Information requirements collected during the session should fit within the scope of the problem definition and the business need. The facilitator should examine each information requirement to make sure it fits with the problem definition domain. You should document the requirements that do not fit as out of scope and add them to an enterprise wish list.

It is important to remember that the enterprise data model will also provide information requirements. Corporate entities, such as CUSTOMER or PRODUCT, should be defined consistently across the enterprise. You will recall from Chapter 1 that the data model must fit within the enterprise model or define a new subject area to add to the enterprise model. The facilitator or modeler should set the expectation that the entity can contain attributes with slightly different names.

TIP

Sample data is actual information that is collected, used, and produced to meet the business need. Users and domain experts are excellent resources to provide sample data. Encourage session participants to provide examples of any existing data, perhaps sample reports or spreadsheets.

Actual data might not be available. Perhaps the business need can only be met by creating data that does not currently exist in the enterprise. In those cases, sample data is contrived. Users and domain experts should work together to define the information that must exist to meet the business need.

The ice cream shop example uses the following information business rules:

- Betty's Ice Cream Shop sells two types of sundaes, banana split and hot fudge.
- A banana split contains three scoops of ice cream, three servings of topping, a banana, whipped cream, and a cherry. A customer can select up to three different ice cream flavors and up to three different toppings.
- A hot fudge sundae contains two scoops of ice cream, hot fudge sauce, whipped cream, and a cherry. A customer can select up to two different flavors of ice cream.
- Toppings are strawberry, raspberry, chocolate, hot fudge, pineapple, caramel, whipped cream, marshmallow, and butterscotch. New toppings are added periodically.

- Ice cream flavors vary constantly, except for the most popular flavors.
- Ice cream flavors are offered at special prices periodically.

After the Session

After the session, you should distribute the information requirements and resulting data model to the session participants for review and feedback. Be sure to communicate the timeframe by which you must receive responses. It is helpful to advise participants that silence is considered agreement.

Distributing the Session Results

The session results for distribution should include a draft of information requirements and a preliminary data model. The data model should include entity and attribute definitions. Publish any parking lot items or issues along the person or group who is responsible for resolution.

Communicating complex activities is not a trivial task. Invite participants to provide feedback within a reasonable timeframe.

Collecting the Feedback

Encourage participants to examine the session results for accuracy and completeness. Be sure to communicate that it is essential to the success of the session that participants review the session results and provide any corrections or enhancements.

Incorporate the feedback received into the information requirements and data model. Participants might provide feedback that appears contradictory or that conflicts with information received during the session. Especially in the case of conflicting information, you should publish all feedback.

Documenting Metadata

Understanding data is critical to the success of an information requirements session, and *metadata* is one of the primary vehicles for understanding data. Metadata is usually defined simply as data about data. There is considerable discussion among IT professionals around when (and if) you should perform metadata tasks. When project deadlines draw near, metadata tasks are some of the first tasks pushed to a future phase. Chances are, metadata documentation might never be completed. This is truly unfortunate. Metadata is a powerful tool for designers, developers, analysts, and end users alike. I strongly encourage collecting, storing, and *using* metadata.

Documenting metadata means collecting and recording facts about the data. Attribute name and attribute description are examples of metadata facts about an attribute. In the sections that follow, I define metadata types and discuss gathering the metadata.

The role of metadata has expanded within the information strategy of the enterprise. Most organizations are developing or enhancing an information architecture that is likely to include operational data stores, an integrated data warehouse, and several data marts. The enterprise increasingly deploys databases that have many of the same data elements but fulfill completely different business needs. Metadata must accurately and consistently describe enterprise information that exists in several databases as if it were residing in a single database.

Another role of metadata is to isolate the user from the complexities of accessing information. When the same information resides in different places, in different formats, users are confronted with precisely the problems that information management was intended to solve: different answers to the same question and inconsistent results.

You should retain two primary types of metadata: technical and business.

Technical Metadata

Technical metadata provides guidelines for designers and developers, as well as the assurance that the information is correct for technical power users of enterprise information. Users that query data structures directly need to understand details, such as when and where data was collected, to ensure that they are using the data correctly. In addition, technical metadata provides the foundation for maintenance and enhancements of the enterprise information. Without technical metadata, the task of analyzing and implementing changes to an information system is considerably more difficult and time-consuming. The following list contains some examples of technical metadata:

- Update frequency or last update, which provide an understanding of the age of the data.
- Systems and processes that also use the data, which provide an understanding of how the data is used elsewhere in the enterprise.
- System of record for the data, which provides an understanding of which system "owns" the data.
- Logical and physical data models, which are conceptual representations of physical data structures and as such are rich sources of information about the data.
- Data stewards, who are the people within the enterprise responsible for the data content, how it is used, and what it represents to the business of the enterprise.

Business Metadata

Business metadata provides the link between the enterprise information and the business users. It supplies directions to assist users in accessing the enterprise information. Business users are often executives or business analysts who have little technical knowledge. Business language metadata completes the link between users and information. Business metadata can define reports, queries, the context in which the information should be used, transformation rules, and locations of the information. For example:

- Update frequency or last update to understand which data will best meet the business need.
- Business definitions for tables and columns to understand the contents of columns and rows in the data structures.
- Rules for drill down to understand the atomic data elements used in roll-ups, summaries, and derivations.
- Logical and physical data models to understand how the data relates to other data.
- Query samples to understand how the business partners use and group the data.

Gathering the Metadata

The two primary types of metadata are explicit and implicit. *Explicit* metadata sources are sources of metadata that have been discussed, documented, and agreed upon by the information managers of the enterprise. Explicit metadata is usually stored in a repository or documents that have a formal maintenance process. It is distributed and recognized throughout the organization. These explicit metadata sources populate both technical and business metadata.

Implicit metadata consists of corporate knowledge, policies, and guidelines that are not recorded in a formal way. This is the information that only certain people know. This type of information is located in the "company consciousness." It might be a note on a key employee's desk or a spreadsheet created and maintained on an employee's desktop. There is probably no formal documentation. However, this knowledge is as valuable as that found in the explicit metadata sources. It is sometimes the most valuable information because it is most clearly and directly business related.

Most of the business metadata is implicit. Therefore, it is critical that this metadata is captured, documented, formalized, and reflected by the enterprise information. This process takes an implicit source of metadata and transforms it into an explicit source. Every organization is different, so it is sometimes difficult to identify implicit sources of metadata. The following list includes the most common types of implicit metadata:

- Data stewards
- Business rules
- Business definitions
- Competitor information
- Transformations and summaries
- Reports and queries

Using a Repository

Not every corporation uses an electronic repository for storing metadata. However, some projects, such as data warehouses and data marts, require a metadata repository as part of their core objectives from the very beginning of the project. You should create this repository using technologically sound architecture, with a primary focus of supporting the users of the information.

To be useful, metadata must have a presentation layer that allows nontechnical business users easy access and navigation of the repository. Even with the given state of the metadata products available, it is difficult to satisfy the needs of business users and technology personnel if building a repository is not a stated goal of the project. The metadata repository significantly aids the enterprise in making the information visible, understandable, and accessible to all users.

Documenting Business Rules

Business rules represent the *way* in which the enterprise conducts business. In technology, these rules define the way the business processes should behave during interactions with the customer or client. The way in which the enterprise uses information to conduct business changes more rapidly than the information that is used. Business is remarkably adept at finding new ways to use information.

The information industry has developed several methodologies for documenting the business. Most of these methodologies tend to focus on business processes as sequential actions performed on information, or, in newer methodologies, as the interaction and collaboration between objects and components.

NOTE

In some respects, the information industry is just beginning to provide support for the rules of business. Business critical functionality is often buried in business rules, deep in lines of procedural code. Business rules that are implemented in code are difficult to find and very expensive, sometimes nearly impossible, to change.

Modeling the information using the properties inherent in the data allows many business processes to use the same information without regard to *how* the information is used.

The sections that follow provide a brief introduction to business rules. For our purposes, the focus is those rules that deal with entities, attributes, and relationships.

Barbara von Halle, in her articles and column in *Database Programming and Design* magazine, has identified the following types of business rules:

- Definition: The definition of a perceived object.
- Fact: A role or relationship between two objects of any complexity.
- Constraint: Some limit on the population or membership of a domain or object type.
- Derivation: A method by which the contents of some object are constructed, calculated, or derived from other objects.

These rule types describe the categories of business rules that you can define using data modeling constructs.

For as long as we have been developing applications, programmers have written business rules in code. Initially, rules were simply buried within the code. However, as relational databases and data modeling become development standards, business information rules are implemented in entities, attributes, and relationships. In a relational database, rules can also be implemented as triggers and stored procedures written in SQL.

Now I discuss how to use entities, attributes, and relationships to represent business rules.

Definition Type

In the preceding chapters, I emphasized the use of good definitions several times. Business rules are represented in the way an entity, attribute, or relationship is defined. It is important that the definitions use business language to define business objects. The business language should reflect the business requirements.

Fact Type

In a data model, fact types are represented by the relationships between entities. Business rules define whether a relationship is identifying or non-identifying, therefore dictating the primary key structure. Business rules also define cardinality, the maximum number of instances that must participate in a relationship, and optionality, the minimum number of instances that must participate in a relationship.

The existence of an entity in a specific subject area of the data model is determined by business rules. Business rules also dictate the placement of an attribute in a specific entity. Although generally not explicitly stated, there is a relationship between an entity and its attributes, as well as between the entity and the subject area.

Constraint Type

Constraints represent the business rules that define the domain of allowable values for an attribute. Business rules define the domain by including or excluding certain values using a formula or list.

It is important to note that some domains are accepted and understood by the industry in which the enterprise participates. You must define constraints that do not conflict with industry standards.

Derivation Type

The information industry has not reached consensus on whether derived attribute values should be included in the data model. It is my opinion that derived attributes should be included in the logical model. Whether or not the data element is actually instantiated, a derived attribute represents an information requirement. It makes sense to include all information requirements in the logical model.

Summary

Gathering information requirements is more than simply collecting a list of data elements. It also includes collecting and documenting the metadata and business rules. Information requirements gathering begins with a problem definition. The problem definition provides the scope for information gathering sessions.

Facilitated sessions are an efficient way to collect information requirements, provided the right participants attend. It is important to distribute information prior to the session. During the session the facilitator must keep the focus on *what* information is needed and not *how* the information will be stored or collected. The facilitator should also keep participants focused and productive, as well as ensure that everyone has an opportunity to express an opinion. The facilitator should introduce modeling concepts to assist participants in defining the information requirements using modeling language. Issues that cannot be resolved should be recorded and assigned to one or more participants for resolution.

After the session, distribute the information requirements, a draft of the logical model, and the issues list, including the person or group responsible for resolution. Encourage participants to provide feedback to the session results within a reasonable timeframe. Be sure to respond to all feedback regardless of whether it is included in the information requirements or not.

In addition to collecting and documenting what information is needed to accomplish the business need, you must also collect metadata. Metadata is "data about data." Metadata can be grouped into two types:

- Technical metadata: Intended for designers, developers, and analysts
- Business metadata: Intended to help business users understand which data elements to use to meet a specific need

Metadata can be explicit or implicit. Explicit metadata has been discussed, documented and agreed upon by the information managers of the enterprise. Explicit metadata is often documented in a repository. Implicit metadata consists of corporate knowledge, policies, and guidelines that are not recorded in a formal way. It is often information that only certain people know. This type of information is located in the "company consciousness." You must make every effort to document implicit metadata and make it available to all users.

The information needed and the metadata that defines it are only part of the picture—you must also collect and document the business rules. Business rules represent the *way* in which the enterprise conducts business. In technology, these rules define the way the business processes should use information during interactions with the customer or client. The way in which the enterprise uses information to conduct business changes more rapidly than the information that is used. Many times business rules are buried within lines of code. However, relational databases and data modeling allow business information rules to be implemented in entities, attributes, and relationships. In a relational database, rules can also be implemented as triggers and stored procedures written in SQL.

After information requirements, metadata, and business rules are collected and documented, it's time to flesh out the draft logical model. In the next chapter, I discuss using ER*win*'s logical model tools and editors to create entities, attributes, and relationships.

8

GATHERING
INFORMATION
REQUIREMENTS

Creating the Logical Model

PART

III

IN THIS PART

Developing the Logical Data Model

The information requirements and business rules provide the information to produce the entities, attributes, and relationships in logical model. Entities represent the "things" about which the enterprise is interested in keeping information. The attributes for each entity and the relationships between the entities are determined by business rules.

This chapter explores the following topics:

- Building the data model in ER*win*
- Creating entities
- Adding attributes
- Using the Key Group Editor
- Using the Domain Editor

First we create a new data model diagram and set the modeling environment. Then we use ER*win*'s logical model tools to create the entities and attributes. ER*win*'s logical model object editors are used to set properties for the diagram, as well as entities and attributes. Lastly, we examine the editors for defining the key groups and the domain dictionary.

Building the Data Model in ER*win*

Remember that an ER*win* data model has two modes, logical and physical. That means a single ER*win* diagram includes both a logical and a physical model. It is important to note that, in ER*win*, the logical model and physical model are tightly linked. Making a change in the logical model automatically includes the same change in the physical model, unless the object is defined as logical only. By the same token, changes to the physical model are reflected in the logical model.

> **NOTE**
>
> Changing the logical name of a logical model object will change the corresponding physical model object, *until* you edit the column or table name directly. Changing the name of a physical model object does *not* change the name of the corresponding logical model object.

In the sections that follow, I explore

- Creating a new ER*win* diagram
- Setting the modeling environment
- Using the Diagram Editor
- Editing on the diagram

Creating a New ER*win* Diagram

Build the logical model for Betty's Ice Cream Shop by performing the following steps:

1. Select the New icon on the toolbar or select File, New.
2. Select the SAMPLE template from the ERwin Template Selection dialog. Figure 9.1 shows the dialog.

Setting the Modeling Environment

Next, you set the modeling environment options for the creation of the Betty's Ice Cream Shop logical model. For the example, this entails setting the ER*win* window display options and selecting the methodology preferences.

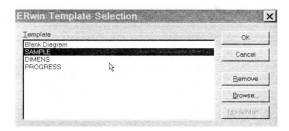

FIGURE 9.1
The SAMPLE template contains a set of predefined options. You can create your own template by using the File, Save As option. Customize one of the templates delivered with ERwin, or use the Blank Diagram option.

Selecting the Window Display Options

To select the ER*win* window display options, select the Window menu and check the following options:

- Stored Display Tabs—The sample template contains a set of example stored displays. You cannot see these tabs until this selection is made.
- Toolbar—The toolbar has icons for commonly used functions, a real time-saver.
- Status Bar—The status of an operation can be valuable information.
- Independent Attribute Browser—Using domains is a best practice. Domains help with consistency and following standards.
- ERwin Toolbox—Displaying the toolbox on the ER*win* desktop is a must.

The Window menu closes each time you make a selection. This behavior is annoying, but keep opening and selecting each option. Note that the ModelMart menu item and the ModelMart toolbar are not available if you are not using ModelMart. The selections shown in Figure 9.2 are my own preferences.

Selecting Methodology

You will use the IE notation for both the logical and physical models. To open the Preferences dialog, shown in Figure 9.3, select Option, Preferences, and on the Methodology tab, choose IE notation for both models. Leave the other options at the default selections.

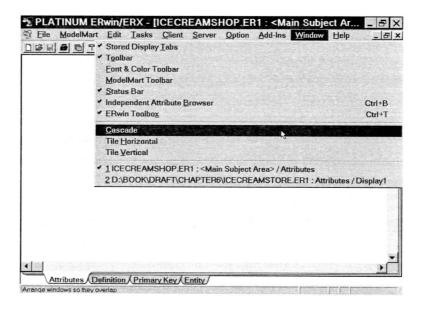

FIGURE 9.2

The ERwin display window allows you to control the look and feel of the diagram workspace. You can elect whether to hide or display the toolbars and toolboxes, as well as display tabs and the status bar.

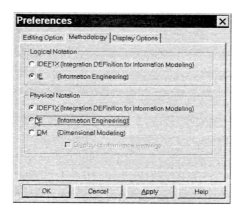

FIGURE 9.3

On the Methodology tab, select the notation ERwin will use for the logical and physical model. IE methodology notation uses "crow's feet" to visually depict the "many" side of a relationship.

Using the Diagram Editor

To use the Diagram Editor, select Edit, Diagram. The Diagram Editor has three tabs for entering information about the diagram (see Figure 9.4):

- General
- Definition
- UDP

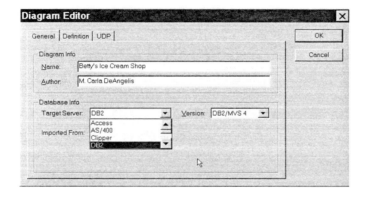

FIGURE 9.4

Note that ERwin provides support for different versions of some target servers, such as DB2. If ERwin supports more than a single version of the target server, the Version drop down list appears.

The General tab is where you enter a name for the diagram and the author, as well as select the database information. I consider it a best practice to name the diagram and provide the author's name as well:

- Name and Author—Enter a name for the diagram and the author of the model. In my model, the diagram is called Betty's Ice Cream Shop, and I entered my name as the author.
- Database Info—It is not necessary to select the Target Server and Version at this time. However, you can select it now if you like. For Betty's Ice Cream Shop, Access 97 is selected as the database platform for a very common reason: It is the program Betty Wilson uses. Availability is often the basis for platform decisions.

It is important to enter a definition for the diagram on the Definition tab. Remember to use business language.

Figure 9.5 shows some ideas for a starter set of information that you can include in the diagram:

- Name of the project: Betty's Ice Cream Shop.
- Date the diagram was created: 11/08/1999.
- Steward of the model: M. Carla DeAngelis.
- A brief restatement of the problem definition or business need for Betty's Ice Cream Shop.
- A reference to the pattern for package configuration and campaign management, which fits the problem domain. Patterns represent well-known modeling concepts used elsewhere within the enterprise.

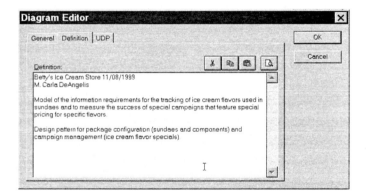

FIGURE 9.5

Use the Diagram Editor, Definition tab to include important information about the diagram itself. I like to include the name of the modeler responsible for creating and maintaining the diagram.

Every diagram object in ER*win* has the option of attaching user-defined properties (UDPs). Creating UDPs and using the UDP Editor is addressed in Chapter 14, "Advanced Features for the Logical Model." For this example, I created a UDP named Modeler with the value MCD, my initials, as shown in Figure 9.6.

Editing on the Diagram

ER*win* has a nice feature that allows you to enter the entity name and attributes without opening an editor. To use on-diagram editing, enter the entity name and press the Enter key. Figure 9.7 shows the on-diagram edit to add an attribute. You can cycle through the attributes by pressing the Enter key to advance the edit mode to the next attribute.

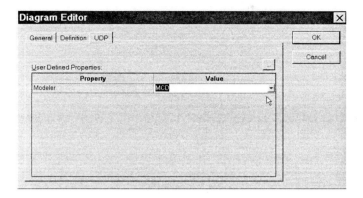

FIGURE 9.6

The Diagram Editor, UDP tab allows you to set properties for user-defined properties that have been attached to the diagram object.

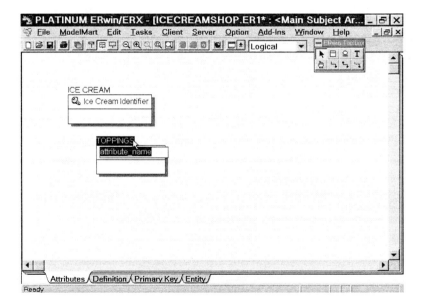

FIGURE 9.7

ERwin's on-diagram editing feature allows you to enter the entity name and attribute names without opening their corresponding editors. However, you will need to use the appropriate editor to set other important properties.

Creating Entities

Entities provide the foundation for a logical model. ERwin allows you to enter entity properties such as name, definition, and notes and attach UDPs.

Recall that a logical model can contain independent and dependent entities. An independent entity is an entity whose instances can be uniquely identified without attribute values from its relationship to another entity. A dependent entity is an entity whose instances cannot be uniquely identified without determining its relationship to another entity or entities. Dependent entities are always child entities where all or part of the primary key contains the primary key of the parent entity. These migrated foreign key attributes are necessary to define a specific instance.

ERwin represents an entity using a rectangular box with a horizontal line that divides the upper half of the box from the lower half. The primary key attributes reside in the upper half of the entity box, and non-key attributes appear in the lower half.

NOTE

When you add a new entity to the diagram, ERwin provides a default name, E/n, where the letter E represents entity and n is a unique number. Figure 9.8 shows a new entity and its E/n default name, E/6.

In the sections that follow, I explore

- Using the entity tool
- Using the Entity Editor
- Adding the name and definition

Using the Entity Tool

To use the entity tool in the ERwin toolbox, click the entity tool and then click the diagram. The mouse pointer changes to provide a visual cue that the entity tool is in use, as shown in Figure 9.8.

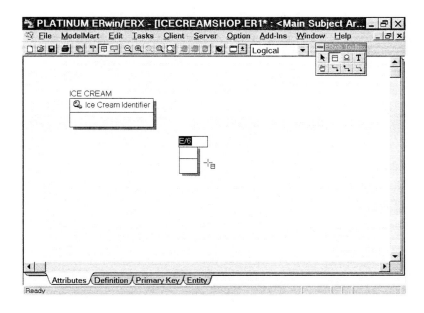

FIGURE 9.8
The Entity tool in ERwin's toolbox allows you to quickly add new entities to the diagram. Notice the mouse pointer changes to indicate that the entity tool is selected.

TIP

As long as the entity tool is selected, a new entity is added each time you click on the desktop.

If you add a new entity unintentionally, you can delete it by clicking the pointer tool, clicking the entity to select it, and pressing the Delete key. Note that ERwin only provides the option to delete from the model. The Delete from Subject Area option is not available for entities with default names.

Enter an appropriate logical name for the entity. Remember to use good naming conventions.

Using the Entity Editor

To use the Entity Editor to add or change an entity's properties, select Edit, Diagram or right-click the entity and select Entity Editor. Figure 9.9 shows the right-click shortcut menu.

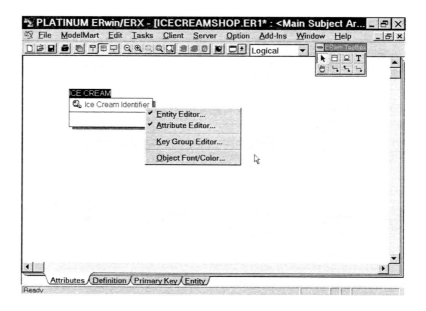

FIGURE 9.9

Right-click an entity to open the Shortcut menu to the editors. Double-click an entity to open the editor that is currently selected.

Use the Entity Editor to enter or change an entity's name and definition. The Entity Editor also allows you to attach three notes to an entity as well as associate an icon with an entity.

The Entity Editor contains the following controls:

- Entity—Here, you see the name of the selected entity. To edit the properties of another entity, select the entity from the drop-down list box.
- Name—Click to change the name of an entity.
- Logical Only—Select this check box to make the entity part of the logical model only. Do not select this check box if the entity is to appear in both the logical and physical models. Entities specified as logical only are not represented by a table in the physical model.

To change the name of an entity, click in the Name edit box and enter the new name. An entity name often appears in all uppercase letters. Select good names that use business language and that are representative of the instances.

NOTE

The Definition tab contains a set of standard editing tool icons, Cut, Copy, Paste to Clipboard, and Print Preview.

The Entity Editor also includes a set of tabs that allow you to enter the following:

- Definition
- Notes
- UDPs
- Icon

The Definition tab is shown in Figure 9.10. The definition in the example is written from the perspective of the business partner or client, Betty's Ice Cream Shop. You should word entity definitions using business terms.

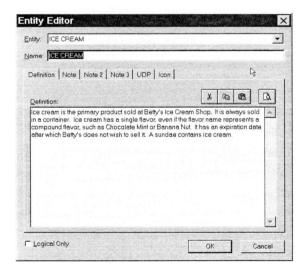

FIGURE 9.10

Use the Entity Editor to change the entity name and add or change the definition. To edit a different entity, select it from the drop-down list. ERwin's drop-down lists allow you to quickly locate a specific list item by typing the first few characters.

The Entity Editor also allows you to attach up to three notes to an entity. These notes are free-form text that can store special information regarding an entity. For example, you can use a note to attach sample data or identify the source system or system of record for the instances of an entity.

Recall that a user-defined property is any useful or important information about an ER*win* object, in this case, an entity. An entity in the logical model and the table in the physical model cannot share a UDP. Using the UDP Editor is covered in Chapter 14.

The Icon tab allows you to attach small and large icons to an entity, as shown in Figure 9.11. You can import bitmaps for use as icons using the Icon Editor. To open the Icon Editor, click the Editor icon. To import a bitmap, click the Import button and browse for the bitmap.

FIGURE 9.11

Use the Icon tab to associate icons with entities. Use the display options to display the icons.

NOTE

You must select the entity icon in the stored display for ER*win* to display the small icon. To display large icons, right-click the diagram and select Display Level, Icon.

Adding Attributes

Attributes represent the information that the enterprise is interested in collecting and maintaining about an entity. Recall that attributes come in two primary types, key attributes and non-key attributes. In ER*win*, key attributes reside above the entity line and non-key attributes are below the line.

You can add attributes to an entity using on-diagram editing or using the Attribute Editor.

Using On-Diagram Editing

To add attributes using ER*win*'s on-diagram editing feature, click the entity once to select it, and once again to use on-diagram editing. Press the Enter key to cycle through the attributes to place the new attribute in the appropriate spot. Figure 9.12 shows the addition of a new attribute using the on-diagram edit feature. Notice that ER*win* assigns a default name of the form attribute_name when you add new attributes using on-diagram editing.

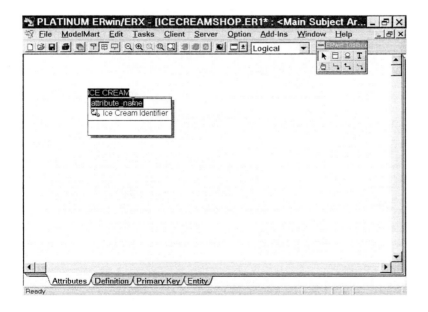

FIGURE 9.12
*You can quickly add attributes to an entity using on-diagram editing. To use on-diagram editing, click the entity once, and then click again. If you perform the second click too quickly, ER*win* will interpret it as a double click, and open the selected editor.*

Using the Attribute Editor

To use the Attribute Editor, select Edit, Attribute or right-click an entity and select Attribute Editor.

The Attribute Editor allows you to add and change attribute properties for all entities in the diagram, as well as specify values for UDPs, as shown in Figure 9.13.

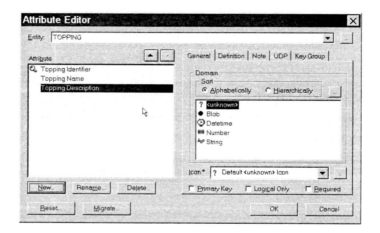

FIGURE 9.13
Use the Attribute Editor to set additional properties for attributes.

The functionality of the Attribute Editor includes

- Entity name—The drop-down control allows you to switch to another entity. You cannot change the entity name from the Attribute Editor. Click the button to the right of the entity name drop-down list to launch the Entity Editor.

- Attribute list—Double-click an attribute to open the Domain Editor. (You'll read more about the Domain Editor in Chapter 14.) When more than a single attribute is present, the up/down icons are active. Click an attribute and click the up or down icon to move the attribute up or down in the list.

- New—To open the New Attribute dialog and add an attribute, click this button. Figure 9.14 shows the New Attribute dialog.

FIGURE 9.14

Use the New Attribute dialog to add a new attribute within the Attribute Editor. ERwin automatically uses the attribute name as the column name.

While adding a new attribute using the New Attribute dialog shown in Figure 9.14, you can select the logical domain, enter the attribute name and column name, and define the attribute as logical only by doing the following:

- Sort—You can select to view the logical domains in alphabetical or hierarchical order. I recommend viewing the domains in hierarchical order because it lets you see the parent domain for any user-defined domains.
- Domain list—Click a domain to select as the domain for the new attribute.
- Attribute Name—Enter the attribute name. Remember to use naming conventions and select a logical name that is indicative of the domain of values.
- Column Name—The column name defaults to the logical name with any spaces replaced by underscores, and ER*win* truncates the name to meet physical database requirements.
- Logical Only—To indicate that the attribute should be present in the logical model only, select this option.

CAUTION

An attribute selected as logical only will not exist in the physical model and will not be created in the database.

- Rename—To open the Rename Attribute dialog (shown in Figure 9.15) and rename an attribute, click this button.

FIGURE 9.15

Use the Rename Attribute dialog to change the name of an attribute. Simply enter the new name and click the OK button.

- Delete—To delete the selected attribute, click the Delete button. Take care; there is no undo facility to give you a chance to take it back. The only option is to cancel all the changes and close the dialog.
- Reset—To reset the properties of the selected attribute, click this button to display the Reset Attribute Property dialog. This dialog allows you to return overridden properties to the default domain settings. Figure 9.16 shows the Reset Attribute Property dialog options.

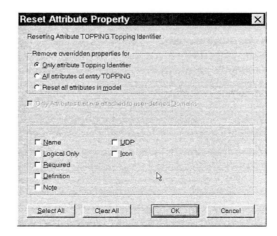

FIGURE 9.16

Use the Reset Attribute dialog to reset the properties of a single attribute, all the attributes in an entity, or all attributes in a model. You can also select which properties to reset.

- Migrate—To select the primary key attribute properties that will migrate to foreign keys, click this button to display the Migrate Attribute Property dialog, shown in Figure 9.17.
- Tabs—To set the logical domain, enter a definition, add a note, assign UDP values, and define the key group attributes, select the appropriate tab.

Reset

ER*win* allows you to attach a domain to a column as well as override the domain properties and assign new properties. Clicking the Reset button displays the Reset Attribute Property dialog, with which you can return overridden properties to the default domain settings.

The Reset Attribute Property dialog contains two primary sets of information. The upper set of options enables you to control the number of attributes whose properties will be reset:

- Only attribute—Select to only reset the properties of the selected column. The name of the selected column appears in the text label.
- All attributes of entity—Select to reset the properties of all attributes in the selected entity. The name of the selected entity appears in the text label.
- Reset all attributes in model—Select to reset the properties of all attributes in the entire model. Making this selection enables the option to only reset user-defined domains.

The lower set lists the attribute properties that can be reset:

- Name—Select this check box to reset the selected attribute name to the logical domain name selected for the attribute.
- Logical Only—Select this option if you want to reset the Logical Model Only property to the value set for the logical domain.
- Required—I assume that this option was intended to allow you to reset the Required property to the default (cleared). I tested this option, and selecting it appeared to have no effect on the model. I do not use this feature, and I could find no information in the online documentation about its purpose.
- Definition—Select this option if you want to reset the definition for the selected columns to the definition for the logical domain. The logical datatypes that come with ER*win* do not include definitions, so the effect might be to clear the definition.
- Note—Select this option if you want to reset the Note property for the selected attribute to the inherited note value for the domain.
- UDP—Select this option if you want to reset the value of the user-defined properties for the selected attribute to the default UDP value.
- Icon—Select this option if you want to reset the icon assigned to the attribute to the one associated with the logical domain assigned to the attribute.

9

DEVELOPING THE
LOGICAL DATA
MODEL

> **CAUTION**
>
> Use caution when using the Reset Attribute Property dialog. Resetting properties such as Name and Definition can result in the loss of valuable business information.

Migrate

ER*win* automatically migrates all primary key attributes as foreign key attributes in a child entity. The Migrate Attribute Property dialog allows you to select the attribute properties that migrate with the foreign key for the relationships in the model.

> **TIP**
>
> The selections you make apply to *all* migrated foreign keys in the model, not just the entity selected.
>
> Migrate all the properties of primary keys to foreign keys unless there is a sound business need to do otherwise.
>
> If you change the name of a foreign key using the Attribute Editor, ER*win* automatically adds the name as a role name in the relationship. These names persist even if the name of the primary key changes in the parent entity.

Click the Migrate button in the Attribute Editor to open the Migrate Attribute Property dialog, shown in Figure 9.17. The following options are available:

- Domain—Select this option to migrate primary key attached domains to foreign key attributes.

- Name—Select this option if you want to migrate the primary key attribute name to a foreign attribute.

- Logical Only—Select this option if you want to migrate the primary key attribute Logical Only property to a foreign key attribute.

- Definition—Select this option if you want to migrate the primary attribute definition to a foreign key attribute.

- Note—Select this option if you want to migrate the primary key attribute note to a foreign key attribute.

- UDP—Select this option if you want to migrate the primary key attribute UDP to a foreign key attribute.
- Icon—Select this option if you want to migrate the primary key attribute icon to a foreign key attribute.

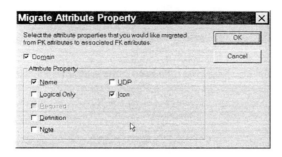

FIGURE 9.17

Use the Migrate Attribute Property dialog to select the primary key properties that will migrate as foreign key properties.

CAUTION

Be careful making changes to the options for migrating properties. ER*win* automatically cascades all the appropriate attribute property information to foreign keys in child entities throughout the diagram and overrides all the properties except name.

The domain of a foreign key can be changed and will remain changed as long as you make no changes to the primary key of the parent entity. However, the foreign key domain reverts to the domain of the primary key if the domain of the primary key is changed.

Attribute Editor Tabs

The Attribute Editor contains the following tabs that allow you to set attribute properties:

- General
- Definition
- Note
- UDP
- Key Group

The General tab, shown in Figure 9.18, allows you to set the following properties:

- Sort—Choose to view the logical domains in alphabetical or hierarchical order. I recommend viewing the domains in hierarchical order because it allows you to see the parent domain for any user-defined domains.

- Domain list—To select a domain for the attribute, click it. Launch the Domain Dictionary Editor by clicking the button marked with the ellipsis to the right of the domain view options. You'll find more information about this in the "Using the Domain Dictionary Editor" section later in this chapter.

- Icon—To associate an icon with the attribute, select an icon from the drop-down list. Launch the Icon Editor, shown in Figure 9.19, by clicking the button marked with the ellipsis to the right of the Icon drop-down list box.

- Primary Key—To indicate that the attribute is part of the primary key, select this option.

- Logical Only—To indicate that the attribute should be present in the logical model only, select this option.

- Required—To indicate that an attribute cannot have a null value, select the Required option.

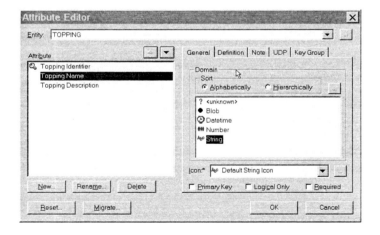

FIGURE 9.18

Use the Attribute Editor, General tab to set some important attribute properties. You can also launch the Domain Dictionary Editor and Icon Editor using the buttons to the right of each drop down.

Icon Editor

ER*win* allows you to associate an icon with an attribute. You can also import new icons as well as rename and delete all icons except the default icons delivered with ER*win*. To launch the Icon Editor, shown in Figure 9.19, click the button marked with an ellipsis to the right of the Icon drop-down list box.

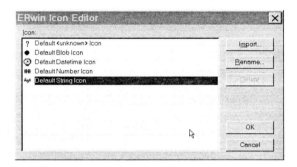

FIGURE 9.19

Use the Icon Editor to import new icons to be included in ERwin's list of available icons.

The functionality of the Icon Editor allows you to

- Import—To import an icon, click this button to open the ERwin Open File dialog and select a bitmap to add to the list of icons in the Icon Editor.
- Rename—To rename an icon, click this button to open the Rename Bitmap dialog and enter a new name for the selected icon. Note that the icon bitmap is renamed only in the Icon Editor; the name of the original bitmap is not changed.
- Delete—To remove the selected icon from the list in the Icon Editor, click this button. Note that the original bitmap is not deleted and that you cannot delete the default icons delivered with ER*win*.

The Definition tab, shown in Figure 9.20, allows you to enter an attribute definition. It contains standard editing functions: Cut, Copy, Paste to Clipboard, and Print Preview.

Print Preview also has standard preview functions: Save (as a .txt file), Print, Find, and Replace, as well as the previously mentioned standard edit functions.

The Key Group tab of the Attribute Editor allows you to select which attributes are included in the key groups for each entity. Primary key groups are based on whether the attribute is a key or non-key. Foreign key groups are based on entity relationships.

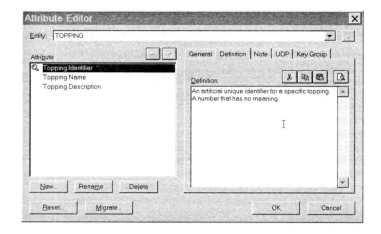

FIGURE 9.20

Use the Definition tab to add or change an attribute definition. Note that the Topping Identifier attribute is defined as an artificial unique identifier, a number with no meaning.

The Key Group tab contains the following:

- Key Group Membership—This lists the key groups defined for the selected entity. An X in the box next to the key group name indicates that the selected attribute is a member. Add an attribute to a key group by selecting the check box next to the key group name. Remove an attribute from a key group by clearing the check box next to a key group name.

- Key Group Editor—To launch the Key Group Editor, click the button marked with an ellipsis.

- Show FK Groups—Select this option to display foreign key groups in the key group membership list. Clear the option to hide foreign key groups.

Using the Key Group Editor

The Key Group Editor, shown in Figure 9.21, allows you to select the member attributes for a key group. You cannot change foreign key group members in the Key Group Editor, but you can add and remove attributes from the primary, alternate, or inversion entry key groups. The options are

- Entity—This indicates the name of the selected entity that contains the key groups. To view the key groups in a different entity, select the entity name from the drop-down list. To open the Entity Editor, click the button marked with an ellipsis to the right of the entity name drop-down list.

- Key Group—This displays the names of all key groups defined for the selected entity.

- Show FK Groups—Select this option to display foreign key groups in the key group membership list. Clear the option to hide foreign key groups.

- New—To add a new key group, click this button to launch the New Key Group dialog, which is discussed in the next section.

- Rename—To rename a key group, click this button to open the Rename Key Group dialog.

- Delete—To delete the selected key group, click this button. This option is not available for a primary key group or foreign key group.

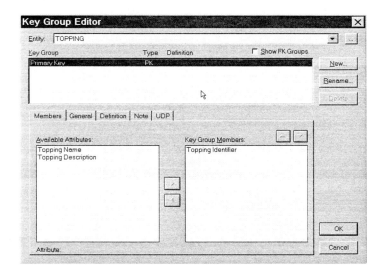

FIGURE 9.21

Use the Key Group Editor to select the members for a key group. You can edit the key groups for a different entity by selecting it from the drop-down list.

NOTE

You can only change foreign key attributes by changing the primary key attributes of the parent entity from which the foreign key group migrates.

New Key Group

The New Key Group dialog, shown in Figure 9.22, allows you to enter or change the name of the key group or index:

- Key Group—Enter or change the logical name for the key group.
- Index—Enter or change the physical name for the key group.

The dialog also allows you to specify the key group type:

- Alternate key (unique)—An alternate key is an attribute that uniquely identifies an instance of an entity but was not selected as the primary key. ER*win* generates a unique index for each alternate key.
- Inversion entry (non-unique)—An inversion entry is an attribute that is used to access instances of entities but that cannot be used to uniquely identify a specific instance. ER*win* generates a non-unique index for each inversion entry.

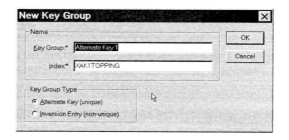

FIGURE 9.22
Use the New Key Group Editor to add an alternate or inversion entry key group.

Adding Members to Key Groups

The Members tab of the Key Group Editor, shown in Figure 9.21, allows you to select the member attributes of most key groups defined for the current entity:

- Available Attributes—Lists the attributes in the entity that do not currently participate in the key group.
- Key Group Members—Lists the attributes in the entity that currently participate in the key group.

To add a new attribute, click an attribute in the Available Attributes list; then click the arrow pointing toward the Key Group Members list.

To remove an attribute, click an attribute in the Key Group Members list; then click the arrow pointing toward the Available Attributes list.

The Key Group Editor's General tab, shown in Figure 9.23, allows you to specify key groups as alternate keys inversion entries. You cannot change the key group type for primary keys and foreign keys in this editor. Key groups are:

- Primary Key—Selected if the key group is the primary key for the entity.
- Alternate Key (unique)—Selected if the key group is an alternate key for the entity. Clicking this button changes an inversion entry key group to an alternate key group.
- Inversion Entry (non-unique)—Selected if the key group is an inversion entry key group for the entity. Clicking this button changes an alternate key group to an inversion entry key group.
- Foreign Key—Selected if the key group is a foreign key for the entity.
- Logical Only—Only available for an alternate key or inversion entry. Select to make the selected key group part of the logical model only. Clear this check box to include the selected alternate key or inversion entry in the physical model as a unique or non-unique index.

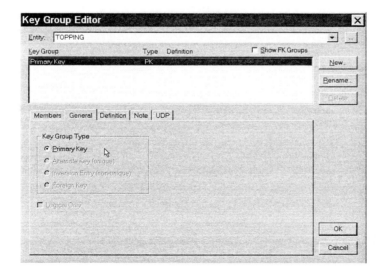

FIGURE 9.23

Use the General tab to change the key type for alternate and inversion entry key groups.

The Definition tab of the Key Group Editor allows you to enter a key group definition. It contains standard editing functions: Cut, Copy, Paste to Clipboard, and Print Preview. Print Preview also has standard preview functions: Save (as a .txt file), Print, Find, and Replace, as well as the standard edit functions.

Similar to the Definition tab, the Note tab of the Key Group Editor allows you to enter a note that is assigned to the key group. The Note tab also contains the standard editing functions.

The UDP tab in the Key Group Editor allows you to assign UDP values to the key group.

Using the Domain Dictionary Editor

ER*win* domains are a flexible tool for defining a set of properties and assigning them to an attribute or column. Using the Domain Dictionary Editor, you can define new domains with logical and physical properties, which can be reused as independent attributes and independent columns. You can also modify the properties of any user-defined domain, as well as all the properties of the five standard domains shipped with ER*win*, except the domain name and domain parent. You can also use the Domain Dictionary Editor to create new domains.

The Domain Dictionary Editor, shown in Figure 9.24, allows you to view and edit the logical properties of a domain. There are two sets of properties: one for the domain itself (non-inheritable properties) and another for the attributes assigned the domain (inheritable properties).

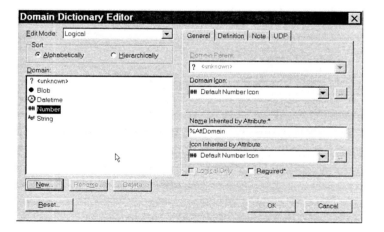

FIGURE 9.24

Use the Domain Dictionary Editor to create and set the properties for user-defined domains.

New Domain

The New Domain dialog in the Domain Dictionary Editor allows you to enter the name for the domain in the logical and physical model. To open the New Domain dialog, click the New button in the Domain Dictionary Editor. Figure 9.25 shows the creation of a new domain called Expiration Date. Figure 9.26 shows the new domain added to the domain list. Note the properties on the General tab for the new domain.

FIGURE 9.25
Use the New Domain dialog to create user-defined domains based on the datatype domains delivered with ERwin.

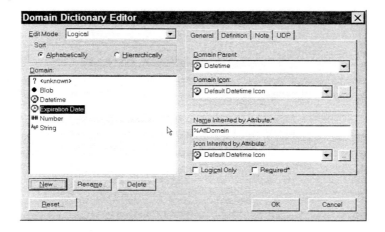

FIGURE 9.26
The New Domain, Expiration Date, uses the Datetime domain to create a specific type of date.

The General tab in the Domain Dictionary Editor allows you to set the following properties:

- Domain Parent—This indicates the parent of the selected domain. To change the parent, select a different domain from the list. This property cannot be inherited.

- Domain Icon—This shows the icon for the selected domain. To change the icon, select a different icon from the list. This property cannot be inherited. Each of the default domains shipped with ERwin is assigned an icon: <unknown>, Blob, Datetime, Number, and String. Click the ellipsis button next to the Domain Icon drop-down box to open the Icon Editor from which you can import bitmap files to use in your ERwin diagram. See the "Icon Editor" section earlier in this chapter for more information.

- Name Inherited by Attribute—Type the name or ERwin macro that the attribute inherits when associated with the selected domain. The ERwin macro %AttDomain automatically migrates the logical domain name to the attribute name.

- Icon Inherited by Attribute—This is the icon that the attribute inherits when associated with the selected domain. To change the icon, select a different icon from the list. Click to open the Icon Editor from which you can import bitmap files to use in your ERwin diagram. See the "Icon Editor" section earlier in this chapter for more information.

- Logical Only—Select this check box if you want the selected domain to appear in the logical model only. Clear this check box if you want the selected domain to be available in both the logical and physical model.

- Required—Select this check box if you want attributes associated with this domain to be a required field in a data entry application. This option corresponds to the NOT NULL option in a physical model.

The Definition tab for the Domain Editor, shown in Figure 9.27, allows you to enter two definitions for each domain: one for the domain itself and another that will be inherited by attributes using that domain:

- Domain Definition—Type or edit the definition for the selected domain. This definition is non-inheritable.

- Definition Inherited by Attribute—Enter the definition that will be inherited by the attributes with the domain.

Similar to the Definition tab, the Note tab for the Domain Dictionary Editor allows you to enter two notes for each domain, one for the domain itself and another that will be inherited by attributes using that domain.

The UDP tab in the Domain Dictionary Editor allows you to assign two sets of UDP values, one for domain itself and one for the attributes using that domain.

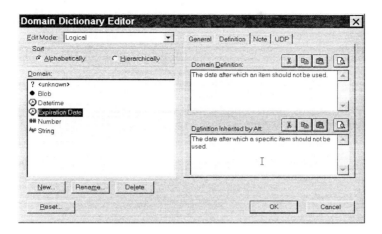

FIGURE 9.27
Use the Domain Dictionary Editor, Definition tab to add a definition for a user-defined domain. Note the definition of the Expiration Date domain.

Summary

Begin developing the logical data model by creating a new ER*win* diagram. To create a new diagram, select an ER*win* template. You can save any model as a template to use as the basis for new diagrams. After selecting the template, set the modeling environment by selecting the ER*win* workplace display options and the methodology notation. The workplace display options allow you to control the toolbars and toolboxes that will be displayed in the diagram. Methodology notation allows you to select the visual notation options for the logical and physical model. Use ER*win*'s Diagram Editor to include important information about the diagram itself.

Using ER*win*'s on-diagram editing features, you can quickly add the entity and attribute names. To open on-diagram editing, click the entity and click again. Press the Enter key to move from the entity name to attribute name. Add entities by selecting the entity tool from the ER*win* toolbox and clicking on the diagram to add an entity. As long as the entity tool is selected, a new entity will be added each time you click on the diagram. Use the Entity Editor to set and edit the properties for entities.

Attributes can be added using ER*win*'s on-diagram editing feature or the Attribute Editor. Use the Attribute Editor to set and edit properties for attributes. You can reset one or more attribute properties to the default using the Reset dialog. The Reset dialog allows you to reset the properties of a single attribute, every attribute in an entity, or every attribute in the model. Use Er*win*'s Migrate dialog to select the primary key attribute properties that migrate to foreign key attributes.

ER*win*'s Key Group Editor allows you to add alternate and inversion entry keys. Alternate keys are one or more attributes that uniquely identify a specific instance of an entity, but were not selected as the primary key. Inversion entry keys are one or more attributes that facilitate the way users will access the data.

ER*win* domains are a flexible tool for defining a set of properties and assigning them to an attribute or column. Using the Domain Dictionary Editor, you can define new domains with logical and physical properties, which can be reused as independent attributes and independent columns. You can also modify the properties of any user-defined domain, as well as all the properties of the five standard domains shipped with ER*win*, except the domain name and domain parent.

Now that you know how to create entities and attributes, you're ready to create the relationships between them. In the next chapter I explain how to create relationships between entities using ER*win*'s relationship tools.

Building Logical Relationships

In previous chapters, you examined the ER*win* tools for creating and editing entities and attributes. You will recall that the logical model is represented in an ERD by entities, attributes, and relationships. A relationship is the association, or link, between two entities.

Relationships might seem simple at first glance. In fact, relationships represent the core of a data model and are the mechanism for implementing many business rules. Take care that the logical relationships reflect the information requirements and business rules. Keep in mind that representing the relationships accurately and completely requires some analysis and might even require additional contact with domain experts for further clarification.

In this chapter, I focus on using ER*win* to model the relationships between the entities defined for Betty's Ice Cream Shop. The sections that follow explore

- Logical relationships in ER*win*
- Using the relationship tools
- Using the Relationship Editor
- Understanding cardinality
- Understanding nullity

ER*win* has features that protect you from making some technical mistakes with relationships. However, it has no way of knowing if you have correctly identified parent and child relationships according to specific business rules. Use caution as you implement relationships, the heart of a relational model.

Logical Relationships in ER*win*

In ER*win*, you can create a relationship between two entities (or an entity and itself) using the relationships tools in the toolbox or the Relationship Editor. In creating the relationship, ER*win* migrates the primary key attributes of the parent entity as foreign key attributes in the child entity. The placement of the migrated foreign key attributes as key or non-key attributes depends upon the relationship type.

A relationship is visually represented in the logical model by

- A relationship line connecting two entities
- A verb phrase that describes how the two entities relate to one another
- End-point symbols that represent cardinality and optionality or nullity

Remember that in the logical model, verb phrases should use business terminology to describe the business rules defining the relationship.

Figure 10.1 shows a preliminary data model of the information requirements for the problem statement defined for Betty's Ice Cream Shop. Note that five relationship types are represented in the relationships between the seven entities. In the sections that follow, I refine these logical relationships.

Unifying Relationships

ER*win* has a feature called *unifying relationships*, where two or more foreign keys with the same name are merged into a single foreign key. The assumption is that foreign keys must be identical if they have the same logical and physical name. Normalization rules do not permit an entity to have two attributes with the same name.

When there are multiple relationships between a parent and child entity, the child entity inherits multiple instances of the same foreign key. By default, ER*win* unifies and displays only one occurrence of the foreign key in the child entity. Because this can be confusing, it is a best practice to use rolenames for these attributes. You'll read more on rolenames in the section "Using the Relationship Editor" later in this chapter.

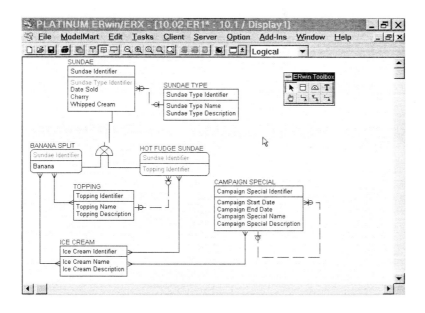

FIGURE 10.1

The preliminary data model for Betty's Ice Cream Shop shows examples of all the relationship types available in ERwin.

Using the Relationship Tools

In ER*win*, follow these steps to create a relationship using one of the relationship tools in the toolbox:

1. Click the relationship tool.
2. Click the parent entity.
3. Click the child entity.

Each relationship tool creates a different relationship type. The mouse pointer changes shape, providing a visual indicator of which relationship tool is in use. A new relationship is assigned a default name of the form R/*n*, where R is relationship and *n* is a unique number.

TIP

ERwin's on-diagram editing feature allows you to enter a relationship verb phrase on the diagram instead of using the Relationship Editor, but you must select the option that displays the verb phrase on the diagram.

Right-click the diagram to display the Diagram Display Option menu. Select Display Options/Relationship, Verb Phrase. This displays the default R/n relationship name. Click once to select the relationship line, and click again to edit the verb phrase using ERwin's on-diagram editing feature. It's a little tricky to get the click just right.

ERwin relationship tools allow you to create the following types of relationships:

- Many-to-many
- Identifying
- Non-identifying
- Subtype
- Recursive

Many-to-Many Relationship

A many-to-many relationship indicates a situation where a single instance of one entity relates to one or more instances of a second entity, and a single instance in the second entity also relates to one or more instances in the first. These relationships are also called *non-specific relationships*.

NOTE

Many-to-many relationships should only exist in the preliminary stage of logical model development. Because many-to-many relationships often hide important business rules or constraints, you should fully resolve them as part of the modeling process.

There is no physical representation for many-to-many relationships. Because these relationships cannot be represented in physical data structures, ERwin automatically resolves many-to-many relationships when the model is changed to physical mode.

In ER*win*, a many-to-many relationship is visually represented by a solid line connecting two entities. There is no migration of foreign key attributes. Using IE methodology, both end points of the relationship line have the crow's foot symbol for many.

Our business rules define an instance of BANANA SPLIT as having up to three different kinds of ICE CREAM and three different kinds of TOPPING. The same kind of ICE CREAM and the same kind of TOPPING can appear in many instances of BANANA SPLIT. Figure 10.2 shows these two many-to-many relationships.

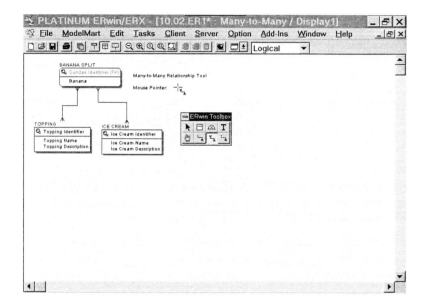

FIGURE 10.2

Many-to-many relationships in IE notation use the crow's foot as a visual indicator of the fact that many instances of one entity can participate. In many-to-many relationships, both end points of the relationship line have crow's feet.

Identifying Relationship

An identifying relationship is a relationship between two entities in which a specific instance of a child entity is identified by values of attributes in the parent entity. In other words, an instance of the child entity is dependent on the parent entity for identity and cannot exist without an instance of the parent.

In ER*win*, an identifying relationship is visually represented as a solid line connecting two entities and the migration of the primary key attributes of the parent entity as foreign key attributes that become all or part of the primary key in the child entity.

> **NOTE**
>
> Identifying foreign key attributes cannot have a null value. Take care to ensure that a value is available for each instance.

Figure 10.3 shows the identifying relationships between a banana split, ice cream, and topping. Also, note that because the relationship type is identifying, the Sundae Identifier primary key attribute migrates from the parent entity to the two child entities, BANANA SPLIT ICE CREAM and BANANA SPLIT TOPPING. These *associative* entities were added to the model to resolve the many-to-many relationship between BANANA SPLIT and ICE CREAM and BANANA SPLIT and TOPPING.

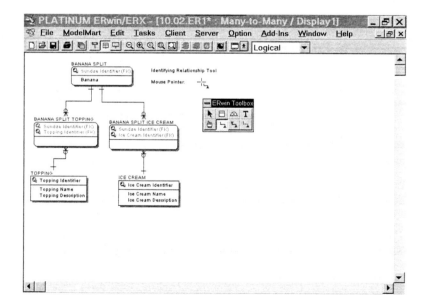

FIGURE 10.3

In ERwin, identifying relationships are represented by a solid line connecting two entities. Notice that the mouse pointer indicates that the Identifying Relationship Tool is in use.

Let's analyze the relationships between BANANA SPLIT, ICE CREAM, and TOPPING. What do you know from the session? You have a definition of a banana split:

> A banana split contains three scoops of ice cream, three servings of topping, a banana, whipped cream, and a cherry. A customer can select up to three different ice cream flavors and up to three different toppings.

The following list represents the clearly stated relationship rules:

- A banana split has three scoops of ice cream.
- A banana split can have up to three different kinds of ice cream.
- A banana split has three servings of toppings.
- A banana split can have up to three different kinds of toppings.
- A banana split has a banana, whipped cream, and a cherry.

Other relationships are not so clearly stated.

In the model snippet shown in Figure 10.3, you can infer the following business rules from the identifying relationships:

- An instance of TOPPING and an instance of BANANA SPLIT are required to identify an instance of BANANA SPLIT TOPPING.
- An instance of ICE CREAM and an instance of BANANA SPLIT are required to identify an instance of BANANA SPLIT ICE CREAM.

Some questions that should arise regarding these relationships follow:

- Does an instance of BANANA SPLIT require at least one kind of ice cream?
- Does an instance of BANANA SPLIT require at least one kind of topping?
- How will the model handle instances of BANANA SPLIT ICE CREAM where the customer elects to have more than one scoop of the same kind of ice cream?
- How will the model handle instances of BANANA SPLIT TOPPING where the customer elects to have more than one serving of the same kind of topping?

The answer to the first question might seem trivial in the example. However, in other, more complex problem domains, this question might reveal important business rules. The answers to the remaining questions will reveal important business rules regarding cardinality. I address the answers to these questions in later sections.

Non-Identifying Relationship

A non-identifying relationship is a relationship between two entities in which an instance of the child entity is not identified through its association with a parent entity. This means the child entity is not dependent on the parent entity for identity and can exist without an instance of the parent.

In ER*win*, a non-identifying relationship is visually represented by a dashed line connecting two entities and the migration of the primary key attributes from the parent entity as non-key attributes in the child entity. Figure 10.4 shows a non-identifying relationship between

SUNDAE TYPE and SUNDAE. Also, notice that the primary key of the parent entity, SUN-DAE TYPE, migrates as a foreign key, non-key attribute in the child entity, SUNDAE.

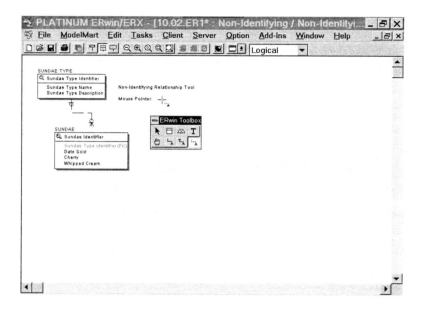

FIGURE 10.4

Non-identifying relationships are represented by a dashed line. Note that the mouse pointer indicates that the Non-identifying Relationship Tool is in use.

In the model snippet shown in Figure 10.4, you can see that Sundae Type does not identify a specific instance of SUNDAE because the foreign key, Sundae Type Identifier, is not included in the primary key. However, the relationship does not answer the following question: Does an instance of SUNDAE require that the SUNDAE TYPE have a value?

Again, the answer to the question might seem trivial in our example. However, in more complex problem domains, this question can reveal important business rules. These and other questions will reveal important business rules regarding nullity and cardinality. I address the answers to these questions in later sections.

Subtype Relationship

Subtype relationships are relationships between a parent entity, sometimes called the supertype, and one or more child entities. Subtype entities almost always have one or more sibling entities.

Subtype relationships are often identified during the normalization of a logical model. Remember that part of the normalization process includes identifying attributes whose value is dependent upon the value of another attribute. An attribute in a parent entity whose value determines the value of attributes in a child entity is called a *discriminator*.

To create a subtype relationship, click the Subtype Tool in the toolbox. Click the parent entity, and then click the child entity. For subsequent child entities, click the subtype relationship symbol, and then click the child entity.

To identify the subtype relationships in the example, the process is fairly straightforward. You can apply the following process to identify complex subtypes as well.

1. Look for strong similarities among attributes that exist in two or more entities. Take care to define attributes clearly and completely to make this part of the process easier.

2. Look for attributes within an entity that depend upon another attribute for a value. These dependent attributes often represent subtypes. The attributes whose value determines the value for dependent attributes are discriminators.

3. Look for attributes within an entity that have null values for some instances. Examine the instances to identify similarities among them. Groups of instances might identify subtypes.

NOTE

IDEF1X defines all subtype relationships as exclusive. This restriction simply does not support the real world. It means that a person cannot be both an employee and a customer! It's not surprising that our government has embraced this methodology.

In IDEF1X methodology notation, subtype relationships have a significantly different meaning. Subtype relationships are *complete* or *incomplete*. A complete subtype relationship is one in which every instance of a parent entity has a corresponding instance in a single child entity. An incomplete subtype relationship is one in which not all instances of a parent entity have a corresponding instance in a child entity.

The subtype entity siblings are related to the parent entity through a subtype relationship that is either exclusive or inclusive using the IE methodology.

Exclusive Subtype

Exclusive subtype relationships indicate that only one child entity is defined by an instance of the parent entity. In other words, an instance of the parent entity does not have related instances in more than a single child entity. Exclusive subtypes represent an "is a" relationship.

In ER*win*, an exclusive subtype relationship is visually represented using the subtype symbol with an X in the center.

Figure 10.5 shows a subtype relationship. To arrive at that relationship, consider the following:

- Domain experts told us that Betty's sells two types of sundaes. Domain experts often identify subtypes during the information requirements gathering.
- Similarities in attributes confirm that banana splits and hot fudge are types of sundaes. Each contains ice cream, toppings, whipped cream, and a cherry.
- Differences in attribute values confirm that although banana split and hot fudge sundaes have similar attributes, they are distinct entities.
- An instance of a sundae can be either a banana split or hot fudge, but not both. This fact confirms that the subtype is exclusive.
- A discriminator, Sundae Type, is recognized and accepted by domain experts, a powerful fact.

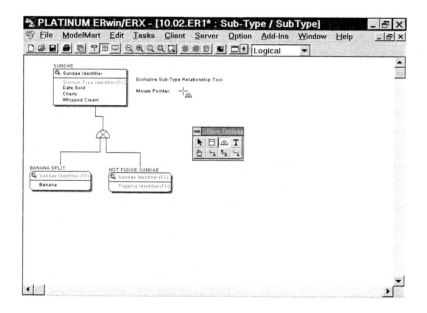

FIGURE 10.5

Exclusive subtype relationships in ERwin use an X in the subtype symbol as a visual indicator that an instance of an entity can only relate to a single child.

Double-click the subtype relationship symbol to launch the Subtype Relationship dialog and select the discriminator attribute. Click the attribute in the Discriminator Attribute Choice list.

Figure 10.6 shows the Subtype Relationship dialog with the Sundae Type Identifier selected as the discriminator in the example.

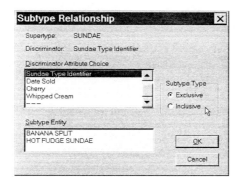

FIGURE 10.6
Use ERwin's Subtype Relationship dialog to select the discriminator attribute and choose the subtype type.

Inclusive Subtype

Inclusive subtype relationships indicate that more than one child entity can be defined by an instance of the parent entity. In other words, an instance of the parent entity has related instances in more than a single child entity.

TIP

In ER*win*, all subtype relationships are initially exclusive when created. To create an inclusive subtype relationship, double-click the subtype relationship symbol to launch the Subtype Relationship dialog shown in Figure 10.6. Change the Subtype Type to Inclusive.

An often-used example of an inclusive relationship is a PERSON. An EMPLOYEE is a subtype of PERSON. A CUSTOMER is also a subtype of PERSON. It makes sense that an enterprise would keep some identical information about EMPLOYEE and CUSTOMER, such as Name and Address. It also makes sense that the enterprise would keep some information about EMPLOYEE that it would not keep about CUSTOMER, such as Pay Rate and Skill Set.

An inclusive relationship allows the model to use a single instance of PERSON and capture additional information about PERSON in the role of EMPLOYEE and CUSTOMER.

Recursive Relationship

A recursive relationship is a relationship between two entities that indicates that an instance of the entity can be related to another instance of the same entity. In a recursive relationship, the parent entity and the child entity are the same entity.

In ER*win*, a recursive relationship is represented by a "fishhook" symbol that begins and ends in the same entity. To create a recursive relationship, select the Non-identifying or the Many-to-Many Relationship Tool, click the entity, and then click the same entity.

NOTE

A recursive relationship can only be non-identifying or many-to-many. Allowing a recursive relationship to be identifying would create a cyclic relationship. A *cyclic* relationship is a relationship that is interdependent.

ER*win* presents an error message if you attempt to use the Identifying Relationship Tool to create a recursive relationship.

Figure 10.1 shows a recursive relationship in the CAMPAIGN SPECIAL entity. The recursive relationship in the example allows us to group campaigns. Admittedly, this relationship is somewhat contrived, but the concept of grouping instances of an entity based on a parent instance is a common modeling construct.

Using the Relationship Editor

The Relationship Editor allows you to define the values for a set of properties for a relationship, such as its verb phrase, cardinality, type, and nullity. You can also use the Relationship Editor to enter a definition, define migrating foreign key attribute rolenames, and define referential integrity trigger actions.

To launch the Relationship Editor, shown in Figure 10.7, select Edit, Relationship, or right-click a relationship and then select the Relationship Editor item on the shortcut menu.

TIP

Select the Relationship Editor once and then simply double-click a relationship line to launch the editor.

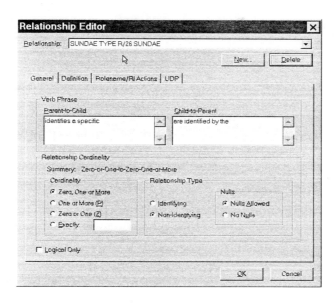

Figure 10.7

Use ERwin's Relationship Editor to set the properties of the selected Relationship. Note that the Relationship drop-down uses the form Entity-Relationship-Entity.

The Relationship drop-down list displays the currently selected relationship. To view and edit the properties of another relationship, select a different relationship from the list.

Clicking the New button opens the New Relationship dialog, which allows you to add a new relationship. Select a parent entity to enable the selection of a child entity, and then select the type. Figure 10.8 shows the New Relationship dialog. Note that when you use the New Relationship dialog to create a relationship, the default type is identifying. If the relationship type is set in error, use the Relationship Editor to change the relationship type. ER*win* automatically handles the foreign key placement.

10

Figure 10.8

Use the New Relationship dialog to create a new relationship between two entities. When you create a relationship, ERwin automatically places the foreign key attributes as key or non-key, depending on the relationship type.

Clicking the Relationship Editor's Delete button deletes the selected relationship. ER*win* displays a warning that the action cannot be undone. Clicking the Cancel button does not undo this action.

> ## TIP
>
> If you delete a diagram object in error, you can close the diagram and not save the changes to revert to the previously saved version. If you've made other changes and you prefer not to repeat the work, use the Save As option to save the diagram using another name. Then, use ER*win*'s feature for copying and pasting model objects between diagrams to save the changes you want to keep.
>
> ER*win* saves the previous version of a diagram as a *.bk1 file in the same directory. To open this file, change the file extension from BK1 to ER1.

Selecting the Logical Only check box indicates that the relationship should appear only in the logical model. Do not select this check box if you want the relationship to appear in the physical model and be created in the physical data structures. Logical-only relationships do not appear in the data model when the model is in the physical mode, but the parent entity's primary key still migrates as a foreign key to the child entity.

The Relationship Editor also includes the following tabs (shown in Figure 10.7):

- General—Add or edit the general properties of a relationship.
- Definition—Add or edit a definition for a relationship.
- Rolename/RI Actions—Enter foreign key attribute rolenames and select referential integrity actions.
- UDP—Provide a value for a user-defined property for the selected relationship. Launch the UDP Editor by clicking the button on the upper-right corner of the UDP tab.

General

The General tab of the Relationship Editor allows you to add and edit the general properties about a relationship, including the verb phrase, cardinality, relationship type, and nullity.

Verb Phrase

Enter a verb phrase that describes the relationship. Use business terminology and be descriptive. Remember that you should be able to read a relationship:

- Parent-to-Child—Enter the verb phrase for the parent-to-child relationship.
- Child-to-Parent—Enter the verb phrase for the child-to-parent relationship.

Cardinality

The relationship cardinality specifies the maximum number of instances of one entity that can be related to the instances of another entity. Cardinality is defined for both sides of a relationship, the originating entity and the terminating entity. Cardinality defines the maximum number of entity instances that can participate in a relationship, whereas optionality, or nullity, defines the minimum number of instances.

The following cardinality options are available for relationships:

- Zero, One or More—Select to specify that an instance of the parent entity is related to zero, one, or more instances of the child entity.
- One or More (P)—Select to specify that an instance of the parent entity is related to one or more instances of the child entity.
- Zero or One (Z)—Select to specify that an instance of the parent entity is related to zero or one instance of the child entity.
- Exactly—Enter an exact number of instances of a child entity that will be related to the parent entity.

Consider the sample model. An instance of BANANA SPLIT must have exactly three instances (servings) of BANANA SPLIT ICE CREAM. An instance of BANANA SPLIT ICE CREAM requires an instance of BANANA SPLIT and an instance of ICE CREAM. These are examples of business rules that can be implemented using cardinality.

ER*win* displays the cardinality for a relationship. To see the cardinality for the relationships in a diagram, set the cardinality display option by right-clicking the diagram, selecting Display Options/Relationships, and then selecting Cardinality.

Relationship Type

Select the relationship type:

- Identifying—Select to indicate that the relationship is an identifying relationship. Remember that no nulls are allowed in identifying relationships.
- Non-Identifying—Select to indicate that the relationship is a non-identifying relationship.

Nulls

Non-identifying relationship foreign key attributes in the child entity that migrated from the parent can have a NULLS ALLOWED or NO NULLS value. A NULLS ALLOWED value means that an instance of the child entity can exist without an instance in the parent. A non-identifying relationship that allows NULLS is also called an *optional* relationship. A NO NULLS value means that an instance of the child entity is dependent upon an instance of the parent entity for its existence. A non-identifying relationship that does not allow NULLS is also called a *mandatory* relationship.

- Nulls Allowed—Select to indicate that the foreign key attributes in the child entity can have nulls. This option is available only for non-identifying relationships.
- No Nulls—Select to indicate that the foreign key attributes in the child entity will not accept nulls. This option is available only for non-identifying relationships.

In the example, there is a non-identifying relationship between SUNDAE TYPE and SUN-DAE. There is a question regarding whether an instance of SUNDAE requires a value for the foreign key attribute Sundae Type Identifier. The Sundae Type Identifier does not uniquely identify an instance of SUNDAE. However, the migrated attribute Sundae Type Identifier was identified as the discriminator that indicates a subtype entity. A discriminator should not be allowed to have a NULL value in SUNDAE.

Rolename/RI Actions

Use the Rolename/RI Actions tab of the Relationship Editor to define attribute rolenames and select referential integrity trigger actions for relationships. Figure 10.9 shows the Rolename/RI Actions tab with the recursive relationship in CAMPAIGN SPECIAL selected.

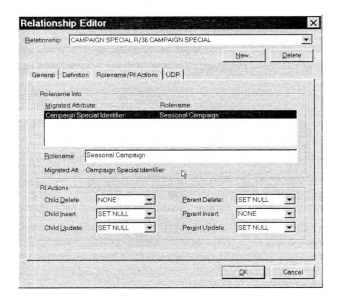

FIGURE 10.9

The Rolename/RI Actions tab allows you to provide a different name for a migrated foreign key. Using a different name can help users understand how the migrating attributes are used in the entity.

Migrated Attribute and Rolename

The Migrated Attribute area displays a list of the primary key attributes that migrated from the parent entity to the child entity. Any rolenames assigned to the migrated attributes in the current relationship are displayed. Note in Figure 10.9, the rolename of Seasonal Campaign is assigned to the migrated attribute Campaign Special Identifier.

Rolename

Enter or edit the rolename for the attribute selected from the Migrated Attribute list.

RI Actions

RI actions are the referential integrity trigger actions that maintain the relational integrity between instances of a parent and instances of child. ER*win* supplies a set of built-in referential integrity actions to implement the business rules that apply to the relationships between instances in parent and child entities. These rules are enforced through referential integrity trigger actions.

You can define the following referential integrity trigger actions for relationships:

- RESTRICT—Defining this action prevents deleting, inserting, or updating an instance in the parent or child entity when there are one or more related instances in the child or parent entity.
- CASCADE—When an instance of the parent entity or table is deleted, inserted, or updated, each related instance of the child entity or table is also deleted, inserted, or updated.
- SET NULL—When an instance in the parent entity or table is deleted, inserted, or updated, the foreign key attribute values in each related instance of the child entity or table are set to NULL.
- SET DEFAULT—When an instance in the parent entity or table is deleted, inserted, or updated, the foreign key attribute values in each related instance of the child entity or table are set to the default value assigned to that attribute.
- NONE—No referential integrity action is required.

NOTE

The list of available RI actions depends on the relationship type and nullity. The RI actions for each relationship type are

- Identifying—RESTRICT, CASCADE, and NONE.
- Non-identifying (no nulls)—RESTRICT, CASCADE, NONE, and SET DEFAULT.
- Non-identifying (nulls allowed)—RESTRICT, CASCADE, NONE, SET NULL, and SET DEFAULT.

10

You can attach the following RI actions to a relationship, instructing the DBMS which action should be taken on an attempt to delete, insert, or update an instance of an entity:

- Child Delete—Select the referential integrity trigger action that should be taken when an instance in the child entity is deleted.
- Child Insert—Select the referential integrity trigger action that should be taken when a new instance is inserted in the child entity.
- Child Update—Select the referential integrity trigger action that should be taken when an instance in the child entity is updated.
- Parent Delete—Select the referential integrity trigger action that should be taken when an instance in the parent entity is deleted.
- Parent Insert—Select the referential integrity trigger action that should be taken when a new instance is inserted in the parent entity.
- Parent Update—Select the referential integrity trigger action that should be taken when an instance in the parent entity is updated.

ER*win* automatically assigns a default referential integrity trigger action to each relationship when you add it to a model based on the default specified using the RI Defaults options set in the Target Server dialog. Relational Integrity defaults are specific to the target server selected and apply to the entire model.

ER*win* displays the referential integrity symbols for a relationship at both the child and parent ends of a relationship line. To see the referential integrity symbols in your diagram, set the referential integrity display options.

Summary

Logical relationships are the core of a relational model and represent the business rules for how the instances of one entity relate to instances of another. In ER*win*, relationships are represented by a line between two entities, a verb phrase that describes the relationship, and end points that indicate cardinality and optionality or nullity. Relationships are defined in terms of type, degree, cardinality, and optionality or nullity.

To create a relationship in ER*win*, select the appropriate relationship tool, click on the parent entity, then click on the child entity. ER*win* has tools that allow you to create five relationship types:

- Many-to-many: Those relationships in which an instance of one entity relates to multiple instances of a second entity, and an instance in the second entity also relates to multiple instances in the first. Many-to-many relationships are logical model concepts that cannot be represented in the physical model.

- Identifying: Those relationships in which an instance of a child entity depends on the parent entity for identity and cannot exist without an instance of the parent. The key attributes that participate in identifying relationships, by definition cannot have null values. ER*win* represents identifying relationships with a solid line connecting two entities.

- Non-identifying: Those relationships in which an instance of the child entity is not dependent on the parent entity for identity and can exist without an instance of the parent. You can specify whether the key attributes that participate in a non-identifying relationship are allowed to have null values.

- Subtype: Those relationships in which a parent or super type entity is related to at least one instance in the child entity. Subtype relationships are either exclusive or inclusive in IE methodology, complete or incomplete in IDEF1X methodology. Subtype relationships are logical model concepts and cannot be represented in the physical model.

- Recursive: Those relationships in which instance of an entity are related to other instances of the same entity. In ER*win* a recursive relationship is represented using a "fishhook" symbol. Recursive relationships can only be created as non-identifying relationships.

ER*win*'s Relationship Editor allows you to set the properties of relationships including adding role names and relational integrity actions. Rolenames allow you to give new names to migrating foreign key attributes that provide insight into how the attributes are used in the entity. Relational integrity actions allow you to specify what should happen on the insert, delete and update actions.

In addition to creating the entities, attributes, and relationships for the logical model, ER*win* provides some powerful features that allow you to organize and enhance the understandability of the logical model. In the next chapter, you learn how to use subject areas, display areas, text boxes and icons.

Organizing and Enhancing
the Logical Data Model

In previous chapters, I described the mechanics of building a logical data model using ER*win*. I explored a process for collecting information requirements and discussed translating information requirements and business rules into an ER diagram. I explained ER*win* tools for creating entities, attributes, and relationships and built a logical model for Betty's Ice Cream. In this chapter, I explore ER*win*'s features for organizing and enhancing the logical data model.

ER*win* provides features that allow you to organize a diagram into subject areas. Subject areas divide large, complex data models into smaller segments that are easier to create and maintain. Subject areas can also include stored displays, which can enhance readability and understandability.

ER*win* supplies several powerful display options that allow you to set properties for all diagram model objects, including the diagram itself. These properties include font size, color, and special diagram objects, such as text blocks and icons, that can significantly improve the appearance and readability of the diagram.

This chapter explores the following topics:

- Subject areas
- Stored displays
- Display options
- Text blocks
- Icons

Dividing a large complex model into subject areas makes it easier to create and maintain. Stored displays allow you to display subject area objects at different levels. Display options allow you to control the appearance of diagram objects. Text blocks and icons allow you to add additional information to make a model more understandable.

Subject Areas

Every ER*win* data model diagram initially includes a single subject area, called the *main subject area*. The main subject area includes all the objects (entities, tables, views, and text blocks) in a data model. You can divide the main subject area into one or more specialized subject areas that focus on a specific business function. For the most part, objects in a specialized subject area should relate to a specific business unit, such as personnel, finance, sales, or marketing.

Working with subject areas is also useful when designing and maintaining a large, complex data model. Dividing the main subject area into a group of smaller, more manageable subject areas lets several different groups within an organization concentrate on the business processes and tasks specific to a particular business area.

NOTE

Although a diagram can contain many subject areas, the main subject area is a core diagram object and cannot be renamed or deleted.

An ER*win* subject area is a set of diagram objects selected from the objects contained in the main subject area. You can add new subject areas to a diagram using the Subject Area Editor. When you create a new subject area, it is added to the subject area list on the ER*win* toolbar and in the Subject Area Editor. To switch to a different subject area, select the subject area name from the list as shown in Figure 11.1.

Organizing and Enhancing the Logical Data Model

CHAPTER 11

223

11

ORGANIZING AND
ENHANCING THE
MODEL

If a diagram contains multiple subject areas, you can create a unique set of stored displays for each subject area. Within a subject area, you can see only the stored display tabs for that subject area. Creating stored displays is covered in the ""Stored Displays" section later in this chapter.

When you create a new subject area for a diagram in logical mode, ER*win* creates the same subject area in the physical model. In other words, subject areas are shared between the logical and physical models. If a diagram object, such as an entity or a text block, is added or removed as a member of a subject area in the logical model, the membership change is reflected in the physical model. However, adding or removing members in one subject area does not affect the members of any other subject areas.

CAUTION

When you delete diagram objects in a subject area, ERwin offers the option of removing from the subject area or deleting from the model. Deleting an object from the model in *any* subject area removes the object from *every* subject area in which is a member.

When you add diagram objects in any subject area, ER*win* automatically adds the object to the main subject area (if you are not currently in the main subject area). Remember, the main subject area includes *all* diagram objects.

ER*win* saves subject areas with the main subject area diagram when the diagram is saved as an .er1 file. However, you must also save the diagram to permanently save all the subject area information along with the rest of the diagram. Canceling changes on the diagram, or closing the diagram without saving, erases any new additions or changes in the subject areas.

You can create new subject areas using the Subject Area Editor. The Subject Area Editor provides features for naming the subject area, setting global options, and selecting the members (diagram objects) to include. In addition, you can use the ER*win* Neighborhood feature to specify how many generations of ancestors or descendants of the members to include in the subject area.

TIP

You can use subject areas as filters during schema generation to limit the creation of data structures to those selected in the subject area. You'll read more on schema generation in Chapter 19, "Delivering the Physical Data Model."

Using the Subject Area Editor

Use the Subject Area Editor to create, modify, and delete subject areas in the diagram. To launch the Subject Area Editor, shown in Figure 11.1, click the Subject Area icon on the ER*win* toolbar or select Edit, Subject Area.

The Subject Area Editor includes the following:

- Subject Area—This displays a list of the subject areas in the diagram. To open a subject area, click on the name and click the OK button.
- New—Click this button to open the New Subject Area dialog, shown in Figure 11.2.
- Rename—Click this button to open the Rename Subject Area dialog and change the name of the selected subject area.
- Delete—Click this button to remove the selected subject area from the diagram. If you delete a subject area in error, press the Cancel button.

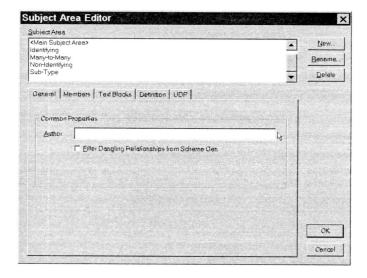

FIGURE 11.1

Use the Subject Area Editor to set the properties for new subject areas. Every diagram contains a <Main Subject Area> that includes every model object and cannot be changed. Subject areas you create can contain only a subset of the available objects.

When you add a new subject area, ER*win* offers an option to copy members from the selected subject area. If you do not copy the members from the selected subject area, the new subject area will contain all the objects in the main subject area. Use the dialog shown in Figure 11.2

Organizing and Enhancing the Logical Data Model

CHAPTER 11

225

11

ORGANIZING AND
ENHANCING THE
MODEL

to add a name for the subject area. As always, use naming conventions and guidelines to create good subject area names.

FIGURE 11.2
In the New Subject Area dialog, provide a name for the new subject area and indicate whether or not to copy the members of the current subject area as the basis for the new one.

The Subject Area Editor also includes the following tabs:

- General
- Members
- Text Blocks
- Definition
- UDP

Figure 11.1 shows the functionality available in the General tab:

- Author—Enter the name of the modeler who created the subject area.
- Filter Dangling Relationships from Schema Gen—Check this box to exclude references to tables in the main subject area that are not in the currently selected subject area during schema generation.

When ER*win* generates the schema for a subject area, it references tables in the main subject area that are not in the current subject area, specifically foreign keys and triggers. ER*win* provides the option of excluding references to these objects in the schema statements. Selecting the Filter Dangling Relationship from Schema Gen box in the Subject Area Editor instructs ER*win* to eliminate foreign key references to tables not included in the currently selected subject area.

NOTE

Selecting the Filter Dangling Relationship from Schema Gen option has no effect on the foreign keys displayed in the subject area. The migrated keys from tables not included in the subject area still appear. Only schema generation is affected.

The Filter Dangling Relationships from Schema Gen box is not available if the currently selected subject area is the main subject area because the main subject area includes *all* diagram objects.

Subject Area Members

Use the Members tab of the Subject Area Editor to select the entities, tables, or views to be included in the subject area. ER*win* provides the option of using the logical model names or the physical model names when selecting subject area members. Figure 11.3 shows the functionality of the Members tab.

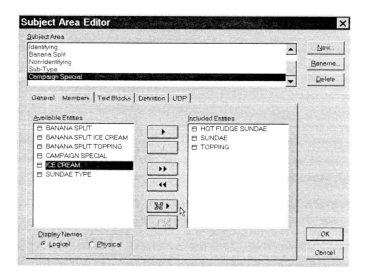

FIGURE 11.3

The Subject Area Editor, Members tab allows you to select the diagram objects that will be included in the subject area. You cannot change the members in the <Main Subject Area>.

Available Entities displays the diagram objects that you can include as members of the selected subject area. Double-click an item to move it from the Available list to the Included list. When the Logical option is selected, the list contains the entities that can be included as members of the subject area. When the Physical option is selected, the list contains the tables and views that can be included as members of the subject area.

Included Entities displays the diagram objects that are currently included as members of the subject area. Double-click an item to move it from the Included list to the Available list. When the Logical option is selected, this list contains the entities that are currently included as

Organizing and Enhancing the Logical Data Model

CHAPTER 11

227

11

ORGANIZING AND
ENHANCING THE
MODEL

members of the subject area. When the Physical option is selected, this list contains the tables and views that are currently included as members of the subject area.

Clicking the single-arrow buttons also moves the selected item to the Available or Included list. Clicking the double-arrow buttons moves all items from one list to the other.

The two buttons below the double-arrow buttons allow you to automatically include or exclude an object's ancestors or descendants when adding or removing subject area objects. Clicking either of these buttons opens the Spanning Neighborhood dialog, shown in Figure 11.4. This dialog allows you to select the level of ancestors and descendants to include for each object in the subject area. The following options apply to ancestors:

- All—Click this button to include all entities that are ancestors (parents, grandparents, great-grandparents, and so on) of the selected object in the subject area.
- Level—Click this button and enter a number that represents the level of ancestors to include in the subject area. For example, enter **2** to include only the parents and grand-parents of an entity. Enter **1** to include only the parents.

You have the following options for descendants:

- All—Click this button to include all entities that are descendants (children, grandchil-dren, great-grandchildren, and so on) of the selected object in the subject area.
- Level—Click this button and enter a number representing the level of descendants to include in the subject area. For example, enter **2** to include the children of the entity (level 1) and the children of the child entities.

FIGURE 11.4
Use the Spanning Neighborhood dialog as a quick way to include related entities in a subject area. The buttons are not available unless the entity selected is related to other entities.

NOTE

The spanning feature is extremely useful when creating subject areas in large, com-plex diagrams. It allows you to quickly and easily include related entities without selecting each one individually.

Use the Text Blocks tab of the Subject Area Editor to select the text blocks to include in the selected subject area. This tab works much the same as the Members tab:

- Available Text Blocks displays the text blocks that can be included as members of the subject area. Double-click a text block to move it from the Available list to the Included list.
- Included Text Blocks displays the text blocks that are currently included as members of the subject area. Double-click a text block to move it from the Included list to the Available list.

NOTE

If a text box contains more text than will fit in the list, use the ER*win* Name Tips feature to display more of the text. Place the mouse pointer over a text block; after a moment, more text appears in the Name Tip box.

Stored Displays

In ER*win*, stored displays provide an alternate way to arrange, view, and work on the objects in a diagram. Each subject area in a diagram can have several different stored displays.

You create stored displays using the Stored Display Editor. The Stored Display Editor contains several options for display levels and several options for the subject area. Diagram objects can be arranged differently in each stored display. For example, a stored display for a business area can contain only entity names with magnification to make the entities easy to see during a presentation.

Initially, a new data model diagram includes one stored display (Display1) and one subject area (the main subject area). For each stored display created, ER*win* adds a stored display tab at the bottom of the diagram window. Switch to a different stored display by clicking its tab. If a diagram contains multiple subject areas, each can contain a different set of stored displays. You see only the stored display tabs for the current subject area.

NOTE

If the stored display tabs are not visible at the bottom of the diagram window, select Window, Stored Display Tabs.

Organizing and Enhancing the Logical Data Model

CHAPTER 11

229

11

ORGANIZING AND
ENHANCING THE
MODEL

When you create a stored display for the logical model, ER*win* automatically creates a similar stored display for the physical model, and vice versa. However, you can set the Stored Display Editor options differently for the logical and physical models in the same stored display.

When you save a diagram as an .er1 file, the stored displays are saved along with the diagram.

Using the Stored Display Editor

The Stored Display Editor allows you to select and save a set of diagram display options and display levels for the subject area. Changes made to a stored display do not affect any other stored display or subject area in the diagram.

To launch the Stored Display Editor, shown in Figure 11.5, right-click the diagram and select Stored Display or select Edit, Stored Display.

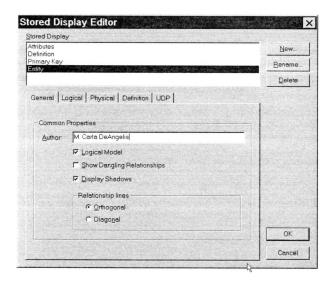

FIGURE 11.5
Use the Stored Display Editor to set the properties of any display level. ERwin automatically creates one stored display, called Display1, for each subject area. Use the rename button to provide a new name for Display1.

Stored Display lists all the stored displays in the subject area. Select a different stored display in this list to view the display options for the logical and physical models. There are three essential buttons at the top of the dialog box:

- New—Click to open the New Stored Display dialog and create a new stored display.
- Rename—Click to open the Rename Stored Display dialog and change the name of the selected stored display.

- Delete—Click to delete the selected stored display.

The General tab options of the Stored Display Editor, shown in Figure 11.5, let you enter information that applies to all the objects in the stored display, both logical and physical:

- Author—The person creating the stored display should enter name and contact information here.

- Logical Model—Although the online documentation indicates that selecting this option limits the use of the stored display to the logical model, I can find no evidence of this behavior.

- Show Dangling Relationships—Click to show relationship lines on the diagram when the related object is not in the view. Sometimes showing the dangling relationships helps users understand the model. Seeing the relationship lines provides a connection point.

- Display Shadows—Select to display the shadow effect for entities, tables, and views in the stored display. Clear this check box to hide the shadow effect for the current stored display.

- Relationship Lines—Select Orthogonal to keep relationship lines straight. Select Diagonal to allow slanted lines.

TIP

Creating a subject area with fewer entities than the main subject area might cause stored displays for that subject area to include dangling relationships. Dangling relationships are those relationships for which the subject area does not include either a parent or child object. The main subject area always includes the complete set of entities, so it cannot include dangling relationships.

ERwin hides the relationship line for a dangling relationship. To display dangling relationship lines in a stored display, select the Show Dangling Relationship check box on the General tab in the Stored Display Editor. When creating a subject area that includes dangling relationships, consider displaying the dangling relationships in one stored display and hiding them in another.

The Logical tab options, shown in Figure 11.6, allow you to specify the display level, entity options, and relationship options for the logical view of that stored display.

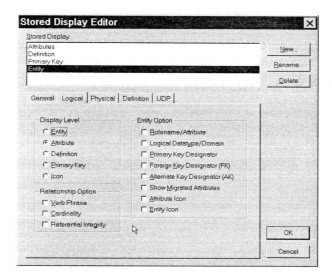

FIGURE 11.6

Use the Stored Display Editor, Logical tab to set the display properties to specify the level of diagram object detail for the logical model.

The Display Level options allow you to control the amount of information shown in the stored display:

- Entity—Select to display only the entity name inside the entity box.
- Attribute—Select to display the primary key and non-key attributes inside the entity box and the entity name outside.
- Definition—Select to display only the entity inside the entity box and the entity name outside.
- Primary Key—Select to display only the primary key attributes inside the entity box and the entity name outside.
- Icon—Select to display the large entity icon associated with the entity and the entity name inside the entity box.

The Relationship Option area allows you to control the amount of information that is displayed:

- Verb Phrase—Select to display verb phrases for relationships in the stored display. Clear to hide relationship verb phrases.

- Cardinality—Select to display cardinality symbols (P, Z, or n) for relationships in the stored display. Clear to hide relationship cardinality.
- Referential Integrity—Select to display referential integrity symbols (D:R, U:R, I:R, and so on) for relationships in the stored display. Clear to hide them.

CAUTION

Selecting options in the Stored Display Editor overrides the relationship display options selected in the Preferences dialog.

The Entity Option area allows you to control the amount of information displayed with the attributes in an entity:

- Rolename/Attribute—Select to display the rolename for the attributes. Clear to hide the basenames of rolenamed attributes. The basename is the attribute name that migrated from the parent entity to the child entity. ER*win* inserts a dot after the rolename and then appends the attribute's basename: rolename.basename. You assign a rolename to a migrating foreign key attribute using the Relationship Editor. The rolename is displayed as the foreign key name.
- Logical Datatype/Domain—Select to display the logical datatype for attributes in the stored display. Clear to hide the datatype.
- Primary Key Designator—Select to display the primary key designator (key icon) for attributes in the stored display. Clear to hide it.
- Foreign Key Designator (FK)—Select to display the foreign key designator (FK) for attributes in the stored display. Clear to hide it.
- Alternate Key Designator (AK)—Select to display the alternate key (AK) and inversion entry (IE) designator for attributes in the stored display. Clear this check box to hide them.
- Show Migrated Attributes—Select to display migrated foreign key attributes in the stored display. Clear this check box to hide migrated attributes that do not have rolenames.
- Attribute Icon—Select to display attribute icons to the left of the attribute name in the stored display. Clear to hide them.
- Entity Icon—Select to display the small entity icons in the stored display. Clear to hide them.

The Physical tab options allow you to specify the display level, entity options, and relationship options for the physical view of the stored display. Physical options are explored in Chapter 16.

The Definition tab options allow you to enter a definition for the stored display. As always, I encourage you to add a definition describing the reason you created the stored display and what it features.

TIP

Use the ER*win* template feature to store display options and settings. Then create new diagrams based on the template to automatically apply the stored display options.

Display Options

ER*win* allows you to change the font and color features to enhance the appearance of diagram objects, making the data model easier to read and understand. For example, when presenting a diagram, you might consider enlarging the font size for entity names or adding an entity fill color to make it easy to identify existing entities that are being reused. Perhaps changing the font color of migrating foreign keys to red can help set them apart from other attributes.

ER*win* allows you to change the default fonts and colors for

- All objects of a specific type in the active diagram by selecting All Objects
- All of the objects of a single type in the current subject area by selecting Current Object Pool
- A single object or a group of selected objects by selecting the objects and then selecting the font and color.
- New objects of a single type in the active diagram by selecting New Objects

When you add a new object to a diagram, ER*win* automatically assigns the default font and color for that object. You can assign a different default color scheme to objects using the All Default Font/Color Editor, shown in Figure 11.7. You can change the color or font of individual objects in the diagram using the Font/Color Editor for the object. To open the Font/Color Editor for a specific object, right-click the object and select the Object Font/Color item from the shortcut menu. You can also use the icons on the Font and Color Toolbar. To display the toolbar, select the Font and Color Toolbar item from the Window menu option.

The color of some diagram objects is related to that of another object. For example, a relationship line is the same color as the relationship name. Some objects, such as foreign key attributes, inherit color from a parent object. For foreign keys, the color is inherited from the primary key attribute of the parent entity.

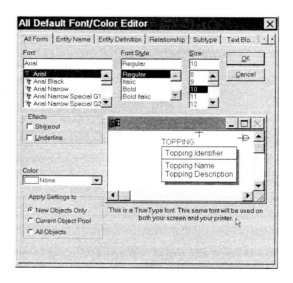

FIGURE 11.7

Use the All Default Font/Color Editor to set the font and color properties for diagram objects. You may need to scroll the tabs to see specific diagram objects.

Some ERwin display options apply to all subject areas in the diagram. For example, changing the background color or the fill color of a specific object applies to every subject area and stored display that includes the object as a member. Setting the width or height of entities, tables, or views to a specific value changes the width and height in every subject area and stored display that includes the object.

NOTE

Initially, all ERwin diagram objects display in black and white. If you add color, be sure that the entity fill color and attribute font color work well together. Also, the mapping of color between your computer monitor and the printer can vary significantly, producing models that are difficult to read.

Height and Width

ER*win* automatically adjusts the size of each entity. The height of each entity is sufficient to display all the attributes. The width of each entity is sufficient to display the complete name. ER*win* gives you the option of setting the height and width to a specific size.

Use the Resize Diagram Objects dialog, shown in Figure 11.8, to specify an exact height and width for an entity, table, or view in a diagram. To launch the Resize Diagram Objects dialog, select Option, Resize Diagram Objects.

The Width area allows you to select the display width of object names:

- Automatic—Select to have ER*win* automatically display the complete name of each entity, attribute, table, and column in the diagram. ER*win* allows up to 255 characters for the entity name.
- Set Width—Select and enter the exact number of characters to be displayed for each attribute name.

The Height area allows you to specify the number of attributes that are displayed in each entity, table, and view:

- Automatic—Select to have ER*win* automatically display all attributes or columns on the diagram.
- Set Height—Select and enter the exact number of attributes or columns to be displayed for each entity, table, and view in the diagram.

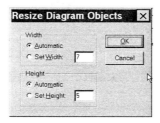

FIGURE 11.8
Use the Resize Diagram Objects dialog to specify the size of entities, tables and views.

> **NOTE**
>
> If the custom height or width entered is not large enough to display all of the attribute names completely, part of the name is hidden from view. You can view the full name in the appropriate editor.
>
> ER*win* does not increase the height of an entity greater than that necessary to display all the attributes in the entity. However, ER*win* does increase the width of entities to the specified width, even if it is wider than the space required to display the complete attribute name.

Text Boxes

You can add text blocks to an ER*win* diagram to identify or describe model elements. Text blocks can contain any text, such as the diagram version, author's notes, and a title.

To create a text block, click the Text Block tool in the toolbox and then click the diagram background. ER*win* adds a new text block and enables text editing, allowing you to type the text directly onto the diagram.

> **NOTE**
>
> You cannot use tab characters in a text block. However, you can use any other keyboard character, including the Enter key to separate text.
>
> If you add a text block to the diagram without entering text, ER*win* displays the empty text block as an asterisk (*) on the diagram. You can select and delete the empty text block or add text at any time.

Using the Text Block Editor

Edit text in the text block using the Text Block Editor. To launch the editor, shown in Figure 11.9, right-click the text block and select Text Block Editor from the shortcut menu.

Change the font size and color in the text block using the Text Block Font/Color Editor. To launch the editor, shown in Figure 11.10, right-click the text block and select Object Font/Color from the shortcut menu.

Organizing and Enhancing the Logical Data Model

CHAPTER 11

237

11

ORGANIZING AND
ENHANCING THE
MODEL

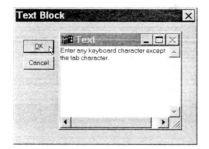

FIGURE 11.9

Use the Text Block Editor to add text to the diagram. The text block can contain any type of meaningful text. Position a text block near the diagram object to which it refers.

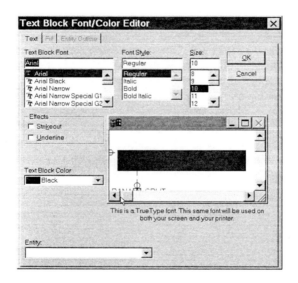

FIGURE 11.10

Use the Text Block Font/Color Editor to add fill and font color, or change the font size to increase readability.

Icons

Icons can be associated with diagram objects to enhance the appearance of logical model. You can use icons to represent entities, attributes, attribute domains, and primary keys. ER*win* provides a set of default icons, and you can also use the Icon Editor to import bitmap files.

The diagram shortcut menu allows you to toggle the following logical object icons on or off:

- Primary Key Designator Display Option
- Entity Icon Display Option
- Attribute Icon Display Option

The menu closes after each selection, which is a little annoying, but just continue to open it and select each option.

Using the Icon Editor

Using the Icon tab of the ERwin Entity Editor, and the General tab of the Attribute Editor and Domain Dictionary Editor, click the button to the right of the icon name to open the ERwin Icon Editor. The Icon Editor allows you to import, rename, and delete icon bitmaps. Once imported, these internal bitmaps exist as icons within ERwin. After an icon is imported, you can assign it to logical model entities, attributes, and domain icons. The options follow:

- Import—Click to launch the ERwin Open File dialog, shown in Figure 11.11, and select a bitmap to import into ERwin. Imported bitmaps appear in the Icon Editor list.

- Rename—Click to launch the Rename Bitmap dialog, and enter a new name for an imported bitmap. The name of the original bitmap does not change; only the instance imported into ERwin changes.

- Delete—Click to delete the selected icon. You cannot delete the default ERwin icons. Deleting an imported icon does not delete the icon from disk; only the instance imported into ERwin is deleted.

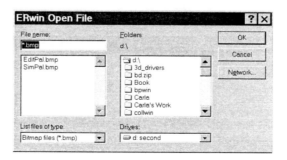

FIGURE 11.11

Use the ERwin Open File dialog to locate bitmaps that can be added to ER's list of available icons.

NOTE

Although it is called the Icon Editor, you cannot use it to make graphical changes to a bitmap. The Icon Editor simply maintains separate bitmaps for the large and small icons imported into ER*win*.

Summary

ER*win* provides several features for organizing and enhancing the logical model to improve understandability. Every diagram automatically includes one subject area, called <Main Subject Area>, which contains all diagram objects and cannot be edited or changed. You can use ER*win*'s Subject Area Editor to create new subject areas that contain a subset of the objects in the <Main Subject Area>.

Each subject area, including the main subject area, automatically includes one stored display, called Display1. You can use ER*win*'s Stored Display Editor to specify the display level options for the logical and physical model.

ER*win* also provides a Default Font/Color Editor that allows you to control the appearance of diagram objects. You can specify the line, font and fill color for model objects. Launch the All Default Font/Color Editor from the Option menu, or use the short cut menu available by right-clicking a diagram object and selecting the Default Font/Color item from the menu. Take care when selecting font and fill color, as color combinations can make the model difficult to read.

You can also add text blocks and use icons to add meaning to the logical model. The Text Block Editor allows you to position a block of text near entities to add additional meaning or record issues. You can specify the font size and color, as well as a fill color for the text blocks. Use the Icon Editor to add new icons to ER*win*'s list of available icons and use the Entity or Attribute Editors to associate an icon.

After creating the logical model and using ER*win*'s features to organize and enhance it, it's time to review the logical model to ensure that it is complete and accurate. In the next chapter, I introduce the concept of logical model reviews.

Reviewing the Logical Data Model

The preceding chapter explained some ER*win* features for organizing and enhancing the readability and understandability of a logical data model. Those features include subject areas, stored displays, various display options, text blocks, and icons. This chapter focuses on using model reviews to ensure that the logical data model fulfills the information requirements and business rules that represent the business objective defined during sessions and interviews.

I explore the model review process from the perspective of the modeling team tasks, as well as those of the reviewer. The modeling team builds the logical model diagram and provides the supporting documentation; the reviewer assesses the quality of the model. In examining the logical review process, I discuss the following topics:

- The characteristics of a quality data model
- When to review the model

- Who should review the model
- Preparing for the logical model review
- Reviewing the logical model
- What happens after the model review

Performing an effective logical model review requires an understanding of the characteristics of a quality logical model. The model should be reviewed by a senior modeler when one or more subject areas nears completion. Steps for preparing for and conducting the review, as well as what should happen after the review, are introduced in the sections that follow.

A Quality Logical Model

What is a good logical data model, and how do you know when you have one? A quality model should exhibit the following characteristics:

- It is technically correct.
- It follows corporate standards.
- It meets the business objective.
- It accurately reflects business rules.
- It fits within the enterprise model.
- It is scalable and extensible.

A logical data model is considered technically correct when it is resolved to (at least) third normal form. Normalization to third normal form places every attribute into an entity such that the value of each attribute is dependent on the value of the primary key, the whole value of the primary key, and nothing but the value of the primary key.

A logical model can be technically correct but fail to follow corporate standards such as naming conventions, completeness requirements, and integration standards. Using a set of modeling standards and guidelines ensures that the models produced within an enterprise are uniformly understandable and relatively consistent, regardless of which modeling team developed the model.

A logical model can be technically correct and follow corporate standards, but if it does not meet the business objective, it fails to achieve its purpose. A data model should manifest the business plans and strategies of the enterprise. This is the goal of business-driven data modeling as defined by the father of Information Engineering, Clive Finklestein.

A logical model that is technically correct, follows corporate standards, and meets the business objective must also reflect the business rules to be useful. A data model that does not accurately

Reviewing the Logical Data Model

CHAPTER 12

243

12

REVIEWING THE
LOGICAL DATA
MODEL

reflect the business rules might supply flawed or inadequate data for making business-critical decisions.

A technically correct logical data model that follows corporate standards, meets the business objective, and accurately reflects the business rules but does not fit within the enterprise model introduces inconsistency and inaccuracy at the enterprise level. Every data model is a view of the larger set of information requirements and business rules for the enterprise. At some level, every model shares concepts. It is essential that the concepts shared by the enterprise be modeled consistently. The ability to share and integrate a model throughout the enterprise is a measure of its quality.

A technically correct model that follows corporate standards, meets the business objective, accurately reflects the business rules, and fits within the enterprise model but is not scalable and extensible will not stand the test of time. A model that rigidly represents only the current information requirements, with no thought for changes that are likely to occur, cannot be considered a quality model. A highly scalable and extensible model should implement the extension of the business rules by adding rows to a table, rather than columns.

Now that you know the characteristics of a quality logical data model, how does a modeling team ensure that a quality model is produced? One way is by conducting model reviews at frequent intervals during the modeling process.

When Should the Model Be Reviewed?

Model reviews are an integral part of the modeling process. Periodic reviews of the model allow the team to make minor adjustments rather than radical change. The number and frequency of reviews vary according to the size of the modeling effort. However, even the smallest modeling project should include at least two reviews, an initial review and a final review. For extensive modeling efforts that span several months, consider reviewing the model at evenly spaced intervals, no more than three to four weeks apart.

The initial model review should occur immediately upon completion of the first draft of a logical model. Conducting the review before the model is fairly stable is a wasted effort because the model will likely experience substantial change. On the other hand, waiting until the logical model is complete can be an expensive delay that might require extensive rework. Problems that could have been corrected with little effort early in the process might result in errors that compound into fatal flaws and put the model on the scrap heap. Even worse, a business-critical application with a flawed model can create years of maintenance nightmares.

The final model review should give the modeling team time to respond to recommendations from the reviewer. The reviewer should make every effort to remain close to the modeling endeavor and perform frequent reviews as the model nears completion. This constant relationship can prevent a flurry of activity in the final stages of the model.

With an understanding of when a model review should occur, let's take a look at who reviews the model, and then at some ways to prepare.

Who Should Review the Model?

The reviewer and the modeling team should work together during the model review. Model reviews are most valuable when conducted by an expert modeler who has considerable experience modeling a broad spectrum of business functions. An experienced modeler should have no difficulty interpreting the business rules represented by the model.

The reviewer works with the modeling team to establish the review frequency. The reviewer is responsible for assessing the model for accuracy and completeness in meeting the problem statement or business objective, using the supporting documentation provided by the modeling team.

TIP

The reviewer must make a determination regarding the quality of the supporting documentation supplied by the modeling team. If the supporting documentation is weak or inaccurate, the reviewer should work with the modeling team to produce good documentation.

The reviewer also provides advice on modeling practices and corporate standards. The reviewer's findings should be documented along with the resolution approach devised in partnership with the modeling team. Although the responsibility for the quality of the review clearly rests with the reviewer, the modeling team plays essential roles in providing the supporting documentation for the model and working with the reviewer to determine the resolution approach. Of course, the modeling team also implements the resolution approaches that are deemed appropriate.

Preparing for the Logical Model Review

The modeling team prepares for the logical model review by assembling supporting documentation. The availability of supporting documentation depends upon the nature of the model effort and the stage of the model itself, as well as the experience of the scribe, facilitator, and participants.

The following list outlines the documentation that supports a logical model review:

- Problem statement or business objective that the model is to fulfill
- Data model diagram
- Report containing entity names and definitions
- Report containing the attribute names, definitions, and logical datatypes
- Process flows, activity diagrams, use case diagrams, data flow diagrams, and so on
- ER*win* model validation reports
- Session notes and meeting minutes
- Issue resolutions and documentation on the decisions made by the modeling team
- Results and responses to any previous model reviews
- Project plan or documentation that indicates the state of the model

It is important to provide as much supporting information as possible to allow the reviewer to make a complete assessment.

CAUTION

A model cannot be accurately assessed without the problem statement or business objective documentation. It is impossible to review a model for accuracy and completeness without a clear understanding of what the model is intended to support.

The reviewer prepares for the review by collecting the latest supporting documentation and works with the team to establish the model review schedule. The reviewer and modeling team discuss any questions regarding the business objective, information requirements, and business rules. They should also discuss the process for communicating the review findings and working together to define resolution strategies.

Once the model documentation is delivered and any new information is collected, the reviewer is ready to begin.

Reviewing the Logical Model

There is no quick, simple way to perform a logical model review. It takes time and demands close attention to detail. The review process requires the reviewer to acquire a clear understanding of the business objective and the information requirements and business rules that support the objective. Then, the reviewer performs a step-by-step examination of the diagram objects (entities, attributes, and relationships) to determine whether the model accurately and completely fulfills the information requirements using the business rules.

The following steps outline a process that organizes the review into a series of high-level tasks:

1. Study the documentation of the problem statement or business objective.
2. Take a quick pass through the logical model diagram.
3. Review the session notes.
4. Understand the stage of the logical model.
5. Select the subject area for review.
6. Organize the subject area into data clusters.
7. Examine the independent entities, their attributes, and the relationships.
8. Examine the dependent entities, their attributes, and the relationships.
9. Compare the diagram objects to the business objectives.
10. Document the review findings.
11. Present the review findings to the modeling team and work with the team to develop a resolution strategy.
12. Document the resolution action taken.
13. Schedule the next review.

The reviewer must study the documentation of the problem statement or business objective to gain a clear understanding of the business function that the model is intended to support. He or she examines the role of the business objective in relation to the rest of the enterprise. She must understand any shared resources or integration with other business objectives. The modeling team helps the reviewer identify dependencies and areas where there might be synergism or overlap with other initiatives. The reviewer compares the business objectives to the goals and strategies of the enterprise to ensure that there is no conflict. She examines the information requirements and business rules to ensure that they completely and accurately support the business objective.

The reviewer makes a quick pass through the logical model diagram to gain an overall understanding of the scope and complexity of the model. She reviews the logical model reports to understand the entities and subject areas.

Using the Session Notes

The reviewer reads the session notes to gain an understanding of the information provided by the domain experts. The session notes should include key discussion topics and a record of the decisions made by the modeling team. While reviewing the session notes, particular attention is paid to the refinement of information requirements and the documentation of business rules, and logical model fragments developed during the sessions are noted. Part of the model review should include an assessment of the quality of the session documentation produced by the scribe. The scribe is the person, or sometimes several people, responsible for documenting the session results. The quality of the session notes depends on the experience and skill level of the scribe.

Session notes should include the following key items:

- The session agenda or documentation of the session objectives.
- List of participants invited to attend the session and a list of actual attendees, roles and responsibilities, and contact information for participants, the modeler/facilitator, and the scribe.
- Key discussion points and decisions made by participants and the modeling team. Important concepts discovered and defined during the session should be carefully documented. Options that were considered and then discarded also should be included. Documenting every option that was considered and the reason the option was discarded can help you avoid rehashing and revisiting the same issues and solutions over again.
- Drawings or diagrams developed during the session, especially model fragments.
- A review by the session participants and the facilitator to ensure accuracy and completeness.

NOTE

The session notes provide the details of the information requirements and business rules that drive the model. The quality of the model is determined by how well it represents the findings of the modeling sessions. The better the quality of the session documentation, the easier the task to determine how well the model produced matches the session findings.

The modeling team prepares documentation that defines the stage of the logical model. The team should identify areas of the model that are fairly well defined, as well as those expected to experience significant change. Entities and attributes should include preliminary names and definitions. Include the state of primary key and alternate key selections. The reviewer must study the documentation provided by the modeling team and understand the level of completeness of the logical model prior to conducting the model review.

The reviewer works with the modeling team to determine the order in which subject areas should be reviewed. Although the decision of where to begin is somewhat arbitrary, it is essential to review the model in manageable segments. The model might have an area that is clearly the core or heart of the model. For some models, it is best to begin by understanding this core subject area. With other models, it might be best begin with a subject area that is well understood by the reviewer. Other considerations include whether the team needs assistance in a particular area. Even more frequently, the implementation schedule might require a subject area be the first reviewed because it is scheduled to be the first area implemented. The important thing is to review the model in manageable chunks.

After the reviewer selects a subject area, she should organize it into data clusters.

Data Clusters

Data clustering is a concept introduced by, you guessed it, Clive Finklestein. A data cluster is a logical group of entities that are tightly coupled by foreign key relationships. The reviewer identifies data clusters by performing a data dependency analysis, also defined by Finklestein.

To group the subject area into data clusters, the reviewer must perform the following steps:

1. Identify a terminal entity.
2. Identify all the parent entities of the terminal entity.
3. Identify any mandatory relationships for the parent entities.
4. Identify any derived attributes that use base attributes not present in the cluster.

A terminal entity is a child entity that has no children. In other words, relationships end at a terminal entity. The terminal entity, also called the end point, represents the beginning of the data cluster. Each terminal entity is likely to become a separate data cluster.

Starting from the terminal entity, the reviewer must trace the lineage of the child back to parent entities using the foreign key relationships until an independent entity is reached. An independent entity is one that has no parent. The reviewer adds all the parent entities to the data cluster.

Next, the reviewer must examine the child entities of each parent entity in the data cluster, to identify any mandatory relationships with child entities. Mandatory relationships are those where the existence of an instance of the parent entity requires at least one instance of the child. The reviewer adds these child entities to the data cluster. He adds all the parents of these child entities to the data cluster as well.

The reviewer identifies any derived attributes in the data cluster with values that are calculated using the values of base attributes that are *not* already in the data cluster. He adds the entity that contains the base attributes to the data cluster.

After the process is completed, the data cluster should contain all entities that exhibit data dependency. Each data cluster represents a tightly integrated logical grouping of entities. Identifying the data clusters within the subject area helps the reviewer examine entities within the context of the logical grouping that defines its interaction domain. Next, the reviewer performs an object-by-object review of each data cluster.

Reviewing the Entities

Data clustering allows the reviewer to focus on a logically complete subset of entities. She assesses the quality of each entity in the data cluster according to its technical correctness and compliance with modeling standards.

The reviewer begins the evaluation of each data cluster object by examining the independent entities. Independent entities are entities that inherit no foreign keys. Beginning with independent entities allows the reviewer to proceed from the general to the specific. After assessing the independent entities, the reviewer examines the dependent entities in the data cluster.

The reviewer evaluates entities by assessing the quality of the following:

- Name and description
- Primary key attributes
- Foreign key attributes
- Non-key attributes
- Relationships between entities

The reviewer must examine the name of the entity. Does the logical name follow naming conventions? Does the name give a good indication of the instances for the entity? For more information on good entity names, see Chapter 2, "Understanding Entities."

The reviewer studies the description of the entity. Does it provide a rich definition of the instances? Does it use business terminology? Is the description complete and accurate? Does the description represent the entity in the context of a single business function or in the context of the role the entity plays in the enterprise?

The reviewer analyzes the primary key to determine whether its values truly identify a unique instance of the entity. She ensures that every attribute in the entity depends on the value of the primary key, the whole key, and nothing but the key. She traces the migration of the primary key attributes to child entities. She examines the non-key attributes to ensure that there is no functional dependence on the value of other attributes.

The reviewer traces the relationships between parent and child entities by examining the primary key attributes that migrate as foreign keys. She evaluates identifying relationships where the primary keys become part of the primary key structure in child entities to determine whether the values of the migrated key are required to identify each instance. The reviewer examines any non-identifying mandatory relationships to ensure that values are always available for the migrating keys.

> **NOTE**
>
> Although it is important to assess each entity, I do not propose that the reviewer examine each entity in isolation. Entities must also be evaluated in groups of three or more. For example, a cyclic relationship involves three entities with dependencies that fail to identify a true parent entity. You might think of the question, "Which comes first, the chicken or the egg?" Unless the reviewer considers the relationships between all three, he might not identify the cyclic relationship.

The reviewer documents any issues or concerns regarding entities in each data cluster and prepares to evaluate how well the objects in each data cluster support the business objective.

Meeting the Business Objective

After reviewing the data clusters for technical correctness and compliance with modeling standards, the reviewer should have a good understanding of the objects in each data cluster. Next, the reviewer must evaluate how accurately and completely the model meets the business objective. An assessment of how well the model represents the information requirements and business rules is not as easy or straightforward as the evaluation for technical correctness and compliance with modeling standards. In fact, the reviewer spends most of the review time performing this assessment.

The ability of the reviewer to measure how well the model meets the business objective relies heavily on the quality of the supporting documentation, particularly the session notes. The documentation supplies the information requirements and the business rules that should be present in the model. Using the documentation, the reviewer must perform the following:

1. Determine whether every information requirement is represented.
2. Determine whether every business rule is accurately reflected.
3. Determine whether the key decisions recorded in the session notes are implemented correctly.
4. Determine whether the model supports the business objective.

Information requirements are usually implemented in the model by attributes whose values represent the information the enterprise is interested in collecting and maintaining. The reviewer should compare the information requirements documented in the session notes with the attributes in each data cluster. Although the review should certainly ensure that all information requirements are represented in the model, the reviewer should also question any extra attributes present in the model that do not appear to map to information requirements.

Business rules are usually represented in the relationships between the entities in data clusters. The reviewer should examine the cardinality and nullity options to determine whether the business rules are accurately represented according to the documentation. The reviewer must also study the relationships between entities to ensure that parent and child relationships do not contain reverse logic. Reverse logic is when a child entity has been incorrectly identified as the parent and vice versa.

The reviewer must determine whether key decisions and explanations documented in the session notes were implemented correctly in the model. Many times, critical issues that were the subject of much discussion in sessions are not reflected in the model simply because they are not listed as information requirements.

> **TIP**
>
> Modeling sessions often include intense debate over certain areas of the model. The reviewer should be cautious when raising issues or concerns in areas that have already been the subject of painful resolution by the team.

Determining whether the model supports the business objective requires the reviewer to step back and consider the logical model from two perspectives. First, the reviewer must determine the precision to which the model meets the objectives within the scope of the specific business objective. Then, the reviewer must consider the role of the model as a part of the larger enterprise model. The strategic goals and objectives of the business objective must align with the goals and objectives of the enterprise. An experienced reviewer might find that the business objective itself is in conflict with the stated objectives of the enterprise. This provides a valuable opportunity to revisit business objectives and make changes and enhancements prior to implementing the system.

The reviewer documents any issues or concerns about how well the model supports the business objective, as well as any issues or concerns regarding the business objective alignment with enterprise objectives.

Documenting the Review Findings

The purpose of the review is not to find errors or to pass judgment on the modeling team. Instead, the review gives domain experts and the modeling team opportunities to ensure that the model meets the business objective as accurately and completely as possible. The reviewer might find alternatives that were not considered by the modeling team.

The reviewer must clearly and completely document each question or concern. The documentation should include references to the entity, attribute, or relationship in question, as well as the information requirement and business rule.

TIP

Keep a historical record of the review findings to provide as input for subsequent reviews. This step is an effective time-saver for the reviewer, as well as an opportunity to ensure that the resolutions to review findings are implemented accurately and completely.

After the Logical Model Review

After completing the review, the reviewer must present the documentation of the review findings to the modeling team and work with the team to develop a resolution strategy. The modeling team must have the opportunity to ask questions regarding the findings to ensure that each question or concern is clear. The reviewer has the opportunity to respond to questions from the modeling team and participate in developing resolutions.

It is important to document the resolution decisions made by the team along with the timeframe in which the resolutions are scheduled for implementation.

NOTE

It is essential that you address and resolve every issue documented in the review report. You must also document and implement every resolution to produce a quality logical model.

After documenting the review findings and working with the modeling team to define resolution strategies, the reviewer remains an integral part of the team and shares responsibility for delivering a model of the highest quality possible.

Summary

The objective of a logical model review is to ensure that the model produced is of the highest quality possible. A quality data model

- is technically correct
- follows corporate standards

- meets the business objective
- fits within the enterprise model
- is scalable and extensible

The logical model review report should document the degree to which the proposed model fulfills each item.

Every logical model should have at least two reviews. An initial review is conducted as soon as a first draft of the logical model is complete. A final review should be conducted near the end of the modeling tasks to allow time for the team to resolve issues.

Reviews are most valuable when performed by an experienced modeler. The reviewer prepares for the review by reviewing the supporting documentation for the model. The supporting documentation includes the information requirements and business rules, logical model diagram and reports on the model objects, session notes, as well as results and resolution of any previous model reviews and any other documentation on the modeling decisions.

The reviewer reports the review findings for each entity, attribute and relationship in the logical model, including references to specific information requirements and business rules. The reviewer and the modeling team develop an implementation strategy to resolve any issues or concerns and schedule the next review.

When the logical model is complete and accurate, you are ready to deliver the logical model. In the next chapter, I examine the activities associated with delivering the logical model and supporting documentation.

Delivering the Logical Data Model

Previous chapters explained the ideas and techniques involved in creating a logical data model. The preceding chapter introduced the practice of using model reviews to ensure the production of a quality data model. This chapter explores delivering the logical model by discussing the following topics:

- Delivering supporting documentation
- Delivering the logical model diagram
- Delivering logical model reports

The supporting documentation provides the record of the production of the logical model. The logical model diagram and associated reports are the representation of the information requirements and business rules.

Delivering Supporting Documentation

Chapter 12, "Reviewing the Logical Data Model," introduced a list of supporting documentation for the logical model. The list is intended to provide examples of the *type* of supporting information that goes into producing a quality logical model. The list is not all-inclusive. For our purposes, this documentation consists of two types:

- Documentation that is produced outside ERwin
- Documentation that is produced within ERwin

Documentation produced outside ERwin provides the information that drives the data model. Examples of supporting documentation produced outside ERwin are

- The problem statement or business objective that the model is to fulfill
- Session notes and meeting minutes
- Issue resolutions and documentation on the decisions made by the modeling team
- Results and response to model reviews
- Process flows, activity diagrams, use case diagrams, data flow diagrams, and so on

Documentation produced within ERwin provides details of the model produced in support of the information requirements and business rules. ERwin has facilities to produce the following supporting documentation of the logical model:

- A data model diagram
- A report containing entity names and definitions
- A report containing the attribute names, definitions, and logical datatypes
- Model validation reports

Delivering a Logical Model Diagram

Delivering the logical model diagram in your organization might involve printing one or more standard views of the diagram. Refer to the methodology selected for use within your organization for descriptions of these views. If your organization's methodology does not include a set of standard logical model views, consider developing a set to include as part of the modeling standards. Remember to use ERwin to develop the standard views and save the resulting model as a template. You can use the template to provide a consistent look and feel across all models.

You might need to divide a large model into several additional subject areas, and each subject area might need several additional stored displays. Subject areas should consist of logical groupings of model objects that support a specific business function or activity. Display levels within the subject area should represent the level of detail appropriate to give different stakeholders a clear understanding of the model objects. In ERwin, printing is performed at the display level, with the option of selecting to print only a single page within a stored display.

ERwin (for the most part) prints a diagram WYSIWYG, "what you see is what you get." That is, the current display of the current subject area is printed.

TIP

Entities near the top or bottom edge of the display might be clipped when printed. If attributes near the top or bottom of the entity or the entity box line appear to be missing, zoom out on the display, drag the clipped entities away from the edge, and print the diagram again.

The size and appearance of the printed logical diagram is heavily dependent upon the printer used to print the model diagram. The diagram should be organized into page sizes that are appropriate for the printer. ER*win* provides features that allow you to control the appearance of the printed diagram: diagram page grid boundary lines and the Print Model dialog.

The paper size and orientation selected in the Print Setup dialog determine the size and orientation of the page grid boundary lines. You can use the page grid boundary lines to control the amount of diagram information printed on each page by determining the print scaling. Using page grid lines shown in the Print Model dialog or in the diagram itself, adjust the objects included on the page by clicking the grid line and dragging to include or exclude diagram objects. Figure 13.1 shows the sample diagram with grid lines during the adjustment process.

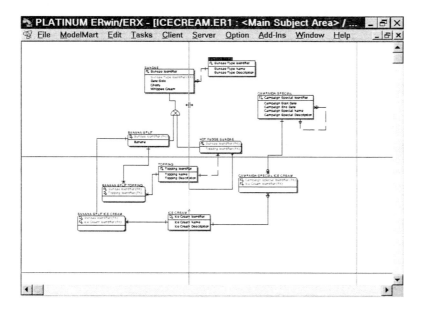

FIGURE 13.1

Diagram page grid boundary lines provide an indication of the number of pages on which the diagram will print.

Adjusting the size of the page grid affects the size of printed diagram objects and fonts. Reducing the size of the page grid enlarges the print scale, making the objects and fonts appear larger when printed. Enlarging the size of the page grid reduces the print scale, making the diagram objects and fonts appear smaller when printed.

NOTE

To see the page grids on the diagram, select the Page Grid item in the Option menu. Hide them by deselecting the Page Grid option.

ER*win* includes the standard Windows Print Setup dialog for selecting printing options. Select the printer and change various print options such as page orientation, paper size, and paper tray source. Remember that the paper size and orientation you select determine the size and orientation for the diagram page grid lines.

Using the Print Model Dialog

ER*win*'s Print Model dialog, shown in Figure 13.2, includes an embedded diagram window that provides a miniature view of the data model. Click in the diagram window to select one or more specific pages to be printed. The page grid lines in the diagram window control which objects print on each page.

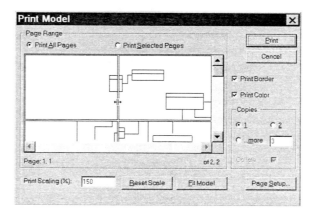

FIGURE 13.2
Note that the number of printed pages is shown below the diagram window in the Print Model dialog.

NOTE

ERwin provides a facility within the Print Model dialog to control the size of the diagram objects on the printed diagram. Adjust the page size by clicking a grid line and dragging the line. When you move the grid line to adjust the page, the diagram's print scale is reduced or enlarged. Use the page grid lines to include or exclude diagram objects.

The ERwin Print Model dialog offers the following functionality:

- Print All Pages—Select to print all the diagram pages.
- Print Selected Pages—Select to print a single page or group of specific pages. Click the page in the diagram to select for printing. Select multiple pages using the Shift or Ctrl key along with the left mouse button. ERwin indicates which pages are selected by highlighting them.
- Print Scaling (%)—The scale of the diagram is displayed here. Specify another print scale by entering a percentage value in the box. Enter 50 to print the diagram at half the normal size.
- Reset Scale—Select to reset the model scale to 100 percent.
- Fit Model—Select to print the entire model on a single page. When using this option, check the Print Scaling to ensure that the printed model will be readable. It is difficult to read a model printed at less that 50 percent.
- Print—Print the diagram using the current specifications.
- Cancel—Clicking this closes the Print Model dialog. Note that printing might continue if the print job is already in the print queue.
- Print Border—Select to print a border around the diagram.
- Print Color—Select to print the diagram using colors defined within the diagram objects. Often, the color palette in the computer does not map to the same color in the printer. Take care that font and fill colors do not combine to make the model difficult to read.
- Copies—Select the number of copies of the model to print. The option defaults to one copy. To print more than two copies, select the more option and enter the number of copies in the box. Selecting to print multiple copies automatically activates the Collate option if you are printing a model with more than one page.

- Collate—Select to collate the copies while they are being printed. This option is automatically activated when you print two or more copies of a model that has multiple pages. To deselect, simply click the check box.
- Page Setup—Select to open the Page Setup dialog and set the page margins and the content of page headers and footers.

The Page Setup dialog opens to display the Margins tab that lets you set all four separate page margins (top, bottom, left, and right) for the current stored display. Simply enter the margin size (in inches) for each margin.

Adding Headers and Footers

The Page Setup dialog also lets you add a customized header and footer to all the pages when printing a diagram. Selecting the Header/Footer tab displays the Header/Footer section of the Page Setup dialog, as shown in Figure 13.3. Use the buttons to insert information that is automatically updated by ER*win* as the diagram changes. You can add static information by clicking in the box and entering the information.

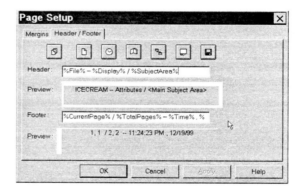

FIGURE 13.3
Use the Header/Footer tab to add a customized header and footer to the diagram. Note that the default options use ERwin's macros to provide header and footer text.

The Header/Footer tab contains two text boxes, one for the header and the other for the footer. A preview area below each text box provides a view of the header or footer information as it will appear on the diagram.

ER*win* automatically inserts the diagram name, stored display name, and subject area name into the header. You can edit the header information to remove one or more of the default selections or change it to include static information that you simply type in.

ERwin automatically inserts the grid page number, time, and date into the footer. You can edit the footer information to remove one or more of the default selections or enter static information by simply typing it in.

The following list describes the information you can insert using each button, from left to right in Figure 13.3:

- Total Page—Select to insert the total number of page grids in the diagram.
- Current Page—Select to insert the current grid page number of the diagram.
- Time—Select to insert the current time.
- Date—Select to insert the current date.
- Subject Area—Select to insert the current subject area name from the diagram.
- Stored Display—Select to insert the current stored display name.
- File Name—Select to insert the ER1 filename.

To insert button information, position the cursor in the text box and click the button that represents the desired information.

Using RPTwin

RPTwin is a fully functional, standalone reporting tool delivered with ERwin. A complete exploration of the functionality of RPTwin is beyond the scope of this text. This section explores the fundamentals of using RPTwin. You can launch RPTwin in one of the following ways:

- Automatically when you create a report in ERwin and export it as a RPTwin data set (.LWD)
- By double-clicking the RPTwin icon in the Windows Program Manager

NOTE

Every RPTwin report must be associated with a data set. When you run reports inside of ERwin, the report data set is created automatically. You can also create data sets using the Export function in the ERwin Report Browser to export the results of a report in RPTwin data set format.

When launching RPTwin using the RPTwin icon and selecting to create a new report, the data set is associated using the Select Data File For Report dialog, shown in Figure 13.4.

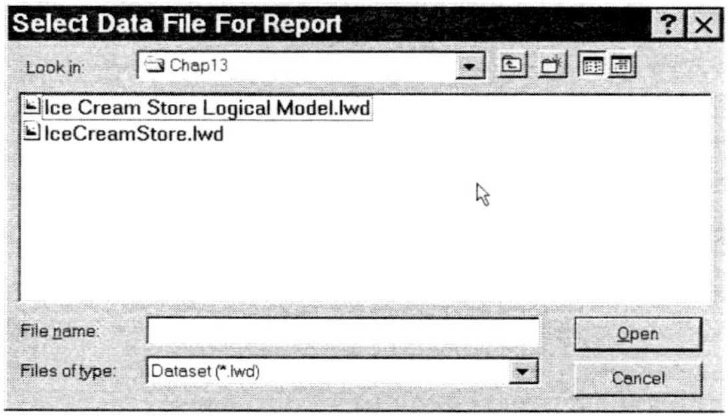

FIGURE 13.4
Use the Select Data File For Report dialog to associate an ERwin RPTwin report with a new data set.

RPTwin provides some predefined reporting functions, Quick Report or Guided Report, or the functionality to create a completely new report. The New Report dialog, shown in Figure 13.5, lets you select the type of report to create.

FIGURE 13.5
Use the New Report dialog to create a new Quick or Guided report.

There are two primary types of reports:

- Quick reports
- Guided reports

Selecting one of the Quick Reports options automatically creates standard report layouts. The three Quick Reports options are

- Columnar—Creates a simple tabular report with data elements represented in columns across the page. The standard columnar report includes all data file objects.
- Vertical—Creates a single column report where each record of data is laid out vertically down the page. The standard vertical report includes all data file objects.

- Blank—Allows you to create a report from scratch using a completely blank report format with no data file object placement. Even for expert report writers, it makes sense to start with one of the standard report formats and make modifications.

Selecting one of the Guided Reports options launches a wizard to guide you through a simple, step-by-step process to create customized reports. The two Guided Reports options are

- Group/Totals—Creates a columnar report with automatic grouping and sorting, including headers, footers, and totals.
- Vertical—Creates a vertical report letting you select which data file objects are included, the order of the data objects, and the options for sorting.

RPTwin saves report files with an .LWR file extension. As mentioned previously, each report contains an association to its corresponding data set (.LWD file). This association is established when the report is created. Each time you open the report, RPTwin searches for the appropriate data set and uses its data for report design.

If RPTwin cannot find the data set associated with the report, it prompts you to locate the correct data set. If you select a data set that does not correspond with the original one (RPTwin detects non-matching column names or datatypes), RPTwin displays a warning dialog. If you use the data set anyway, you might need to adjust the formulas in the report so that they refer to the appropriate columns in the new data set. If the words "Bad Formula" appear in a formula, it likely needs adjustment to work with the new data set.

Understanding Report Bands

RPTwin reports are divided into several horizontal sections called bands. You create or edit a report by adding elements (text, data, lines, and so on) to the appropriate bands in the report layout. It is not necessary to use all the sections in every report. All bands, with the exception of the Detail band, are optional. Simple reports might have only the Detail band and not use the header or footer sections at all.

Each band includes a border at the top containing its name and a band layout area underneath the band border, where you insert data or text. The available bands are

- Report Header—Appears once at the top of the first page of the report. The name of the data set file is inserted in the Report Header. In the sample report shown in Figure 13.6, "Ice Cream Store Data Elements" appears in the Report Header.
- Page Header—Appears at the top of each page of the report. In the sample report, the Page Header includes the labels for the report columns, Entity Name, Entity Definition, Attribute Name, and Attribute Definition.

- Group Header—Appears at the beginning of each group of data specified in the Group/Sort editor. The sample report shown in Figure 13.6 was grouped by Entity Name (BANANA SPLIT, BANANA SPLIT ICE CREAM, and so on).

- Detail—Appears once for every row of data in the data set. In the sample report, the data appears in the Detail band. Every report must include a Detail band even if it contains nothing else.

- Group Footer—Appears following each group of data specified in the Group/Sort editor. In the sample report, the Group Footer displays the number of attributes in each entity.

- Page Footer—Appears at the bottom of every page. The sample report shown in Figure 13.6 adds the page number.

- Report Footer—Appears once at the bottom of the last page of the report. The sample report adds the number of records.

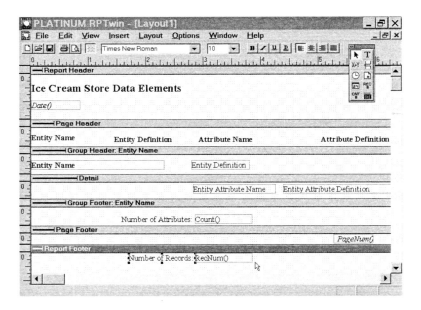

FIGURE 13.6

Report bands divide a RPTwin report into sections that can be customized or removed.

Rulers appear along the left and top of the design window. Use the rulers to align and size items in the report layout. You can set the unit of measurement for the rulers to inches or centimeters using the Preferences item in the Options menu. To use different units for a specific report, use the Current Layout item in the Options menu.

You can turn the rulers on or off by clicking the Ruler item in the View menu. Note that each band in the report has its own ruler. Also, notice that when you click the mouse button in a band or move a field, the position is highlighted on both the top and side rulers. Rulers are especially useful if you know the exact dimensions of the report layout or you want to position a field in an exact location. Rulers indicate dimensions inside the margins of the report, not paper size. The rulers provide guidelines to help you appropriately position report elements.

The Insert menu lets you add the following report elements to any band:

- Data Fields—Data fields contain the actual data in the report. This data can come from the columns in the data set file or from formulas.
- Text Fields—Add extra text such as titles or labels to the report.
- Page Break—Determine the placement of page breaks at specific locations in the report.
- Formula Fields—Add calculations that are based on the values of other fields.
- Special Fields—Insert a frequently used field such as date, time, or page number.
- OLE (Object Linking and Embedding) Objects—Place graphical objects such as bitmaps in the report and link them to an OLE server application, such as Excel or Word.

The two primary field types in RPTwin are data fields and text fields. You generally place data fields in the Detail band of the report, but you can also place them in headers and footers. For example, formulas such as sums and averages often appear in Group Footers and the Report Footer.

Data fields can be stationary in the report or can move to adjust to the needs of the report. There are two movement options available:

- Can Move Down
- Can Slide Left

The position of the selected field does not change in the band layout area in the Design window, but the output is positioned appropriately in the printed report:

- If Can Move Down is selected, the field automatically moves down when the data in the field above it expands.
- If Can Move Down is not selected, the field stays in a fixed position and cannot move down, even if the field above it expands downward. If this happens, the expanded field might overlap the field below it.
- If Can Slide Left is selected, the field automatically moves to the left until it encounters either another field or the left margin of the report. In other words, if there is empty space between the selected field and the left margin or any other field on its left, that space is removed and the selected field is placed to the immediate right of the margin or the previous field.

13

DELIVERING THE
LOGICAL DATA
MODEL

You create formulas in RPTwin using the Formula Editor. To create a new formula, click the X+Y tool in the toolbox. To change or add to a formula in an existing data field in the report, double-click the data field. RPTwin opens the Data Field Properties dialog. Then, click the Formula Editor button in the upper-right corner of the Properties dialog to open the Formula Editor.

Build the formula by adding a combination of data set columns, functions, and operators. Use the numeric keypad and edit buttons to insert numbers and use cut, copy, and paste techniques. Add a data set column, function, or operator by double-clicking the item in the list. The chosen item appears in the formula window at the top of the Formula Editor.

Using the RPTwin Toolbox

The RPTwin toolbox, shown in Figure 13.7, contains icons that represent tools you use to place report elements within the report bands. Open the toolbox by choosing View, Toolbox. Close the toolbox by clicking the close box in the upper-left corner.

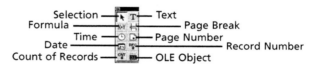

FIGURE 13.7
Use the RPTwin toolbox to place report elements within the report bands of a customized report.

The toolbox floats in the design window, and you can move it anywhere in the report window by clicking the top bar of the toolbox and, continuing to hold the mouse button down, dragging the toolbox to the desired location.

To add a report element, select one of the buttons in the toolbox to choose the type of element; the mouse pointer changes to provide a visual indicator of which tool is currently in use. Then, click the band in the location to add the report element to the report layout at the cursor position.

The report layout tools available in the RPTwin toolbox are

- Selection—Use this tool to select or change the location of existing elements. This is the default tool, and it becomes active again automatically after you add a report element using any of the other tools.
- Text—Add a text field and open the Text Properties dialog to enter the text.
- Formula—Add a data field and open the Formula Editor to define a formula for that data field.

- Page Break—Add a page break.
- Time—Add a special data field that displays the time of day the report was printed.
- Page Number—Add a special data field that displays the number of each page on the printed report.
- Date—Add a special data field that displays the date the report was printed.
- Record Number—Add a special data field that displays the current record number.
- Count of Records—Add a special data field that displays the count of records processed in the current group. If the report does not use groups, the Count function shows the number of records for the entire report.
- OLE Object—Add an OLE object to the report and open the insert object dialog to define the specific object server application. Most Windows applications are OLE object servers. For example, you can generate a Microsoft Word document as part of the report in any location. The new document is embedded in the report but is a Word formatted document linked to Word.

Sorting and Grouping

Sorting determines the order in which the rows of data in the report are arranged. The order can be ascending or descending and sorted on multiple levels. Grouping separates the report data into categories. Reports can have any number of groups and subgroups, each of which can have its own header and footer.

> **NOTE**
>
> Grouping only makes sense when the report data is also sorted. You cannot group report data without sorting it; however, you can sort it without grouping it, which essentially eliminates group headers and footers.

To sort or group the report data, select Sorting and Grouping from the Layout menu. RPTwin opens the Sorting/Grouping dialog, shown in Figure 13.8.

The DataSet Columns list on the left of the Sorting/Grouping dialog shows all the column names in the data set file. Double-click an item in the list to place the item into the Sort/Group On list on the right. You can also highlight the item and click the Add button. RPTwin sorts first on the first entry, and within the first sort, sorts on the second item, and so forth. To change the sort order, click an item in the Sort/Group On list and drag it to the appropriate position.

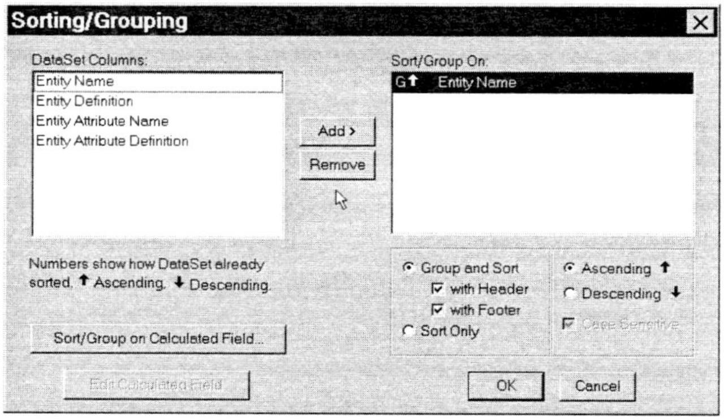

FIGURE 13.8
Use the Sorting/Grouping dialog to specify the sorting and grouping of elements.

Use the controls beneath the Sort/Group On list to specify Group and Sort or Sort Only. Selecting Group and Sort also selects the with Header and with Footer options. Select the appropriate box to uncheck the item. Select to sort items in Ascending or Descending order.

NOTE

If a number appears to the left of a column name in the Sorting/Grouping dialog, the number indicates the order in which the data will be sorted. The arrow to the right of the "G" in the figure indicates whether the data is sorted in an ascending or descending order. You can change the sort or grouping order, but using the current sort order might be useful to save time. A lengthy report runs more quickly if a new sort or grouping order is not required.

The Guided Report called Groups/Totals automatically populates group headers and footers and totals for every numeric field in the report.

The RPTwin reporting tool contains many powerful features, I encourage you to take the time to explore them.

Summary

Delivering the logical data model means to deliver the logical model diagram and the supporting documentation. Documentation can be divided into two types: that produced outside of ER*win* and that produced inside of ER*win*. Documentation produced outside of ER*win* includes the problem statement or business objective, information requirements and business rules, session notes and meeting minutes, and any other documentation that records the decisions of the modeling team.

Documentation produced inside of ER*win* includes the logical model diagram, and reports on the details of diagram objects. You can use ER*win*'s page grids and scaling options to print the model diagram. Use the Print Model dialog to print selected pages of a larger diagram and use the Header/Footer tab to add or change the default model information that is automatically included in the diagram header and footer.

ER*win* allows you to print reports directly from the Report Browser, or use RPTwin. RPTwin is a fully functional standalone-reporting tool that allows you to create customized reports. Each RPTwin report must be associated with a data set. When you create a new report, or change the data set associated with an existing report, RPTwin will prompt you to select a new data set. When a new data set is associated with an existing report, RPTwin will present a warning if report elements do not match the data set elements. Use the RPTwin toolbox to add report elements to the report bands that divide the report into sections.

Delivering the logical model diagram and supporting documentation ends the logical modeling activities. In the next chapter I introduce some of ER*win*'s advanced features for the logical model, such as user-defined properties, domains, and the model dictionary for managing models.

13

DELIVERING THE
LOGICAL DATA
MODEL

Advanced Features
for the Logical Model

So far in this part of the book you learned the principal steps of developing, reviewing, and delivering the logical data model using ER*win*. This chapter explores some of ER*win*'s advanced features by discussing the following topics:

- User-defined properties (UDPs)
- Domains and independent attributes
- Model storage in the dictionary

User-defined properties allow you to add details to diagram objects that extend ER*win*'s ability to record information specific to your organization. Domains and independent attributes allow you to define and use the base properties of attributes consistently across the enterprise. If your organization does not have a repository that handles versioning, you can create a model storage dictionary using the model delivered with ER*win*.

User-Defined Properties

A user-defined property (UDP) can be anything that is considered useful or important for managing a specific class of model object. UDPs allow you to attach additional information to logical and physical model objects. UDPs extend ERwin's ability to define model objects.

For example, consider an environment where several different modelers have the responsibility for creating and maintaining specific objects within the enterprise model. Using the UDP Editor, you can easily and quickly create a user-defined property that allows each modeler to select his or her name from a drop-down list box to indicate the person responsible for the object.

Another example is to include a UDP that allows modelers to add the date that a subject area within a logical model is scheduled for review, and another that records the date the review is completed.

NOTE

UDPs do not translate into physical database objects; they are *not* created in the database. UDPs are simply tools that allow you to more easily manage the complexity of a data model. You can use UDPs for UDP macros. In the Report Browser you can include UDPs in model object reports and report on UDP definitions.

The diagram, subject area, stored display, and relationship objects span the logical and physical models and can share UDPs across the logical and physical models. However, UDPs cannot be shared between objects that are specific to the logical and physical model. For example, entity and table object classes cannot share UDPs; you must create them for each using the appropriate editor.

There are two parts to using UDPs, creating them and assigning values. You create UDPs using the UDP Editor and attach them to the appropriate model object class. You assign values using the appropriate model object editor.

Using the UDP Editor

You can create UDPs for any ERwin object class using the UDP Editor. To launch the UDP Editor, select Edit, UDPs or click the UDP Editor button in any object editor. Using the UDP Editor, you can assign the name, datatype, default value, and description for a new or existing UDP. Afterward, the UDP tab in the appropriate object editor displays the properties defined in the UDP Editor to allow you to enter or select the values.

The UDP Editor, shown in Figure 14.1, contains the following functionality:

- Class—The UDP you create is assigned to the model object class you select in the drop-down list.
- Name—As always, I encourage the use of good conventions for naming and defining a UDP. As with all modeling objects, good names and definitions are a best practice.
- Type—Select a datatype for the UDP.
- Default—Enter a default value that will appear as the UDP default.
- Description—Enter a definition of the UDP.

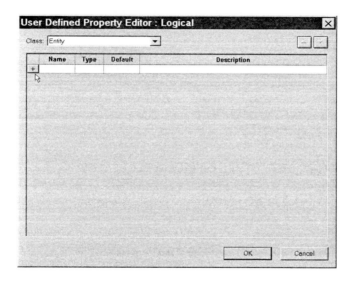

FIGURE 14.1
Use the User-Defined Property Editor: Logical to create new properties and attach to model object classes. Each UDP is specific to the model object to which it is attached and cannot be shared by other objects.

Use the Class drop-down list to select the class of ERwin object to which you want to assign the UDP. The model object class defaults to the diagram object from which the UDP Editor is accessed. For example, the model object class selected is the entity class if you open the UDP Editor using the UDP Editor button in the Entity Editor.

The edit grid contains columns that allow you to enter the name, type, default, and description for the UDP. The information entered here is displayed later in the UDP tab for the object editor for the class of object to which the UDP is assigned.

> **NOTE**
>
> The up and down arrows above and to the right of the edit grid allow you to orga-
> nize the UDPs. Select the UDP and click up or down to move the UDP to the appro-
> priate location.
>
> After you add a UDP, the + sign at the left side of that row in the edit grid changes
> to a × sign. Clicking the × deletes that UDP and all values assigned.

To enter the name of the UDP, click the + sign in an unused name field and type the name. If you do not enter a name, ERwin assigns a default name of UDP. Each successive UDP is named UDP#, where # is the next available consecutive number. Use good conventions for naming and defining UDPs.

UDP Datatypes

ERwin assigns a default datatype of text to all new UDPs. You can select a new datatype for the values assigned to specific instances of the model objects that will use the UDP by clicking inside the Type column of the edit grid. The available UDP datatypes are

- Command
- Date
- Int
- Real
- Text
- List

Note that selecting command as a datatype and attaching an executable as the default provides a facility to launch applications using the ERwin editor's UDPs. The object to which the UDP is attached displays a button with the UDP name that, when pressed, launches the default application. Figure 14.2 shows the UDP Editor using the command datatype to create a UDP that launches Microsoft Word as a UDP.

Use the date datatype to define the UDP values as a valid date in MM/DD/YY format. This datatype provides several options for assigning values, such as a spin control and a calendar control.

Use the int datatype to define the UDP values as whole numbers. This datatype provides no error checking to ensure that the value entered is a whole number. Although negative numbers are allowed, a decimal or fractional value is automatically truncated to a whole number.

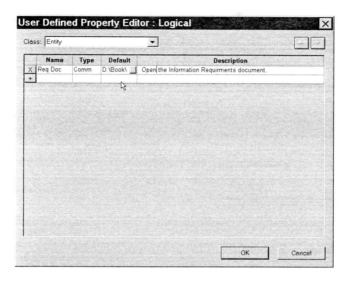

FIGURE 14.2
Using the command datatype UDP to launch an application from within ERwin.

Use the real datatype to define the UDP values as decimal numbers. As with the int datatype, no error checking is performed. The value entered can be a whole number (integer) or a decimal number.

Use the text datatype to define the UDP values as text. I have entered well over 255 characters of text as a UDP value. There might be a limit to the number of characters that you can enter as a value, but the documentation does not specify any such limit.

Use the list datatype to create a list box that constrains the values to a list of selections. Use the Default column to enter the selection choices. Separate each list item with a comma (,) and designate the default list item by preceding it with a tilde (~). You must enter default values because the list datatype requires a list of selection choices.

Use the Default column to define a default value for new instances of model objects that use the UDP. Default values are optional for all datatypes, except the list data type, which requires a list of default values. If you provide a value and later delete it, the default value will not be assigned. Separate the list items with commas. Indicate the default item in a list by preceding it with a tilde (~).

TIP

Default values can be an invitation to erroneous data or a real time-saver. Take care that your defaults add value.

Use the Description column in the edit grid to add a good definition of the UDP. I cannot place too much emphasis on including definitions for all modeling objects. The value of UDPs will likely be lost if you do not use good names and definitions.

Assigning UDP Values

Each ERwin object editor has a UDP tab you can use to assign values for UDPs as well as open the UDP Editor to create new UDPs. For example, after you create a UDP and attach it to the entity class in the UDP Editor, you can easily specify the property value for a specific entity using the UDP tab of the Entity Editor.

The functionality of the UDP tab includes the following:

- Property—Displays the name of the UDP. When you point to the property name, the UDP description displays in a tooltip.
- Value—If a default value was defined when the UDP was created, the property default value is automatically populated.

In addition, you can launch the UDP Editor from this tab.

When the command datatype is defined for a UDP property, the box where the property name displays becomes a button that you can click to launch the file or application specified in the Value text box. If a default application was not specified, you can enter a command or click the button to browse for a file or executable program. For example, you can type or select `C:\entity.doc` to launch the Microsoft Word document entity.doc, provided you have an association between files with a file extension of DOC and Microsoft Word.

For int, real, and text datatypes, simply enter a value or use the designated default value if appropriate. Remember that no error message appears if you enter a character in an int or real datatype. Text values can be as long as necessary. A scrollbar is displayed if needed for longer values.

The date datatype provides different options for assigning a value:

- Type in the value.
- Use the spin control.
- Use the calendar drop-down list.

The date datatype includes a spin control (the up/down arrow). To use the spin control, click in the portion of the date to change—month (MM), day (DD), or year (YY)—and then click the up arrow to move the date forward in time or the down arrow to move the date backward in time. To use the calendar control, select the drop-down list and use the arrows to move forward or backward in time. Figure 14.3 shows an example of a Date UDP named Scheduled Model Completion Date and displays the calendar control option.

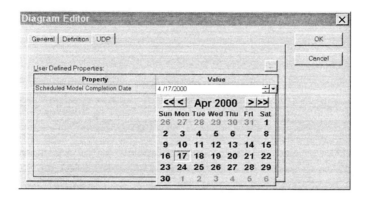

FIGURE 14.3
Creating a UDP using the Date datatype calendar feature allows modelers to easily select the date the model is scheduled to be completed.

Select a value from the drop-down list of choices for the list datatype. For example, you can create a UDP to allow the selection of the modeler responsible for maintaining a specific modeling object from the Value list. Figure 14.4 shows a list UDP that allows a modeler's name to be associated with a specific model object.

UDP Macro Functions

Use the UDP macro functions to display UDP values in an ER*win* diagram object. A macro is available for each ER*win* model object class that supports UDPs, as shown in Table 14.1.

TABLE 14.1   ER*win* Logical UDP Macros

Object Class Name	Object Class Macro
Diagram	%DiagramProp(*UDPName*)
Subject Area	%SubjectAreaProp(*UDPName*)
Entity	%EntityProp(*UDPName*)

continues

14

ADVANCED
FEATURES FOR THE
LOGICAL MODEL

TABLE 14.1   Continued

Object Class Name	Object Class Macro
Key Group	%KeyGroupProp(*UDPName*)
Relationship	%RelLogProp(*UDPName*)
Domain	%DomainLogProp(*UDPName*)
Attribute	%AttProp(*UDPName*)

FIGURE 14.4

Creating a UDP using the list datatype UDP to allow users to select from a list of options to provide a value for the UDP.

The argument for the UDP macro is the UDP name defined in the UDP Editor. For example, to define the business unit, you can create an entity UDP called Unit and assign a list of business units as UDP property values that can be associated with an entity. Then, use the %EntityProp(Business Unit) macro to display the UDP business unit value on the diagram. Macros can make diagrams more descriptive as well as tailored to meet the specific needs of the enterprise.

The ER*win* Report Editor allows you to include the values assigned to model objects as part of a new or predefined ER*win* report. To include UDPs, open the UDP folder and select the UDP check box.

You can include UDPs in reports for the following ER*win* logical objects:

- Diagrams
- Subject areas
- Stored displays
- Entities
- Relationships
- Domains
- Key groups
- Attributes

TIP

The UDP report option is only available for those object classes to which UDPs have been assigned.

Domains

Using domains as part of the data modeling process can be a significant time-saver for the data modeler in designing the logical model, as well as developing the associated physical data model. The logical data modeler can assign a domain to attributes in the logical model without regard to the domain's physical column properties. A domain that is assigned to logical attributes automatically includes physical model column properties based on the domain assigned in the logical model. Domains allow you to define and use logical and physical properties consistently across the enterprise.

For example, if the data model contains multiple columns for cost centers (general_ledger_cost_center, service_cost_center, and so on), you can create a new domain named Cost Center for which the datatype is defined as smallint. You can then attach a list of valid cost centers to the domain using a validation rule (100, 200, 300, and so on) and assign the general ledger cost center as the default value (100). You can also assign a display format that inserts parentheses around the cost center. When you assign the Cost Center domain to a column that stores cost center code information in the database, it automatically inherits the complete set of inheritable domain properties defined in the Domain Dictionary Editor.

An ER*win* domain is an independent model object that you can use to quickly assign properties to an attribute or column. You can define both logical and physical domains in the Domain

14

ADVANCED FEATURES FOR THE LOGICAL MODEL

Dictionary Editor. Unlike model objects that are only associated with either the physical or logical data model, a domain can be defined once and then used in both the physical and logical models. Using domains can significantly reduce the database design process time, as well as make the data model much simpler to maintain. You can assign domains to attributes to enforce business rules regarding datatype. Using additional physical model characteristics assigned to the domain can also reduce the time needed to create the corresponding physical model. Rather than assign constraints to each specific column individually, you can create an ERwin domain and use it to set multiple properties for a column in a single step. If the column property needs to change later, instead of changing the property setting for each and every column, you can simply change the domain to automatically update all the columns assigned that domain.

Using domains involves two tasks: defining the domain in the Domain Dictionary Editor and assigning the domain using the Independent Attribute (or Column) Editors, as described in the following sections.

Using the Domain Dictionary Editor

ERwin comes with five predefined domains that are available in the logical model. The <unknown> domain is the root domain in the logical domain hierarchy. ERwin automatically assigns the <unknown> domain to all new attributes when they are created. The Blob, Datetime, Number, and String domains are all children of the <unknown> domain. You can assign a domain to an attribute in the logical model to define a logical datatype for that attribute.

Using the Domain Dictionary Editor, you can define new domains with logical and physical properties for reuse as independent attributes and independent columns. You can also change the properties of user-defined domains, as well as the properties of the five standard domains shipped with ERwin, except the domain name and domain parent.

To launch the Domain Dictionary Editor, shown in Figure 14.5, select Edit, Domain Dictionary. The Domain Dictionary Editor functionality follows:

- Edit Mode—A drop-down list indicates whether the model is in logical or physical mode. Select Logical to add or edit logical domain properties in the tabs, or select Physical to add or edit physical domain properties in the tabs.

- Sort—The Alphabetically option sorts the domains in alphabetical order; the Hierarchically option sorts the domains in hierarchical order, showing the parent domain of each.

- Domain—A list displays all the domains available in the model. When a domain in the list is selected, ERwin displays the properties specified for the selected domain in the tabs. You can change the properties of several domains without closing the Domain Dictionary Editor.

- New—Click to open the New Domain dialog and add a new domain.
- Rename—Click to open the Rename Domain dialog and edit the name of the selected domain.
- Delete—Remove the selected domain from the model.
- Reset—Click to open the Reset Domain Properties dialog and reset one or more domain properties to the domain's default setting. For example, if the null option was changed for a new domain from NULL (a value inherited from the parent domain) to NOT NULL, you can use the Reset Domain Properties dialog to reset the value to the default NULL setting.

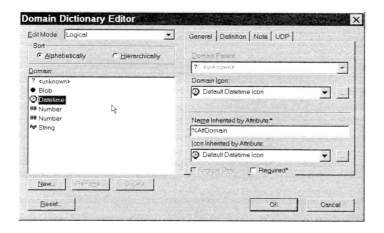

FIGURE 14.5
Use the Domain Dictionary Editor to create user-defined domains customized to meet the particular needs of your organization.

Changes made to a domain are implemented within the model when you click the OK button or select a different domain name in the Domain list. When the Domain Dictionary Editor closes, ER*win* automatically cascades all changes made to a domain to all columns attached to that domain throughout the diagram.

The Domain Dictionary Editor also contains a set of tabs for the logical mode:

- General
- Definition
- Note
- UDP

The General tab in the Domain Dictionary Editor allows you to set the following properties:

- Domain Parent—Indicates the parent of the selected domain. To change the parent, select a different domain from the list. This property cannot be inherited.

- Domain Icon—Indicates the icon for the selected domain. To change the icon, select a different icon from the list. This property cannot be inherited. Each of the default domains shipped with ERwin is assigned an icon.

- Name Inherited by Attribute—The name or ERwin macro that the attribute inherits when associated with the selected domain. The ERwin macro %AttDomain automatically migrates the logical domain name to the attribute name.

- Icon Inherited by Attribute—The icon that the attribute inherits when associated with the selected domain. To change the icon, select a different icon from the list. Click the ellipsis button to open the Icon Editor from which you can import BMP files to use in your ERwin diagram.

- Logical Only—Indicates whether the selected domain appears in the logical model only. Clear this check box if you want the selected domain to be available in both the logical and physical model.

- Required—Indicates whether attributes associated with this domain are required fields in a data-entry application. This option corresponds to the NOT NULL option in a physical model.

The Definition tab for the Domain Editor allows you to enter two definitions for each domain: one for the domain itself and another that is inherited by attributes using that domain:

- Domain Definition—Type or edit the definition for the selected domain. This definition is non-inheritable.

- Definition Inherited by Attribute—Enter the definition that is inherited by the attributes with the domain.

The Note and UDP tabs function in exactly the same way in all the ERwin object editors.

Using the Domain Dictionary Editor, you can define user-defined datatypes for all target servers that support user-defined datatypes. Support is provided for the following:

- DB2/CS and DB2/UDB distinct types
- SQL Anywhere, SQL Server, and Sybase user datatypes
- Rdb and Interbase domains

Once you create a user-defined datatype, you can assign it to columns in the model the same way that you assign an ERwin domain.

TIP

A user-defined datatype is simply an alias of an existing datatype. Similar to a domain, a user-defined datatype specifies the datatype and other column properties for a column. For example, a commonly used user-defined datatype is money. This datatype allows you to quickly define the characteristics of all columns with values in dollars and cents. The money datatype could alias a decimal (10,2) along with a comment such as, "A numeric value representing United States dollars with 2 decimal places representing cents."

When you create a new domain, ER*win* adds the domain name to the domain list, indents it below its parent domain to clarify the domain hierarchy, and adds it to the pool of independent attributes and independent columns. To facilitate reusing domains throughout the model, ER*win* displays all logical domains in the independent attribute browser and all physical domains in the independent column browser.

Using the Independent Attribute Browser

The independent attribute browser contains a list of reusable independent attributes that you can place in any entity in your model. Independent attributes are created in the Domain Dictionary Editor as logical domains. You can drag any domain from the browser and drop it into an entity or table to quickly create an attribute or column owned by that entity or table. The owned attribute or column inherits all of its properties from the domain on which the independent attribute or independent column is based. Use this drag-and-drop method to quickly populate the entities and tables in the diagram.

TIP

The independent attribute browser displays in the logical diagram window automatically the first time ER*win* is launched.

If you cannot see the independent attribute browser, select Window, Independent Attribute Browser or simply press Ctrl+B.

Once an owned attribute or column is created, you can change its name using ER*win*'s on-diagram editing feature. You can modify other properties using the Attribute Editor.

The functionality of the independent attribute browser, shown in Figure 14.6, follows:

- Sort—The Alphabetically option sorts the independent attributes in alphabetical order. The Hierarchically option sorts the independent attributes in hierarchical order under the parent domain.

- Independent attribute list—The logical domain name appears in this list. Click an independent attribute and drag it into an entity to create a new attribute in that entity. The new attribute inherits all of its properties from the parent domain.

FIGURE 14.6

The Independent Attribute Browser contains all the domains and user-defined datatypes. You can drag and drop to create a new attribute, and then edit the name.

Double-click any item in the independent attribute list to open the Domain Dictionary Editor in the logical edit mode. A newly created domain is immediately available as an independent attribute in the independent attribute browser upon closing the Domain Dictionary Editor.

The ER*win* Dictionary

ER*win* provides a simple but powerful facility to save an ER*win* diagram in a database using the ER*win* dictionary. The ER*win* dictionary allows you to store models in a special database that supports check-in/check-out version control and diagram sharing. Using the dictionary allows you to store data models in a central location and modelers to check out a model, make changes, and check it back in. Storing and versioning models enables you to maintain a production version of a model and, at the same time, begin modeling enhancements while keeping the production version pristine.

You can create the ER*win* dictionary on any target server supported by ER*win* simply by generating the ER*win* metamodel to the selected target server.

The ER*win* metamodel defines the data structures needed to store properties such as definition, location, font, color, and other important information about the entities, relationships, attributes, and other objects in ER*win* diagrams. The ER*win* metamodel is defined in the

Erwmeta.er1 file installed in the Model subdirectory in the ER*win* program directory. The metamodel provides the internal database definition information that ER*win* needs to generate the ER*win* dictionary as a physical database on a target server. After the data structures are generated, you can use ER*win*'s Dictionary Manager features to save ER*win* diagrams to this database.

CAUTION

Not all database platforms can store the ER*win* dictionary. You cannot use the following databases: AS/400, Ingres/OpenIngres, Interbase, Paradox, Rdb, and Red Brick.

Other database platforms can present unexpected difficulties unless they are accessed using an ODBC connection. You should access the following databases using an ODBC connection: Clipper, dBASE, and FoxPro. Read the ER*win* online documentation regarding using these DBMSs as the dictionary platform.

In the sections that follow, I explore the steps for creating a model dictionary, using the dictionary, checking in and checking out a model, and understanding model version history.

Creating a Model Dictionary

To store ER*win* diagrams on a target server, you must first create an ER*win* dictionary. To create the dictionary, you simply open the metamodel file in ER*win* and use the forward-engineering feature to generate the ER*win* metamodel schema to the target server.

The information in the ER*win* dictionary metamodel is divided into the following subject areas:

- Main subject area—Includes all the tables in the metamodel.
- Schema—Includes only the tables required to create the ER*win* dictionary on a target server. Remember, when generating schema from the metamodel, be sure the Schema subject area is the current subject area.
- Relevant—Includes several entities that are not included in the Schema subject area and therefore are not generated when creating the dictionary, but contain important information that is helpful in understanding the metamodel.
- Text-related—Contains entities that store lengthy text values such as descriptions or notes.

If you use an ODBC or direct connection to the system catalog to access the target server, the dictionary database that is generated from the ER*win* metamodel is created as a set of tables in the server database. The database can store multiple diagrams and multiple versions of each diagram. However, if you are using dBASE, FoxPro, or Clipper target servers and use a direct connection instead of an ODBC data source to access the server, the dictionary is generated as a set of .DBF files, which can store only a single version of a single diagram.

For the sample dictionary created in this section, shown in Figure 14.7, I used Microsoft Access as the target database. I performed the following steps:

1. Created a directory to hold the dictionary database.
2. Created a blank Access mdb.
3. Made a copy of the Erwmeta.er1 file into that directory (just to be safe).
4. Opened the Erwmeta.er1 file in ER*win*.
5. Changed the Target Server database to Access 97.
6. Selected Forward Engineer/Schema Generation from the Tasks menu.

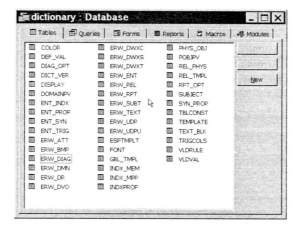

FIGURE 14.7

The ERwin Dictionary data structures created in MS Access. Creating the dictionary in Access can provide an opportunity to become familiar with its features and functionality.

> **TIP**
>
> When generating a dictionary from the metamodel, make sure the Schema subject area is the current subject area and that the model is in physical mode. Be sure that the Access mdb is *not* created exclusive. Check the username and password (if appropriate).

After you generate the ER*win* dictionary schema to your target server, you can begin storing ER*win* diagrams in that database.

Using the Dictionary Manager

When storing ER*win* diagrams on a server, ER*win* uses a check-in/check-out system that helps prevent multiple users from making changes to the same diagram at the same time. This process provides a simple means of version control by treating the diagram as if it were checked into and out of a library. When a diagram is checked in, you can save it with a new name or overwrite an existing copy stored on the server. When you check out a diagram from the server, ER*win* records the check-out status of the diagram, listing you as its current user.

To save a diagram and store it on the target server, you must use the Dictionary Manager option on the File menu instead of the Save or Save As options. Figure 14.8 shows the Dictionary Manager dialog.

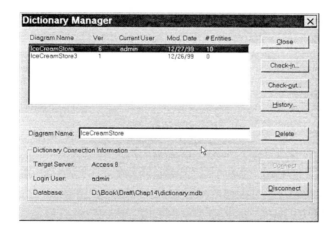

FIGURE 14.8

To launch the Dictionary Manager dialog, select it from the File menu options. You will need to select the Target Dictionary Storage DBMS and connect ERwin.

The functionality of the Dictionary Manager follows:

- Diagram Name/Ver/Current User/Mod. Date/# Entities—A list displays the ER*win* diagrams stored in the dictionary database, the diagram version number, the name of the current user for each diagram, the most recent modification date, and the number of entities in the diagram when it was last checked out.

- Diagram Name—Enter a name for the current diagram. You use this control in conjunction with the Check-in button for storing new diagrams in the dictionary.

- Dictionary Connection Information—This area displays the target server, login user, and fully qualified pathname to the dictionary database. You cannot change this information.
- Close—Close the Dictionary Manager dialog and save any changes.
- Check-in—Click to open the Check-in Diagram dialog.
- Check-out—Click to display the Check-out Diagram dialog and open the selected version of the diagram in ER*win*.
- History—Click to open the Version History dialog to view and update information on versions of the selected diagram.
- Delete—Remove the selected diagram version.
- Connect—Click to open the Connection dialog and open a different ER*win* dictionary. The Connect button is not available (grayed out) if you are connected to a dictionary. To enable the Connect button, you must first disconnect, using the Disconnect button.
- Disconnect—Click to log out of the current ER*win* dictionary.

Checking In a Diagram

The Check-in button is available under two conditions:

- The active diagram was previously stored in the dictionary and was checked out of the dictionary during the current modeling session.
- The active diagram was not previously stored in the dictionary, but a name was entered in the Diagram Name text box.

To check in a diagram under a new name, simply enter the name in the Diagram Name text box and click the Check-in button to start the export from ER*win* into the dictionary.

When checking in an updated version of a diagram, your server login name is displayed, as the Current User of the diagram, in the list box at the top of the Dictionary Manager dialog. To check in, click the diagram name in the list box and then click the Check-in button. ER*win* saves the diagram file on the server with a new version number. Figure 14.9 shows the Check-in Diagram dialog.

The diagram versioning in the dictionary assigns a version number to a diagram each time it is checked in. The diagram version number is displayed in the Dictionary Manager list box and in the upper-right corner of the Check-in Diagram dialog. ER*win* assigns version numbers sequentially, beginning with number 1. Each time a diagram is checked into the dictionary, the version number is incremented. You can enter a different version number for the selected diagram in the text box if you prefer to use a different number. You can also add detailed notes to each version, which can describe and identify the particulars of how the current version is different from the previous version.

The Dictionary Manager displays only the newest version of a specific diagram. To view previous versions of a diagram, click the History button to open the Version History dialog.

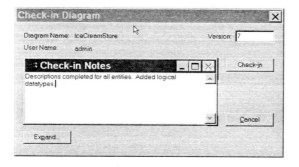

FIGURE 14.9
Use the Check-in Diagram dialog to add your models to the dictionary.

Checking Out a Diagram

When checking out a diagram from the dictionary, ER*win* records the check-out status of the diagram and lists your server login name as the diagram's current user. ER*win* then retrieves the selected diagram information from the dictionary tables in the target server database and displays the information in an ER*win* diagram.

The Diagram Check-out Warning dialog appears if someone attempts to check out a diagram in Read/Write mode while the diagram is currently checked out in the same mode by another user. You can elect to override this warning and continue by selecting Yes or cancel, or return to the Dictionary Manager by selecting No. If you choose Yes, ER*win* automatically selects the Read Only check box to prevent changes to the diagram while another user is updating it. Although you have the option to clear this check box and open the diagram in Read/Write mode, take care to use this option wisely because some changes might be overwritten.

NOTE

To check in or check out a diagram stored on a SQL database server, you must have UPDATE permission on the ER*win* Diagram table (ERW_DIAG) and SELECT permission on all of the ER*win* dictionary tables.

To open a diagram stored in the ER*win* dictionary, select the model, and then click the Check-out button in the Dictionary Manager. The Check-out Diagram dialog, shown in Figure 14.10, allows you to open diagrams that are stored in the dictionary on the target server database.

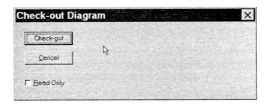

FIGURE 14.10

Use the Check-out Diagram dialog to extract a version of a model. ERwin will warn you if the diagram is already checked out.

The following list describes the functionality of the Check-out Diagram dialog:

- Check-out—Clicking this opens the diagram in ER*win* and updates the check-in/check-out information in the dictionary to indicate that the diagram is checked out.
- Cancel—Close the dialog and cancel any changes.
- Read Only—Select this check box to open the diagram in ER*win* only for viewing, without saving any changes back to the dictionary. Clear this check box to check out the diagram for updating.

Version History

The Version History dialog allows you to view a list of all previous versions of a diagram saved to the dictionary. Use the Version History dialog to check out a version in read-only mode and then view and modify the notes associated with each diagram version or to delete diagram versions from the dictionary.

To view or update a diagram version history in the dictionary, select a diagram in the Dictionary Manager list box and then click the History button to display the Version History dialog, shown in Figure 14.11.

The following list describes the functionality of the Version History dialog:

- Diagram Name—Displays the name of the diagram whose versions are displayed.
- Version—Lists the versions of the selected diagram stored in the ER*win* dictionary in numeric order.
- Check-in Date—Displays the date that the diagram version was checked into the dictionary.
- Check-in User—Displays the server login name of the user who checked the diagram version into the dictionary.
- Current User—Displays the server login name of the user (if any) who currently has the diagram checked out of the dictionary.

- Check-in Notes—Displays the check-in notes for the selected diagram. The text can be edited. To save changes, click the Update Notes button.
- Close—Closes the Version History dialog and saves any changes.
- Extract—Opens the selected diagram version in ER*win* in read-only mode.
- Update Notes—Writes any changes to the Check-in Notes text box to the dictionary for the selected diagram version.
- Delete—Removes the selected diagram version.

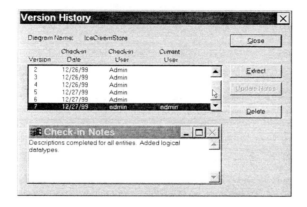

FIGURE 14.11

The Version History dialog allows you to manage the versions of a diagram. You can view and modify the diagram notes, or delete versions.

NOTE

For enterprises that require stronger support and control in a multiuser environment, Computer Associates provides the ModelMart. ModelMart supports diagram locking, circulating multiple diagram versions for team design environments, and automatic methods for merging differences within multiple versions of a model.

14

ADVANCED FEATURES FOR THE LOGICAL MODEL

Summary

ER*win*'s advanced features for creating and managing data model diagrams include

- User-defined Properties (UDPs)
- Domains
- Model Storage Dictionary

User-defined properties (UDPs) allow you to add details to diagram objects that extend ERwin's ability to record information specific to your organization. Although UDPs will not be created in the database, they can be used to record important information about any model object. UDPs can be created and attached to any model object class, including the diagram itself. After using the UDP Editor to create a UDP and attach it to a specific class, you can assign a value to a UDP using the appropriate model object editor.

Domains and independent attributes allow you to define and use the base properties of attributes consistently across the enterprise. Domains are created using the Domain Dictionary Editor and are based on the datatypes supported by the target server selected. Domains can be used to set the properties of a column, as well as constrain the set of values that can be contained by a column. User-defined datatypes can be created in the database for target servers that support them.

ERwin's also includes a facility for creating a model storage dictionary using ERwin's meta-model. The model storage dictionary can be created on many target servers, although there are limitations for some. After creating the model dictionary, you can use check-in and check-out features for versioning. You can add a note to each version to record important details. ERwin also provides a facility that allows you to manage the version history of models, adding new notes and deleting when appropriate.

The introduction to some of ERwin's advanced features concludes Part III, "Creating the Logical Model." In Part IV, "Creating the Physical Model," you learn about collecting usage requirements and using them to define the physical model.

Creating the Physical Model

IN THIS PART

Developing the Physical Model

In Part I, "Modeling Concepts," I introduced modeling essentials, including using facilitated sessions for collecting information requirements and business rules. In Part II, "Introducing ER*win*," I provided an overview of installing ER*win* and introduced ER*win*'s menus and tools. In Part III, "Creating the Logical Model," I built a logical model by translating the information requirements and business rules into ER diagram objects and reviewed ER*win*'s features for organizing and enhancing the readability and understandability of a logical data model. I introduced the concept of using model reviews to ensure you produce a quality data model, discussed ER*win*'s facilities for delivering the logical model, and completed the introduction to logical modeling by reviewing some of ER*win*'s advanced features.

This chapter begins Part IV, "Creating the Physical Model," by exploring the preparation tasks associated with physical modeling using ER*win*. In the sections that follow, I discuss physical modeling activities by covering the following topics:

- Understanding the physical model
- Understanding usage requirements
- Setting the physical modeling environment

Once the logical model diagram is accurate and complete, it's time to make a relational database management system (RDBMS) platform decision and create the physical model. Database platform selection should be based on data usage requirements and the architecture strategies of the enterprise. I use Microsoft Access as the database platform for the same reason that many RDBMSs are selected: I am familiar with Access and I own a copy.

Understanding the Physical Model

The physical model should represent the precise design of the physical database, such as denormalized tables, column datatypes and constraints, indexes, and other physical properties of the database generated using the schema for the target server selected.

In ER*win*, the physical model is a graphical representation of the database that is actually implemented. The design of the physical data model is heavily dependent upon the RDBMS platform selected for implementation and the data usage requirements. Obviously, a physical model for IMS looks considerably different than one for Sybase. A physical model for dimensional reporting looks considerably different than one for online transaction processing (OLTP).

The Relationship Between the Logical and Physical Models

The components of a physical data model are tables, columns, indexes, and so on. The entities in the logical model probably become tables in the physical model. The attributes become columns. The logical relationships become relational integrity constraints and triggers.

In ER*win*, there is a link between the logical and physical models (see Table 15.1). Changes made in the logical model are reflected in the physical model unless they are defined as logical only. In previous versions of ER*win*, the logical and physical models were more tightly coupled. In version 3.5.2 (the version used in this text), diagram objects can belong to both the logical and physical models, the logical model only, or the physical model only.

TABLE 15.1 ER*win* Logical and Physical Model Objects

Logical Model	Physical Model
Entity	Table
Attribute	Column
Logical datatype (text, number, datetime)	Physical datatype (int, decimal(10,2))
Key group	Index
Primary key	Primary key (PK) index

Logical Model	Physical Model
Foreign key	Foreign key (FK) index
Identifying relationship	FK in PK index
Non-identifying relationship	FK not in PK index
Many-to-many relationship	Associative table
Subtype relationship	Denormalized table
(No logical object)	View
Referential integrity	Insert, update, and delete triggers
Cardinality	Insert, update, and delete triggers

NOTE

Some logical model objects cannot be implemented in the physical model. For example, many-to-many and subtype relationships cannot be represented by physical model objects and must be represented using associative and denormalized tables.

Also note that some physical objects, such as views, cannot be represented in the logical model.

The data modeler and the database administrator (DBA) use the logical model, usage requirements, and enterprise architectural strategies to develop the physical model. You can denormalize a physical model to improve performance and create views to support usage requirements.

Understanding Usage Requirements

You might have gathered some usage requirements during previous information requirements facilitated sessions and interviews. However, those sessions generally focused on *what* information is needed; usage requirements generally focus on *how* information is used. Usage requirements define and document, as completely as possible, how the users intend to use the data.

Examples of usage requirements include

- Access and performance requirements
- Concurrent users
- Volumetrics
- Calculated or derived data
- Reporting requirements and standard queries
- Logical groupings

Access and performance requirements are estimations of the critical nature of the information to the business processes of the enterprise. For example, users might indicate that they need access to the data 24 hours a day, 7 days a week, with subsecond response time. When you hear access and performance needs of this nature, it's time to start managing user expectations! Ask questions that will identify the critical business need that mandates such requirements. Because every database needs some maintenance down time, 24×7 access requirements are expensive and require special solutions.

> **TIP**
>
> All other usage requirements have an impact on access and performance requirements. Be sure to let users know when they are providing other usage requirements that make their access and performance requirements difficult to meet.
>
> For example, access to large volumes of historical data by many concurrent users might make subsecond response time requirements difficult to achieve. Let users decide whether they prefer to compromise on the amount of data or the response time.

The number of concurrent users is an estimation of the number of users who will be accessing the data *at the same time*. Don't confuse concurrent users with the total number of users who will access the data, although this is important information as well. A good estimation of the maximum number of concurrent users accessing the data helps you construct the database to provide acceptable performance levels.

For example, suppose your enterprise spans the United States from the East to West coasts and users will access the data during working hours from 8:00 a.m. to 5:00 p.m. in their respective time zones. East-coast users will access the data beginning at 8:00 a.m. Eastern time. Because this is 5:00 a.m. on the West coast, West-coast users will not begin accessing the data until 11:00 a.m. Eastern time. Counting the number of users during the middle of the day when all time zones are within working hours (peak hours) should provide a fairly good estimate of the maximum number of concurrent users.

The remaining usage requirements are often gathered by conducting facilitated sessions. These sessions gather together the design and development teams with end users to define and document how the data will be used. The sections that follow provide some guidelines for productive facilitated sessions.

Facilitated Sessions

You should conduct the usage requirements session as the logical model nears completion. In Chapter 1, "Understanding Data Modeling Concepts," I introduced facilitated sessions, and in Chapter 8, "Discovery: Gathering Information Requirements, Metadata, and Business Rules," I provided details for gathering information requirements. In general, the process is the same for the usage requirements gathering sessions.

Remember, the single most important activity is including the appropriate attendees. Examples of attendees are

- Facilitator—The facilitator is responsible for keeping the attendees focused and productive, as well as ensuring that all attendees participate.

- Scribe—The scribe is responsible for documenting the results of the session. For large sessions with 10 or more attendees, you might want to consider having more than one scribe.

- Data modeler—The data modeler is responsible for answering any questions about the logical data model and documenting the physical model design in ER*win*.

- Database administrator (DBA)—The DBA should lead the discovery session and introduce the topics that will provide the usage information needed to produce a physical design that meets the business and technical needs of the enterprise.

- Data architect—The data architect is responsible for ensuring that the physical model aligns with the technical architecture direction of the enterprise.

- Application development team—The application development team responsibilities vary depending on the how the data will be loaded and accessed. It might be responsible for producing a graphical user interface (GUI) or an application programming interface (API) or extracting and loading data.

- End users—The end users include business partners, analysts, and others who will use the data to meet a business need. End users are responsible for providing sample reports, common queries and ad hoc query examples.

As always, the usage requirements of the information's end users, including the development team, should have the highest priority. It is here that the enterprise realizes the bottom-line value of information. Good design and implementation should meet a significant portion of the business needs of end users. End users are responsible for identifying the business needs that are satisfied by meeting the information and usage requirements.

15

DEVELOPING THE PHYSICAL MODEL

> **TIP**
>
> Discussions with attendees should include user requirements for historical data. The length of time that data is retained has a significant impact on the size of the database. Often, older data is kept summarized and the atomic-level data is archived or removed.

Prepare for the session by distributing the information requirements and business rules documentation and the logical data model. Participants should provide sample reports and queries to include in the distribution prior to the session. The development team and end users should be encouraged to come to the session prepared to discuss how they will use the data and the business needs that will be met.

I recommend a pre-session meeting to help participants prepare for a productive session. Review the goals and objectives of the session to ensure that participants come prepared to accomplish them. Invite participants to make recommendations for additions or changes. The list that follows provides some concepts that should help participants organize their usage needs:

- Conceptual data groupings
- Standard reports
- Commonly used queries
- Ad-hoc queries

Finding Conceptual Data Groupings

Conceptual data groupings are the rows and columns that are accessed to represent a specific business concept. A logical model normalized to third normal form will likely separate the data into several entities. For example, Betty's Ice Cream Shop has a business concept called a banana split. This single concept is represented in the logical model in several entities: an instance of SUNDAE, an instance of BANANA SPLIT, three instances of ICE CREAM FLAVOR, and three instances of TOPPING.

The development team and end users should define the business concepts of interest within the scope of the problem domain. The data architect will ensure that the business concepts fit with the technical architecture of the enterprise. The data modeler will ensure that the business concepts fit within the enterprise data model.

You can implement conceptual data groupings and user requirements for accessing data by using denormalization or planned redundancy or by designing views. Denormalization combines the attributes from two or more entities into a single table. Planned redundancy duplicates the same column in more than a single table. The DBA determines whether the usage requirements should be met using denormalized persistent data structures, planned redundancy, or views.

TIP

Views are generally considered virtual objects, objects that are created upon request and that exist only during the time they are accessed. However, views that meet the needs of many users or that are frequently accessed are often implemented as persistent data structures.

Persistent views differ from other data structures in that they do not contain historical data. Instead, they contain current data that is refreshed on a regular schedule.

Defining Standard and Common Queries

Reporting requirements and standard queries help the DBA construct indexes. Users should bring sample queries and reports to the session. Reports must be well defined and should include the atomic values for any summaries or roll-ups. Usage needs for summarized data, roll-ups, and other calculated or derived data might indicate a need for additional data structures and columns. For example, if users generally sum a set of columns and then average the result, consider storing the result in a table—particularly if the summarization and averaging process is time-consuming. The DBA should guide the decisions in this area.

TIP

A centralized library of reports and queries can be an asset to the enterprise by allowing development teams and end users to leverage previous analysis and design efforts.

If a library exists in your enterprise, a quick check can save hours of analysis and design. If not, now is a good time to create one, using the reports and queries from the current effort.

Reports and common queries are often implemented using views (persistent or virtual) that assist users by performing joins or filtering data. Developers and end users are likely to have queries that support specific business functions. Even if they are not implemented as data structures or views, DBAs certainly consider them as candidates for indexes.

Defining Ad-Hoc Queries

Ad-hoc queries are user-defined queries that are run on an irregular basis to answer a specific business question or to respond to a particular business request for information. Although ad-hoc queries are by nature nonstandard and difficult to predict, you can often identify a pattern or series of patterns.

Understanding ad-hoc queries can also provide candidates for indexes or physical organization of the data. Be aware that today's ad-hoc queries often become the standard queries of tomorrow. Consider including ad-hoc queries in the enterprise report and query library.

Estimating Volumetrics

Volumetrics are estimations of the volume of data that is retained over a period of time. These estimates give database administrators an idea of the physical size of the database. Determining volumetrics is not a trivial task. Experienced DBAs are likely to have a series of questions that will help estimate volumetrics.

ER*win* provides a feature to assist in estimating volumetrics, allowing you to calculate the size of tables, indexes, and physical storage objects in the database. In Chapter 16, "Building the Physical Model in ER*win*," I describe how to add volumetrics information to physical tables.

In ER*win*, you can calculate the size of any table in its initial state or project its growth over a period of time. Calculating all table sizes in the database allows you to easily estimate the size of the entire database.

NOTE

When estimating the size of your database, ERwin uses the specific datatypes that exist within the RDBMS you selected as the target server.

ER*win*'s volumetrics features allow you to

- Change RDBMS column values such as NULL and variable-width columns that can affect table size estimations.
- Include index objects in database size estimations and select appropriate physical storage objects for each table.
- Manipulate parameters that can affect database size estimations, such as the number of bytes per character or the amount of space overhead allocated for each row, and add a log space factor to include the database log space in size estimates.

You can use the ER*win* Report Browser to print volumetrics reports by physical object, database, and table with appropriate size estimates. You can also modify table calculation settings within the Report Browser and have the Report Browser estimate the database size on-the-fly.

Setting the Physical Modeling Environment

Although previous versions of ER*win* supported both logical and physical objects, version 3.5.2 allows you to create a logical model that appears different but is still closely related to the physical model. For example, objects in the logical model can be defined as logical only so that ER*win* does not represent them in the physical model. Physical objects can be defined as physical only so that they do not appear in the logical model. Using ER*win*'s options for defining diagram objects as logical only or physical only, you can develop a fully normalized logical model and denormalize the physical model to meet usage requirements or improve performance.

After you create a logical model in ER*win*, you can view the corresponding physical model by selecting the Physical Model option from the Logical/Physical Model option list in the ER*win* toolbar. You must select the target database for the model to allow ER*win* to appropriately activate the physical editors and options that define the properties of physical model objects.

ER*win* tailors the options available in the physical model based on the selected target database. For example, column-level properties, such as supported datatypes and null options specific to the target server, appear in the Column Editor. Once this model is defined, ER*win* can directly generate the diagram objects in the target database using the correct syntax.

Setting the physical model environment involves selecting the target server and the physical modeling notation. The sections that follow describe the process for each.

Selecting the Target Server

Before you create physical table and column names, datatypes, or other physical properties, you must choose the target database management system (DBMS) where ER*win* creates the physical schema. You must also specify the default datatype, nullity options, and default values ER*win* should use when generating columns.

If you select the target server before you begin developing the physical model, ER*win* defines the physical characteristics specific to the RDBMS, such as datatypes and name-length warnings. Selecting the target server before you start to work on the physical model can prevent significant physical design rework.

You do not have to choose the target server before beginning the physical model design. ER*win* allows you to select a different RDBMS or change default settings at any time.

However, you can get unexpected results when changing between certain target servers. For example, changing from Sybase to DB2 might cause physical names to be truncated, because Sybase supports long names and DB2 limits names to 18 characters.

The Server menu option is only available when the diagram is in the physical mode. Figure 15.1 shows the Server menu options. Figure 15.2 shows the Target Server options.

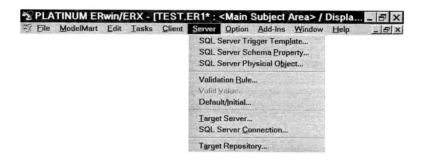

FIGURE 15.1

ERwin's Server menu contains different options depending upon the Target Server selected.

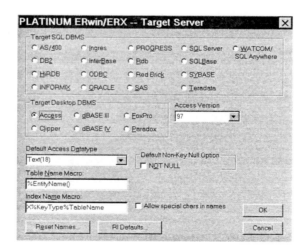

FIGURE 15.2

Use the Target Server options dialog to select your target server from the list of SQL and Desktop DBMSs that are supported by ERwin. The available options vary depending on the target server selection.

The Target Server dialog allows you to select the target server as well as set physical model options for ER*win*, including

- Target SQL DBMS—Click the target server name to select it for the physical model.
- Target Desktop DBMS—Click the target server name to select it for the physical model. You will also need to select the version.
- Default Access Datatype—The default datatype assigned to a new column in the model. Change the default datatype by selecting a different datatype from the drop-down list and entering arguments for precision and scale.
- Table Name Macro—The macro that ER*win* uses to generate table names. The default macro is `%EntityName()`. This macro uses the entity name to generate the default name for the corresponding table in the physical model.
- Index Name Macro—The macro that ER*win* uses to generate index names. The default macro is `%KeyType%TableName`. This macro generates an index name that includes the key type and table name.
- Reset Names—Click to open the Globally Reset DBMS Property dialog and reset the names of all physical model objects.
- RI Defaults—Click to open the Referential Integrity Default Editor dialog and set the default referential integrity rules.
- Default Non-Key Null Option—Select the default null option to be assigned when new columns are added.
- Allow special chars in names—Select to allow the use of special characters and spaces in the physical names of database tables. Clear to prevent the use of special characters and spaces in database table names.

Selecting the Physical Model Notation

You should normalize a logical model to third normal form to define the information requirements accurately and completely. The physical model is developed in response to the usage requirements and must meet access and performance needs.

As I mentioned earlier, a physical model for online transaction processing (OLTP) looks considerably different from one for a decision support system (DSS). OLTP physical models are generally optimized for inserts and updates. DSS physical models are generally optimized for data retrieval and queries. ER*win* provides support for DSS modeling using dimensional modeling. Dimensional modeling is also referred to as a star schema or snowflake.

ER*win* allows you to select the notation for the logical and physical data models separately. You need not select the same notation for both. ER*win* supports three options for the physical model: Integration Definition for Information Modeling (IDEF1X), Information Engineering (IE), and Dimensional Modeling (DM). ER*win*'s default notation for both the logical and physical models is IDEF1X. If you select DM (Dimensional Modeling) for the physical model, you can take advantage of ER*win*'s data warehouse support features and enforcement of star schema diagramming standards.

Summary

The physical model should represent the precise design of the physical database, including denormalized tables, column datatypes and constraints, and indexes specific to the selected RDBMS. The design of the physical model is determined by the logical model, the enterprise data model, the technical architecture strategies of the enterprise, and the usage requirements. A physical model looks different depending on the primary purpose of the information. A physical model for online transaction processing (OLTP) looks different from one for a decision support system (DSS).

You can gather usage requirements during facilitated sessions. Session participants should include a facilitator, one or more scribes, data modeler, database administrator (DBA), data architect, design and development team, and end users. Examples of usage requirements include access and performance requirements, the number of concurrent users, standard reports and queries, calculated or derived data, volumetrics, and logical data groupings.

ER*win* lets you relate the physical model to the logical model yet design them differently. You can define diagram objects as logical only or physical only. You should select the target server (RDBMS) prior to beginning work on the physical model. ER*win* supports three options for physical modeling notation: Information Engineering (IE), Integration Definition for Information Modeling (IDEF1X), and Dimensional Modeling (DM).

Collecting the usage requirements and setting the physical modeling environment prepares you to document the physical model design in ER*win*. In the next chapter, I explore using ER*win*'s tools for building the physical model.

Building the Physical Model in ER*win*

In Chapter 15, "Developing the Physical Model," I defined the components of the physical model, reviewed the relationship between the logical and physical model, and set the physical modeling environment in ER*win*. In this chapter, I explore building the physical model using ER*win*'s physical modeling tools.

In the sections that follow, I discuss physical modeling activities by covering the following topics:

- Using ER*win*'s Table Editor
- Setting a table's physical properties
- Using ER*win*'s Column Editor
- Setting a column's physical properties

Previous versions of ER*win* enforced a strong link between the logical and physical models. The version used in this text, 3.5.2, allows you to create a logical model that appears different but is still closely related to the physical model. You can define objects in the logical model as logical only so that ER*win* does not represent them in the physical model, and define physical objects as physical only so that they do not appear in the logical model. Using ERwin's options for defining diagram objects as logical only or physical only, you can develop a fully normalized logical model and denormalize the physical model to meet usage requirements or improve performance.

You can view the physical model by simply selecting the Physical Model option from the Logical/Physical Model option list in the ERwin toolbar. As I said in Chapter 15, I use Microsoft Access as the target server platform for developing the physical model for Betty's Ice Cream Shop. Selecting the target database prior to building the physical model allows ERwin to appropriately activate the physical editors and options that define the properties of physical model objects specific to Access.

Creating Tables in the Physical Model

Like a logical model, a physical model contains independent tables and dependent tables. An independent table is one in which an instance can be uniquely identified without an instance in another table. A dependent table is one in which an instance cannot be uniquely identified without an instance of another table or tables. A dependent table, also called child table, includes the primary key of the parent table in its primary key and relies on migrated foreign key column values for identity.

A table's type is determined by its relationships with other tables in the diagram. When you first create a table, it is represented as an independent table. When you create a relationship to another table using one of the relationship tools in the toolbox, ERwin determines whether the table is independent or dependent, based on the relationship type. If the table is a child table with an identifying relationship, it appears as a dependent table (rectangular box with rounded corners) in the diagram. All other tables appear as independent tables (rectangular boxes with sharp corners).

You can add tables to a physical model by

- Reverse engineering from an existing database—Recall that reverse engineering means to create a model in ERwin using DDL or connecting directly to a database.
- Adding entities to the logical model (that are not defined as logical only)—If entities are added to the logical model, a corresponding table is added to the physical model.
- Unresolved many-to-many relationships in the logical model—If you leave a many-to-many relationship in the logical model, ERwin automatically creates an associative table with an identifying relationship to each of the two tables involved in the relationship.
- Adding tables using the Table tool in the ERwin toolbox—Click to select the Table tool from the toolbox, then click the diagram to create a table. A corresponding entity will be created in the logical model, unless the table is defined as physical only.

You can create tables in the physical model in the same way you create tables in the logical model. ERwin provides a single tool in the ERwin physical modeling toolbox for creating both independent and dependent tables. When you add a table to the physical model, ERwin names the table E_n, where E stands for table (and entity) and n is the next available unique number. ERwin draws the table with a horizontal line dividing the box. You enter the primary keys in the box above the line and non-keys below the line. You can choose to have keys migrate to either the primary or non-key area of the box.

> **NOTE**
>
> Each table you add to the physical model is automatically added as an entity in the logical model. If you want a table to appear only in the physical model, select the Physical Only option in the Table Editor.

Setting Table Properties

Using the Table Editor, you can set properties such as table names, volumetrics, comments, UDPs, synonyms, aliases, validation rules, stored procedures, and scripts. The Table Editor allows you to view and update the properties for each table in the physical model, as well as open editors for creating validation rules and physical storage. To open the Table Editor (see Figure 16.1), choose Edit, Table or right-click a table and select Table Editor from the shortcut menu.

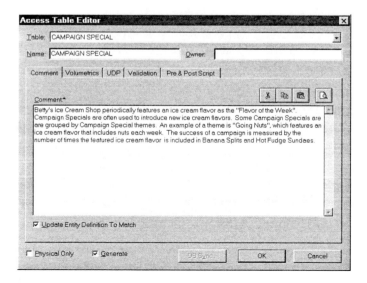

FIGURE 16.1

You have the option of updating the entity definition to match the table comment or keeping the physical comment separate.

The properties you can set in the Table Editor include

- Table—This displays the name of the currently selected table in the drop-down list. To view the properties of another table, select the table name from the list.
- Name—Change the name of the currently selected table.
- Owner—You can enter an owner name or use the name of the user generating the schema.
- Physical Only—Select this check box to cause the selected table to appear only in the physical model. Clearing this check box causes a corresponding entity to be created in the logical model.
- Generate—Select this check box to generate a CREATE TABLE statement for this table in the schema-generation script.

NOTE

To the best of my knowledge, the DB Sync button is disabled in the Table Editor.

If PowerBuilder is selected as the client target, a PB Sync button is displayed. You can click it to synchronize extended table attributes in the physical model with the PowerBuilder dictionary.

Using Access as the target server, Table Editor includes the following tabs:

- Comment—Enter a comment for the selected table. You have the option of updating the entity definition to match or keeping the physical comment separate.
- Volumetrics—Enter table size information by estimating the number of rows initially, the number of maximum rows, and the number of new rows each month.
- UDP—User-defined properties work the same in every object editor. Use this tab to specify a value for any UDPs that have been associated with the Table class of objects. Use the UDP Editor to create, modify, and delete UDPs. For more information on UDP's, see Chapter 14, "Advanced Features for the Logical Model."
- Validation—Attach validation rules to the columns in the selected table.
- Pre and Post Script—Create and edit scripts attached to the tables in the model.

> **TIP**
>
> I cannot overemphasize the importance of adding comments and definitions for every model object. (See Figure 16.1 for an example.) Enhancement and maintenance tasks often represent as much as 80 percent of the activities associated with data modeling. Adding comments and definitions to model objects, particularly physical model objects, can significantly decrease the effort required to support these activities.

Adding Volumetrics

To collect the volumetrics information, work with end users to estimate the initial number of rows in each table. Use trending information to estimate the number of new rows that will be added each month. Combine the number of initial rows and the estimated number of new rows each month and use the length of time that historical data is kept to estimate the maximum number of rows that will be present in the table.

Use the Volumetrics tab to enter the table volumetric estimates, the initial rows, the rows that will be added each month, and an estimate of the maximum number of rows.

> **TIP**
>
> Use the ER*win* Report Browser to print volumetrics reports by physical object, database, and table with appropriate size estimates.
>
> You can also modify table calculation settings within the Report Browser and have the Report Browser estimate the database size on-the-fly.

ER*win* also provides a Volumetrics Editor for maintaining volumetrics information; I introduce it in the section "Using the Volumetrics Editor" in Chapter 17, "Building Physical Relationships." ER*win* also provides additional volumetrics features at the column level. I cover these features later in "Setting Column Properties."

Attaching a Validation Rule

You can attach a validation rule to a table when the rule involves more than a single column. For example, in the Betty's Ice Cream Shop physical model, you can attach a rule to the

CAMPAIGN SPECIAL table to specify that the value entered in the Campaign Start Date column must come before the value entered in the Campaign End Date column. One way to enforce this constraint is to create a validation rule called Check-Date that creates the server expression `CMPGN_STRT_DT <= CMPGN_ND_DT`. If you try to enter a Campaign End Date that comes before the Campaign Start Date, the server returns an error message.

Use the Validation tab, shown in Figure 16.2, in the Table Editor to attach validation rules to tables in the physical model. The Validation tab also allows you to open the Validation Rule Editor to create new rules. I explore the process for creating a new validation rule in Chapter 17.

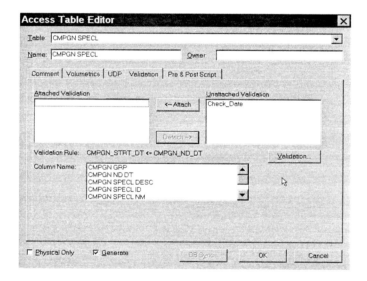

FIGURE 16.2

The Table Editor Validation tab allows you to attach one or more validation rules to tables in the physical model.

The following list describes the functionality available on the Validation tab in the Table Editor:

- Attached Validation—Lists the validation rules that are currently attached to the selected table. To detach a validation rule, select it from the Attached list and click Detach to remove it.

- Attach—Attaches the selected validation rule to the table. It is unavailable if you have not selected a validation rule from the Unattached Validation list box.

- Detach—Detaches the selected validation rule from the table. It is unavailable if you have not selected a validation rule in the Attached Validation list box.

Building the Physical Model in ER*win*

CHAPTER 16

315

16

BUILDING THE
PHYSICAL MODEL
IN ER*WIN*

- Unattached Validation—Lists the validation rules that are available in the physical model. To Attach a validation rule to the table, select it from the Unattached list and click Attach.
- Validation Rule—Displays the SQL statement for the selected validation rule.
- Column Name—Lists the columns in the selected table.
- Validation—Opens the Validation Rule Editor to create a new validation rule. Creating a new validate rule is covered in Chapter 17.

Pre and Post Script

Pre and post scripts are SQL (Structured Query Language) scripts that you can choose to run before or after certain statements in the schema generation script. ER*win* supports pre and post scripts for

- Tables
- Views
- Schema generation

You can create a script that is included before or after the CREATE TABLE statement in the schema-generation script. ER*win* allows you to create scripts using templates (see Figure 16.3). Templates can include both SQL code and ER*win* macros. You can use ER*win* macros to add the names and properties of diagram objects in the script template. I discuss using one of ER*win*'s macros in the next section.

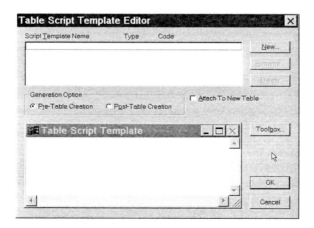

FIGURE 16.3

*ER*win*'s Script Template Editor allows you to attach an SQL script that you can elect to run before or after the table is created.*

Specific Client/Server Functionality

For other target server and client server selections, these tabs are also included in the Table Editor:

- Physical Props—Associate tables to predefined physical storage devices.
- Partitions—Specify physical partition values. Only available if Oracle 8.x is selected as the target server.
- Synonym—Specify synonym names for tables in the physical model. Only available if the selected target server supports synonyms.
- Stored Procedure—Manage the stored procedures that are attached to the tables in the physical model.
- PowerBuilder—Use to specify PowerBuilder-extended attributes for tables in the physical model. Only available if PowerBuilder is selected for the target client.

NOTE

The Table Editor might not display all the tabs that are available. You can scroll to see additional tabs by using the spin control.

Creating Physical Table Names

You should create table names using enterprise naming conventions that follow a set of standards and guidelines. Standards and guidelines should include a list of approved abbreviations for every word or common phrase used to identify the information of importance to the enterprise. Use this list of standard abbreviations to create the physical table names that represent the logical entity names.

NOTE

Using naming standards and guidelines to create entity names makes it easier to create table names. The table name should be an abbreviation of every word in the entity name. Users should be able to look at the abbreviated name and get a good idea of the entity name.

Do not use abbreviated names that are different from logical names. If necessary, change the logical name.

You can use ER*win*'s macro features to add table name abbreviations from a text file. The text file must contain rows with a word and then the abbreviation for that word, separated by a comma. Be sure to end each word/abbreviation row with a return. The text file I used looked like this:

```
Ice, IC
Cream, CREM
Start, STRT
End, ND
Date, DT
```

ER*win*'s Lookup macro finds the logical name in the file and uses the abbreviation as the physical column name.

Select Server, Target Server to open the Target Server dialog, shown in Figure 16.4. The default table name macro is %EntityName, which simply uses the entity name as the table name. ER*win* substitutes underscores for spaces and truncates the name depending on the target server selected.

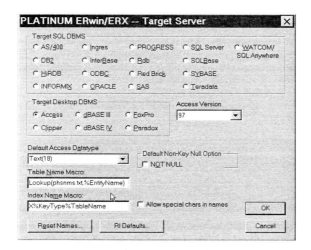

FIGURE 16.4
The Lookup *macro reads a text file of logical names and abbreviations and replaces the entity name with an abbreviated physical name.*

The syntax for using the Lookup macro to find table names is

%Lookup(*filename*.txt,%EntityName)

Note that you must enter the fully qualified path (c:\directory*filename*.txt) to the text file and substitute the name given to the file that contains your approved abbreviation list.

Setting Column Properties

Adding and maintaining columns in a table is more than just entering the column name and datatype. You must assign additional physical properties to the column to complete its description, such as the null option, default values, validation rules, volumetrics, comment, and display properties. You assign and manage all column properties in an ER*win* physical model using the Column Editor. Using the Column Editor, you can view and update the properties for the column in each table in the physical model. You can also launch editors that allow you to create default values, validation rules, and domains. In Chapter 17, I cover creating validation rules and default (initial) values.

Launch the Column Editor, shown in Figure 16.5, by selecting Edit, Column or right-clicking a table and selecting Column Editor on the Table shortcut menu. The Column Editor contains the following features:

- Table—Displays the name of the table that owns the columns in the column list. You can view the columns in another table by selecting a different table name from the drop-down list. Click the button to the right to open the Table Editor.

- Column—Displays the names of all columns in the selected table. Click the up and down arrows above the list to move the selected column up or down a single position.

- New—Click to open the New Column dialog to add a new column to the table. Note that you add the attribute name as well as the column name.

- Rename—Click to open the Rename Column dialog to change the name of the selected column.

- Delete—Click to remove the selected column from the table.

- Reset—Click to open the Reset Column Properties dialog and reset column properties to the default settings defined by the domain assigned to the column.

- Migrate—Click to open the Migrate Column Properties dialog. Use this dialog to change the properties that migrate along with (FK) columns.

- DB Sync—Click to start the Complete Compare task. Complete Compare allows you to synchronize the columns in the physical model with those on the target server.

CAUTION

If you make changes to column properties and then select a different column in the column list, you can still cancel the changes by selecting the Cancel button.

However, if you change to a different table (select a different table from the drop-down list), the column changes are saved in the model and cannot be canceled. Your only option is to close the model without saving it.

Building the Physical Model in ER*win*

CHAPTER 16

319

16

**BUILDING THE
PHYSICAL MODEL
IN ER*WIN***

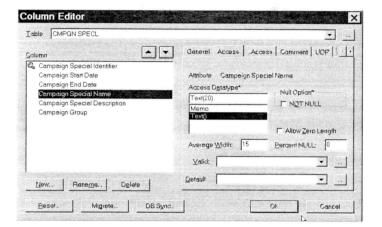

FIGURE 16.5

The number of tabs and the functionality of some tabs in the Column Editor change depending on the target server.

The Column Editor also includes a set of tabs that vary depending upon the target server selected:

- General—Manage the domain, primary key, and logical or physical model display properties for the selected column.
- *Target Server*—Select and maintain the datatype, null option, validation rule, default values, and volumetrics properties for the selected column. The name of this tab depends on the target server selected. In my examples, the tab displays Access.
- Comment—Enter a comment (definition or description) for the selected column. Note that you have the option of updating the attribute definition to match the column comment.
- UDP—Specify a value for a user-defined property that has been attached to the column object class.
- Index—Specify the index membership for the selected column.

NOTE

Note that Figure 16.5 shows two Access tabs. The second allows you to specify a caption name, format, and mask. AS/400, Progress, and Teradata target servers have an additional tab as well.

You can use the controls in the *Target Server* tab of the Column Editor to view and update RDBMS-specific information about the column. The server tab displays the name of the target server. For the examples used in this text, I selected Access as the target server, so Access is shown in the labels and dialogs that contain target server information.

The properties and functionality available in the Access (*Target Server*) tab, shown in Figure 16.5, are

- Attribute—Displays the name of the corresponding attribute in the logical model.
- Access Datatype—Displays the datatype of the current column. You can change the datatype for the column by selecting a different datatype from the list.
- Null Option—Displays the nullity option that is defined by the business rules for this column.
- Valid—Displays the name of the validation rule attached to the column. To attach a different validation rule, select it from the drop-down list of available validation rules. You can create, modify, and delete validation rules using the Validation Rule Editor. Click the button to the right to open the Validation Rule Editor.
- Default—Displays the name of the default rule attached to the column. To attach a different default rule, select it from the drop-down list of available default rules. You can create, modify, or delete a default rule using the Default Editor. Click the button to the right to open the Default/Initial Editor.

NOTE

Access also offers an additional option: Allow Zero Length. If you want to store a string of zero length in the column, select this check box. Clear the check box to prevent zero-length strings.

In addition to setting column properties using the Column Editor, you can also assign the datatype, edit masks, and other column properties using the ERwin Domain Dictionary. You can define a domain with specific set of column properties that you can use to quickly and consistently define properties.

You attach a domain using the Independent Column Browser. You can drag the independent column from the Independent Column Browser, drop into a table, and then change the name using the Column Editor or ERwin's on-diagram editing feature. You can also use the Column Editor to attach the domain to the column.

The sections that follow describe setting particular column properties using ERwin's macros to set column names, setting column volumetrics, adding constraints, and using options specific to Access.

Using the Lookup Macro to Set Column Names

If you used the object/modifier/class word attribute-naming convention to create your logical attribute names, then the column names will, by default, use the same form. This creates a three-part column name. The object portion, also called the subject or prime word, is often the table name. The modifier can be a single term or a group of terms. If the column name is burdensome for the user or cannot be abbreviated to meet database-platform restrictions, you must make compromises to the three-part attribute name.

The root part of the column name is the class word, which classifies the type of information being represented by the attribute. Some commonly used class words and abbreviations are listed in Table 16.1.

TABLE 16.1 A Selection of Class Words

Class Word	Abbreviation
Identifier	ID
Code	CD
Date	DT
Number	NUM
Amount	AMT
Quantity	QTY
Rate	RT

You can use ERwin's Lookup macro to find the approved abbreviation for a word and use the abbreviated word or words as the column name, similar to the process used with table names. This step saves a lot of typing, reduces the chance of error, and enforces consistency by using a list of approved abbreviations.

To use the Lookup macro, open the Domain Dictionary Editor, shown in Figure 16.6, by selecting Edit, Domain Dictionary or double-clicking a column name. Note the option on the General tab: Name Inherited by Column. The default is to inherit the attribute name, using the %AttName macro. To use the Lookup macro, simply enter the following:

```
%Lookup(filename.txt, %AttName)
```

The Lookup macro requires two parameters:

- filename.txt: A text filename (including the fully qualified path to the file) that contains pairs of values separated by commas, with a return at the end of each row.

- %AttName: Another macro that says to use the attribute name to identify a specific row in the file.

The class word/abbreviation example is how the (filename.txt) text file should look. I also include a sample text file along with Betty's model.

The Lookup macro instructs ER*win* to use the text file to look up the attribute name and substitute the value after the comma for the column name.

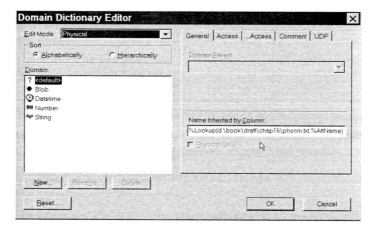

FIGURE 16.6

Use ERwin's Domain Dictionary Editor to set the Name Inherited by Column option to use the Lookup *macro and a text file of approved abbreviations to create the column names.*

Setting Column Volumetrics

You can enter numeric values for average width and percent NULL for some columns. The options are not available (they are dimmed, as shown in Figure 16.5) if the column datatype does not support variable width for the selected target server. ER*win* automatically knows which column datatypes can vary in width and in size, with or without NULL assignments, for a specific target server.

When available, the options have the following functionality:

- Average Width—Enter a numeric value for the estimated average width for the column. For example, in the Betty's Ice Cream Shop, I have several Description columns that are assigned a datatype of text(80). I can enter 50 as the average character width of the column to use in volumetrics estimations and then use the Volumetrics Editor to calculate table and database size estimates based on these and other values.

- Percent NULL—Enter a numeric (whole number) value for the estimated percentage for the column. For example, Betty's estimates that only about half of the campaign specials will have a value for campaign group. You can estimate that the Campaign Group column will be NULL about 50 percent of the time and use the Volumetrics Editor to calculate table and database size estimates.

Attaching a Constraint

In Chapter 17, I discuss using the appropriate editors for creating constraints. This section introduces constraints and how to attach a constraint to a column. Depending on the target database you have selected, ERwin supports constraint information using column defaults, initial values, and validation rules:

- The default provides a value for a column if no value is supplied when a new record is inserted into the table. Each column can have a default value associated with it.

CAUTION

Take care when defining default values. There is no way to know whether a value was supplied or a default value was used unless you include a column that indicates the source of the value.

- An initial value specifies the value that you want to appear in a screen form in a client application that supports such a feature.
- A validation rule can specify a list of valid values for a particular column or use an expression to define some form of data validation code for a column or table.

Validation rules and default column values are generated with the appropriate data definition language for the target RDBMS, either directly to the system catalog or to a DDL script.

> **CAUTION**
>
> ERwin does not perform consistency checking between constraints and default values attached to a column. Take care that constraints and default values do not conflict with one another.

Caption, Format, and Mask Options

Because Betty's is using Access as the target server, you have an additional tab that allows you to specify

- Caption—This provides a label for column values in an Access application. By default, ERwin uses the column name with an appended colon (:).

- Format—This shows the display format assigned to the column. The display format controls how data is displayed in Access applications. For example, mm/dd/yyyy is a date format that displays a date value as 09/12/1999. To change the display format name, select a different display format name from the list of available display formats. Click the button to the right to launch the Display Format Editor.

- Mask—Enter a string of symbols to control how data is entered and displayed in Access applications. For example, the input mask (###) ###-#### lets you enter only the numbers for a common U.S. telephone number. The parentheses around the area code, the space after the area code, and the hyphen after the second three numbers appear automatically.

You can create, modify, or delete display formats using the Display Format Editor. To launch the Display Format Editor, select the second Access tab in the Column Editor and click the button to the right of Format.

Summary

ERwin version 3.5.2 allows you to control the link between the logical and physical model. You can define diagram objects as logical only or physical only. Logical-only objects are not represented in the physical model, and physical-only objects are not represented in the logical model. This way, you can have a logical model normalized to third normal form and a physical model denormalized to meet usage and performance requirements.

ERwin's Table Editor allows you to set the physical properties of the tables in the physical model. Using the Table Editor, you can set properties such as table names, volumetrics, comments, UDPs, synonyms, aliases, validation rules, stored procedures, and scripts. The options and properties available in the Table Editor depend upon the target server selected. You can use ERwin's Lookup macro to create table names using a set of standard abbreviations.

ERwin's Column Editor allows you to set the physical properties of the columns in the physical model. Using the Column Editor, you can set properties such as column names, datatype, nullity, default values, validation rules, volumetrics, comment, and display. You can also use ERwin's Lookup macro to create column names using a set of standard abbreviations.

Although you perform the bulk of physical modeling tasks using the Table and Column Editors, there's much more to building a good physical model. In the next chapter, I discuss denormalization, introduce ERwin's features for estimating volumetrics and creating constraints, and discuss modeling views.

Building Physical
Relationships

In the previous chapters of Part IV, "Creating the Physical Model," I reviewed the physical modeling environment and introduced physical modeling tools. In this chapter, I explore building additional physical objects.

In the sections that follow, I discuss physical relationships in these topics:

- Denormalizing normalized data structures
- Using the Volumetrics Editor
- Creating constraints using validation rules and valid values
- Creating additional indexes to support access requirements
- Building views to support data groupings

In ER*win*, you can designate diagram modeling objects as logical only or physical only. You can use ER*win*'s physical editors to manage volumetrics information and create constraints using validation rules and constrain values to a specific list. ER*win*'s physical editors also allow you to create indexes and views to support usage requirements.

Selecting Microsoft Access as the target database for Betty's Ice Cream Shop prior to building the physical model means ERwin can appropriately activate the physical editors and options that define the properties of physical model objects specific to Access.

Understanding Denormalization

Normalization is the process of separating attributes into entities such that each fact is represented by a single attribute; there is a value for every attribute that is dependent on the value of the primary key, the whole primary key, and nothing but the primary key. Denormalization is the process of decomposing normalized entities into physical tables that group columns according to usage requirements. Denormalization can also use planned redundancy to duplicate one or more columns in more than a single table.

A logical model represents the information requirements and business rules, irrespective of how the data will be used or the database platform selected for implementation. A physical model is based on the logical model but also represents the usage and database platform requirements. ERwin has features that allow you to create a physical model that appears different but is still closely related to the logical model. Using ERwin's options for defining diagram objects as logical only or physical only, you can develop a fully normalized logical model and denormalize the physical model to meet usage requirements or improve performance.

TIP

The DBA will determine whether the usage requirements can best be met using denormalized persistent data structures, planned redundancy, or views.

The modeler should work with the DBA to document denormalization and to ensure that business rules represented in the logical model data structures are not lost in the physical implementation.

Denormalization and Planned Redundancy

In Chapter 15, "Developing the Physical Model," I discussed using conceptual data groupings and usage requirements to determine opportunities for denormalization or planned redundancy in the physical model. Let's look at usage requirements for Betty's Ice Cream Shop and determine whether denormalization is needed to meet the requirements.

Building Physical Relationships

CHAPTER 17

329

17

BUILDING
PHYSICAL
RELATIONSHIPS

To make this a non-trivial exercise, I assume the following design decisions:

- The collection of the ice cream flavors selected for banana splits and hot fudge sundaes will be implemented as an enhancement to an existing OLTP sales system.
- The management and tracking of campaign specials will be implemented as a decision support system (DSS).

These design decisions will likely produce physical models that are linked but look considerably different.

Betty's has two primary usage needs:

- Collect the ice cream flavors selected for banana splits and hot fudge sundaes.
- Track the success of campaign specials that feature a particular flavor of ice cream.

Betty's usage requirements include

- Access and performance requirements—The system must be available to collect sales information during business hours, 10:00 a.m. to 10:00 p.m. EST, seven days a week.
- Concurrent users—Betty's has two computerized cash registers that record sales information and one sales manager who manages campaign specials. Therefore, the system has the potential for three concurrent users.
- Volumetrics—Betty's sells an average of 158 sundaes each day and intends to keep historical information in the sales system for two calendar months. Campaign specials are run weekly with historical sales information kept in detail for one year, and summarized information for two additional years.
- Calculated or derived data—Campaign specials use summarized information regarding the ice cream flavors selected for sundaes.
- Reporting requirements and standard queries—Betty's requires monthly and weekly reports of daily sales of ice cream flavors, grouped by sundae type from the OLTP system. Campaign management reports measure the success of campaign specials, including trending reports.
- Logical groupings—Betty's has identified sundae and campaign as logical groupings. A sundae includes selected ice cream flavors and toppings. A campaign includes an ice cream flavor.

In preparation for building the physical model, I created two new subject areas in the ER diagram for Betty's:

- OLTP collection—To contain the physical model for the enhancements to the existing system.
- DSS campaign management—To contain the physical model for the new DSS.

I began with the OLTP collection subject area and excluded the CAMPAIGN SPECIAL and CAMPAIGN SPECIAL ICE CREAM entities from the subject area. I set ERwin's logical-only property in the following diagram objects:

- BANANA SPLIT
- BANANA SPLIT ICE CREAM
- HOT FUDGE SUNDAE
- Many-to-many relationship between HOT FUDGE SUNDAE and ICE CREAM

NOTE

ERwin automatically creates the HOT FUDGE SUNDAE ICE CREAM table in response to the unresolved many-to-many relationship between HOT FUDGE SUNDAE and ICE CREAM.

The associative table is still created even after you define the HOT FUDGE SUNDAE entity as logical only. You must define the many-to-many relationship as logical only to prevent the creation of the table.

I created two denormalized tables that I defined as physical only: SUNDAE ICE CREAM and SUNDAE TOPPING. Figure 17.1 shows an example of a proposed physical model for the enhancements to the existing OLTP sales system at Betty's. Note the addition of a SUND IC CREM ID to ensure uniqueness if a customer chooses two servings of the same ice cream flavor.

Creating the physical model for DSS campaign management involves a slightly different approach. I began by organizing the subject area. I removed the entities not involved in campaign management:

- SUND TYP
- SUND TPNG
- TPNG
- SUND

I used planned redundancy to duplicate the DT SLD column (Date Sold attribute) of the SUND table (SUNDAE entity) in the SUND IC CREM table. I left the IC CREM table to facilitate the association of an ice cream flavor with a campaign special by creating a new row in CMPGN SPCL IC CREM.

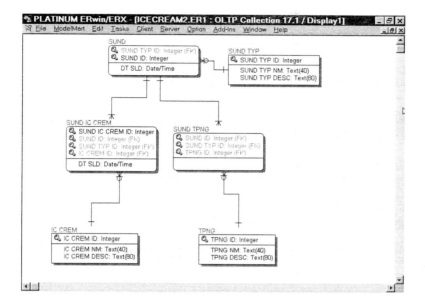

Figure 17.1

The physical model records the ice cream flavors and toppings selected for each sundae, as well as the date the sundae was sold.

The physical model for the DSS campaign management allows the creation of new campaigns and the association of a campaign with zero, one, or many ice cream flavors (see Figure 17.2). The DT SLD column (planned redundancy) allows reporting on the ice cream flavors selected for sundaes and comparisons to the STRT DT (start date) and ND DT (end date) of a CMGPN SPCL.

TIP

The "one to zero, one, or many" relationship between CMPGN SPCL and CMPGN SPCL IC CREM allows a row to exist in CMPGN SPCL prior to selecting the ice cream flavor (or flavors). The "one to zero, one, or many" relationship between IC CREM and CMPGN SPCL IC CREM allows a row to exist in IC CREM that is never associated with any row in CMPGN SPCL.

Think carefully about the implications of optionality. For example, changing the relationship optionality between IC CREM and CMPGN SPCL IC CREM to "one to one or many" would require every row in IC CREM to be associated with at least one CMPGN SPCL. That would mean an ice cream flavor could not exist unless it was included in a campaign special.

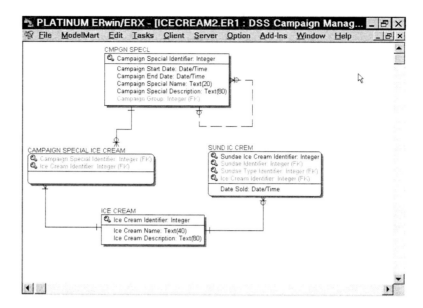

FIGURE 17.2

The proposed physical model allows the creation of new campaign specials and allows reporting to measure the success of campaign specials.

Using the Volumetrics Editor

You can use the volumetrics property in ERwin's Table Editor, as described in Chapter 16, "Building the Physical Model in ERwin," or the Volumetrics Editor to set volumetrics properties for each table in the physical model. I recommend waiting until denormalization tasks are completed because volumetrics estimations are affected by changes in the physical tables.

Using ERwin's volumetrics features, you can accurately calculate the potential size of the database. You can select which database objects to use when calculating database size. ERwin allows you to include indexes and, for some platforms, physical storage objects in your size estimates.

Calculating database size and growth allows you to

- Estimate database initial size and growth requirements
- Evaluate hardware
- Perform hypothetical analysis using different configurations of column and table estimates

In ER*win*, you can estimate the size of any table according to initial state and projected growth. After estimating all table sizes in the database, you can easily estimate the approximate size of the entire database.

> **NOTE**
>
> When calculating the size of a table, ER*win* uses the datatype sizes that are native to the server selected as the target platform.

ER*win*'s Volumetrics Editor, shown in Figure 17.3, has features that allow you to

- Change RDBMS column values such as NULL and variable-width columns that can affect table size estimations.
- Include index objects in database size estimations and (when appropriate) select physical storage objects for each table.
- Manipulate parameters that can affect database size estimations, such as the number of bytes per character or the amount of space overhead allocated for each row, and add a log-space factor to include the database log space in size estimates.

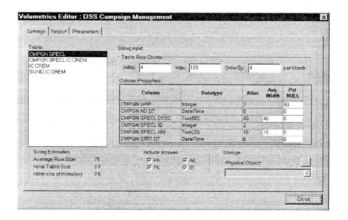

FIGURE 17.3

The Volumetrics Editor allows you to estimate the size requirements for each table, as well as for the entire database.

Creating Constraints

Constraints represent the business rules that specify the set of values that a column can contain. ER*win* provides editors that allow you to create constraints. Because not all database platforms support constraints, ER*win* documents constraints without producing the DDL (data definition language) that will create them.

Depending on the target database selected, ER*win* supports constraint information using

- A validation rule that specifies a list of valid values for a particular column or an expression that defines data validation code.
- A default that provides a value for a column if no value is supplied when a new record is inserted into the table. Each column can have a default value associated with it.
- An initial value that specifies the value that you want to appear in a screen form in a client application that supports such a feature.

The sections that follow describe using ER*win*'s editors to create validation rules, default values, and initial values.

Creating Validation Rules

ER*win*'s Validation Rule Editor allows you to create constraints as an expression or a list of valid values. You can use it to construct a check constraint or validation rule. A validation rule is an expression that specifies the range of values which can be stored in a column. The Validation Rule Editor allows you to attach validation rules to columns that enforce business rules. For example, in the Betty's diagram, the value supplied for the CMPGN ND DT column must be later than the CMPGN STRT DT (see Figure 17.4).

To launch the Validation Rule Editor, select Server, Validation Rule or click the button to the right of the Valid control on the Column Editor.

ER*win* allows you to specify the scope of the each validation rule:

- Client—Select to apply the validation rule to client-side applications.
- Server—Select to apply the validation rule to the target server.

You can specify both Client and Server as the scope for the validation rule.

The Validation Rule Editor provides several controls for creating expressions. ER*win* generates the corresponding validation rule using the appropriate syntax for the selected target server:

- Min—Type a value that you want to specify as the minimum value for a table column.
- Max—Enter the value that you want to specify as the maximum value for a table column.
- Range—Enter both a Min and Max value to specify a range of values for the constraint.

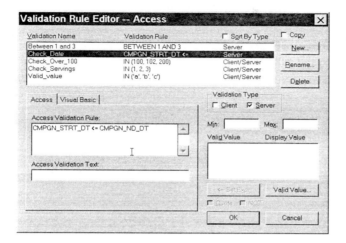

17

BUILDING
PHYSICAL
RELATIONSHIPS

FIGURE 17.4
The Check_Date constraint enforces a business rule that requires the value of the CMPGN ND DT to be later than the value of the CMPGN STRT DT.

NOTE

Click the Set Expr button to generate the validation rule using the Min and Max values you supplied.

Invert an expression (allow all values *except* the ones defined by the expression) by selecting the Not check box, which instructs ER*win* to include the word "NOT" in the expression. For example, using the expression BETWEEN 1 AND 100 allows the column to contain any value between 1 and 100. Selecting the Not check box causes ER*win* to change the expression to NOT BETWEEN 1 AND 100, which allows any number *except* those between 1 and 100.

Some target servers require the items in a valid value list to be enclosed in single quotation marks. ER*win* does not automatically enclose each value in quotation marks. Select the Quote check box to automatically enclose each value in a list of valid values in single quotation marks. Clear this check box if you do not want ER*win* to use quotation marks.

The Validation Rule Editor also includes two tabs (if you have selected a target client):

- Server—The Server tab label is the name of the selected target server. The validation rule and validation text is displayed in the controls on the tab.
- Client—The Client tab label is the name of the selected client server, and the syntax for the validation rule is displayed using ER*win*'s macros for the column name.

Creating Default Values

The Default/Initial Editor allows you to create a default value that is supplied by the server if no value is provided. You can also create an initial value that is provided by the client. An initial value is not a default value, although it often has the same effect. The default value assigned to a column generally represents the most common value stored in a column. ER*win* tailors the controls and properties in the Default/Initial Editor appropriately for the target server selected. In my examples, I use Access as the target server.

CAUTION

> Take care when defining default values. There is no way to know later whether a value is a default value unless you include a column that indicates the source of the value.

For example, in the SUND table in the physical model for Betty's, the SUND SLD DT column might be assigned the system date as the server default value. Then the server would provide the current date as a value if no value is specified.

To launch the Default/Initial Editor, shown in Figure 17.5, click the button to the right of the Default drop-down list.

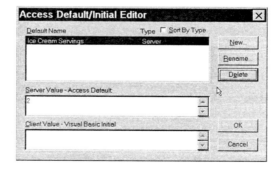

Figure 17.5

The Default/Initial Editor allows you to create a set of default values that can be assigned to columns using the Column Editor.

After you create a default value, you can assign it to one or more columns using the Column Editor. To attach a default value, open the Column Editor, select the column to which you want to attach the server default value, and then select the server default value from the Default list.

Using Valid Values

Use the Valid Value Editor to create a list of the acceptable values that can be stored in a column and to assign it to a validation rule. If you define a valid value list and assign it to a column, only those values can be stored in the column. You can use the "NOT" check box on the Validation Rule Editor to exclude a list of values from those a column can be assigned.

NOTE

You must create a validation rule before you can create a valid value list. A valid value list must be attached to a validation rule.

To launch the Valid Value Editor, shown in Figure 17.6, click the Valid Value button in the Validation Rule Editor. After you create a valid value list, you can select Server, Valid Value to edit the valid value list.

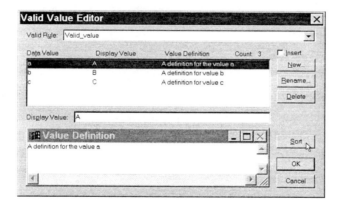

FIGURE 17.6

The Valid Value Editor allows you to attach a list of valid values to a validation rule.

To enter the values, click the New button. ER*win* also allows you to specify a display value that you want to appear in the client application. You can enter a definition for each value in the list.

To insert a new value within a list of values, select the value below the point where you want to insert the new value and select the Insert check box. You can also drag and drop a list item to a new position in the list. By default, ER*win* adds new values to the bottom of the list.

> **TIP**
>
> Consider using a user-defined domain rather than a list of valid values. Domains are reusable and can be defined at the enterprise level. Valid values are database platform–dependent and not as easily reused.

Creating Indexes

An index is a special type of object used in relational databases to provide fast data retrieval. Similar to the way the index in this book helps you find specific information quickly by listing the pages where a topic appears, an index on a table points to all of the rows where a particular column value is stored.

ER*win* automatically creates indexes in the physical model based on the key groups you define in the logical model. ER*win* supports four index types:

- Primary Key (PK)—There can be only one primary key index for a table. A primary key index is unique to ensure the indexed columns cannot have duplicate values. ER*win* automatically creates a primary key index for each table that has one or more columns you have identified as primary keys in the logical model. The default name for a primary key index is XPK*TableName*, where *TableName* is the physical name given to the table.

- Foreign Key (IF)—A foreign key index is an index on one or more foreign key columns in a table. ER*win* automatically creates a foreign key index for each set of foreign key columns that migrate. The default name for a foreign key index is XIFn*TableName*.

- Alternate Key (AK)—An alternate key index is an index on a set of columns in a table not defined as the primary key. As in a primary key, duplicate values in the indexed columns are not allowed. If you create an alternate key in the logical model, ER*win* automatically creates a unique index for the table using the columns. The default name for a unique index is XAKn*TableName*.

- Inversion Entry (IE)—An inversion entry index is an index on a set of columns. An IE index allows duplicate values to promote quick retrieval without requiring unique values. If you create an IE key in the logical model, ER*win* automatically creates a non-unique index for the table. The default name for a non-unique index is XIEn*TableName*.

When you create a database script, or create data structures by connecting directly to the database, ER*win* automatically creates indexes on the primary key, alternate keys, foreign keys, and inversion entries on each table. You can create new indexes using ER*win*'s Index Editor and change the properties of existing indexes, as explained in the following section.

Using the Index Editor

The Index Editor is named according to the target server selected. In my examples, Access is the target server, so the Index Editor is named Access Index Editor. Use the Index Editor to create unique alternate key and non-unique inversion entry indexes for tables in the physical model. After you create an index, use the Index Editor to modify its properties:

- Name

- Column members

- Comment

- UDPs

To launch the Index Editor, shown in Figure 17.7, right-click a table and choose Index on the shortcut menu.

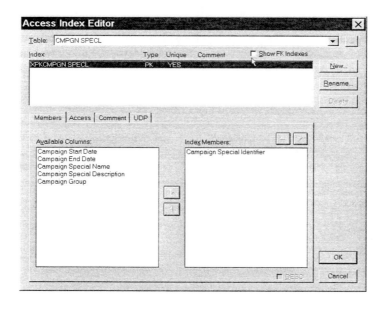

FIGURE 17.7
The Index Editor allows you to create new alternate and inversion entry indexes. To display foreign key indexes, select the Show FK Indexes check box.

The Index Editor tabs allow you to edit index properties:

- Members—Create a new index and select the column members.

- *Target Server*—In my examples, this is Access. This tab contains the properties of an index specific to the selected target server.

- Comment—Add a comment for an index.
- UDP—Set the value for a user-defined property assigned to the index class of diagram objects.

Use the controls in the Members tab of the Index Editor to assign columns to an index. Key groups created in the logical model become indexes in the physical model. In ERwin, the columns in each foreign key index include all of the columns that migrate from the parent table. If a child table has foreign keys from two different parent tables, ERwin creates a foreign key index for each parent table.

Building Views

A view is an SQL query that is stored in the database. The result of executing the view query is a "virtual" table. A virtual table does not exist until the query is executed and it only exists while it is being used. To users, a view looks like a table, with columns and rows of data. Unlike a table, a view is not a persistent set of data values. The rows and columns of data in the view are the results of the query that defines the view. Views allow you to

- Create customized data sets.
- Limit access to a specific subset (columns and rows) of data.
- Tailor data sets to meet particular needs.

When you generate a data definition language (DDL) script, or create data structures directly in a database, ERwin generates the SQL code that creates the view and stores it. When you reverse engineer a database that contains views, ERwin reads the view syntax and creates relationships to the tables referenced by the view. You can also use the View Tool in the physical toolbox to create a view, as described in the following section.

Using the View Tool

In ERwin, views are physical model objects and are only displayed when the diagram is in physical mode. ERwin represents a view as a rectangular box with rounded corners, drawn with a dotted line. A column in a view can be a reference to a column, a reference to a column in another view, or a user-defined expression. View relationships are displayed as a dotted line between a view and a table or between two views, indicating that the view references one or more of the columns from that other object.

To create a new view, click the View Tool in the ERwin toolbox and then click the diagram. To create a relationship between a new view and a table (or another view), click the View Relationship Tool to select it, click the parent table (or view), and then click the new view.

Creating a view relationship between a table and a view causes all of the columns in that table to migrate to the view. You can use the View Editor to remove columns from a view or drag the columns out of the view. By default, the name assigned to a view column is the same as the name of the source column. However, ER*win* allows you to change the view column name using the View Editor, or you can edit the view column names directly, using ER*win*'s on-diagram editing feature. You can also drag a column from a table into a view.

NOTE	

Deleting a column referenced by a view automatically deletes the view column as well. Deleting a table referenced by a view automatically deletes all the view columns referencing that table as well.

ER*win* provides three editors that allow you to create and set the properties for views:

- View Editor
- View Column Editor
- View Relationship Editor

ER*win* includes most of the functionality required to create and manage views in the View Editor. I focus on the View Editor, with the understanding that similar functionality is available in the View Column Editor and View Relationship Editor.

Using the View Editor

The View Editor allows you to create and manage views. You can use it to specify the properties of a view. Using the editor, you can select a view to edit, change the name of a view, add and remove columns, and edit the column names, as well as other properties. You can also indicate whether ER*win* should generate the view SQL code during database creation or synchronization.

To launch the View Editor, shown in Figure 17.8, right-click a view and select the View Editor item on the shortcut menu.

You must select the Generate check box to instruct ER*win* to generate a DDL statement to create the view. If the check box is cleared, ER*win* does not include the view in schema generation.

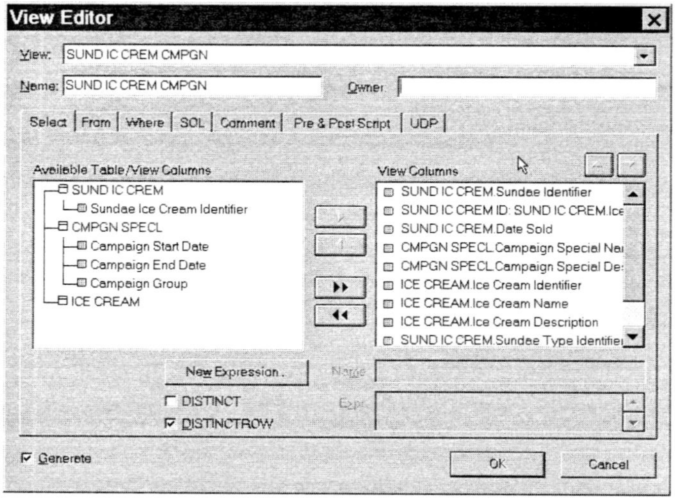

FIGURE 17.8

Views can have relationships with tables and with other views.

NOTE

As in most of ERwin's physical editors, the tabs and controls available for setting properties are specific to the target server selected. For example, if you select a target server that supports stored procedures, ERwin includes a tab to allow you to attach them. Figure 17.8 does not show a stored procedure tab.

The View Editor also includes a set of tabs that allow you to

- Select—Select the columns to be included in a view.
- From—Select the source tables for a view.
- Where—Specify constraints for a view.
- SQL—View and edit the SQL code for a view.
- Comment—Enter or edit a comment for a view.
- Pre & Post Script—Attach a pre-script or post-script to a view.
- UDP—Specify a value for a user-defined property that has been attached to the view class diagram object.

Use the Select tab of the View Editor to specify the columns to be included in the view. You can create column references to any table column or view column in the physical model. In addition to creating references to existing columns, you can create new columns using view expressions.

A view expression is a user-defined function that is stored as a view column. To create an expression, click the New Expression button. You can create simple expressions using operators or functions based on the values of existing columns, to set the value for the created view column.

Select the DISTINCT or DISTINCTROW check box to specify a view that automatically eliminates duplicate rows.

TIP

Check the documentation for the target server for the correct syntax to use when creating expressions and functions.

The From tab of the View Editor allows you to select the tables or views that provide the columns for the view. The source tables or views are referenced by the view for its columns. You can specify the order that sources are displayed as well as an alias name that is indicative of how the source is used in the view.

The Where tab of the View Editor, shown in Figure 17.9, allows you to specify constraints on the rows that are included in the view.

ER*win* uses the text you enter on the Where tab to generate the WHERE clause in the SQL code for the selected view. Other options on the Where tab include

- Use Group By to enter the criteria to group the rows returned by the view query. ER*win* uses the text you enter to generate the GROUP BY clause in the SQL code for the view.

- Use Having to enter the condition that filters out rows that fail to meet the condition. ER*win* uses the text you enter to generate the HAVING clause in the SQL code for the view. Note that this option is only available if the selected target server supports the HAVING clause.

- Use Order By to enter the criteria to sort the rows returned by the view. ER*win* uses the text to generate the ORDER BY clause in the SQL code for the view. Note that this option is only available if the selected target server supports the ORDER BY clause.

- Select WITH CHECK OPTION to specify that the DBMS must check to ensure a row satisfies the condition in the WHERE clause before inserting or updating rows in the source tables. If you check this option, ER*win* adds the WITH CHECK OPTION to the SQL code generated for the view.

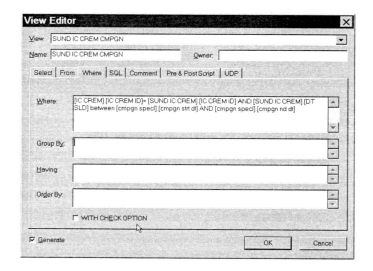

FIGURE 17.9

The Where tab in the View Editor allows you to specify the rows that appear in a view. In this example, the WHERE *clause uses the syntax for Access.*

The SQL tab of the View Editor allows you to view the SQL code that ER*win* maintains for the selected view. You can select the User-Defined SQL option to create the SQL by hand. However, if you choose this option, ER*win* does not maintain the relationships to source tables. ER*win* stores user-defined SQL as a block of text, not an integrated model component.

Summary

Creating the physical model is more than creating technical names and specifying physical datatypes. The physical model should represent the data structures that are actually created in the database. It can look very different from the logical model because the physical model also considers usage requirements and database platform requirements in implementation.

Usage requirements can identify opportunities for the physical model denormalization. Denormalization can take the form of combining normalized entities into a single table or using planned redundancy to create duplicate columns. Use conceptual data groupings and access requirements as guidelines for denormalization.

After denormalization, you should estimate the space requirements for the database. Use ERwin's Volumetrics Editor to estimate the size of each column and table and to select the physical objects that you want to include in the estimates. You can run "what if" scenarios to determine the effect of various database objects on the total size requirements for the database.

The physical model can also include the creation of additional physical objects such as constraints, indexes, and views. ERwin supports constraints in the form of validation rules, default values, and valid value lists and provides an editor for creating each. Validation rules are user-defined expressions that must be created with an understanding of the syntax of the target server. Use caution when creating default values because the users of the data might have difficulty determining whether values were supplied by the server or an application. Consider using domains rather than valid values because domains are reusable across database platforms and valid values are defined within a specific database.

ERwin automatically creates the primary key and foreign key indexes for the key groups defined in the logical model. You cannot change foreign key indexes unless the primary key group is changed. However, you can define additional alternate or inversion entry indexes using ERwin's Index Editor. Consider standard reports and queries when determining the need for additional indexes.

You can create views to support usage requirements and to create specific groupings of data that limit access to particular columns and rows. Although views look the same as tables to users, you create views using an SQL query that returns a virtual table. A virtual table does not exist in the database until it is called, and although you can use it to update columns in persistent tables, it has no persistence itself. ERwin's View Editor provides the functionality to create and manage views in the physical model.

Like the logical model, the physical model should be reviewed for accuracy and completeness. A review is essential to ensuring that no business rules were lost or changed in the translation from logical to physical. In the next chapter, I discuss the process of reviewing the physical model.

Reviewing the Physical Data Model

In the previous chapters of Part IV, "Creating the Physical Model," I discussed collecting usage requirements and setting the physical modeling environment in ER*win*. I introduced some of ER*win*'s physical modeling tools and editors and used them to create physical model objects. In this chapter, the focus is using reviews to ensure that the physical data model fulfills the information requirements and business rules, meets the usage requirements, and meets the platform specifications.

I show you the physical model review process from the perspective of the modeling team and the DBA, as well as the reviewer. The modeling team documents the physical model and provides the supporting documentation, the DBA ensures technical correctness, and the reviewer assesses the quality of the implementation model.

In exploring the physical model review process, I discuss the following topics:

- The objectives of the physical model review
- When to perform the physical model review

- Preparing for the physical model review
- Reviewing the physical model
- What happens after the physical model review

A quality physical model is technically correct and uses enterprise standards. It fulfills the business objectives and the usage requirements. It aligns with the enterprise model and integrates with existing data structures. It is scalable and extensible, with the flexibility to support changing business needs.

Objectives of the Physical Model Review

The primary objective of the physical model review is to measure the degree to which the proposed data structures and database objects meet the specific business objectives and the strategic goals and objectives of the enterprise. In addition, the physical model review should ensure that the proposed physical model

- Is technically correct
- Follows enterprise standards
- Supports the usage and access requirements
- Fits within the enterprise model
- Is scalable and extensible

A physical model is considered technically correct when the physical database objects use the syntax of the target database platform. ER*win* configures the physical model tools and editors to ensure that the physical model objects are produced using the appropriate syntax.

The physical model should follow enterprise standards such as standard abbreviations and datatypes. Using a set of physical modeling standards and guidelines ensures that the data structures produced for use within an enterprise are uniformly understandable and relatively consistent.

The physical model must accurately reflect the business rules that are implemented. In the translation from logical to physical model, business rules that were represented in logical structures might not be represented in physical structures. These business rules might be implemented in applications to ensure that the information supplied for making business critical decisions does not contain flawed or inadequate data.

The physical model must fit within the enterprise model to ensure that it does not introduce inconsistency and inaccuracy at the enterprise level. Every physical model represents a part of the larger set of physical data structures that contain information for the enterprise. At some level, every set of physical structures represents shared concepts.

It is essential that the physical data structures representing concepts shared across the enterprise be stored consistently. The ability to share and integrate information consistently throughout the enterprise is a measure of the quality of its physical data structures.

To the extent it is possible, the physical model should be scalable and extensible to allow for enhancements. A physical model that rigidly represents only the current information requirements, with no thought for changes that are likely to occur, cannot be considered a quality model. A scalable and extensible physical model should be able to implement extensions of the business rules with minimal impact to core data structures.

Given an understanding of the objectives of the physical data model review, let's begin by discussing the physical model review process.

Conducting the Physical Model Review

Similar to logical model reviews, physical model reviews should be an integral part of the modeling process. The physical model should be reviewed periodically to allow the team to make minor adjustments rather than radical change. The number and frequency of reviews varies according to the size of the modeling effort. However, even the smallest project should include at least two physical reviews, an initial review and a final review. For extensive modeling efforts that span several months, consider reviewing the physical model at evenly spaced intervals, no more than two to three weeks apart.

The initial physical review should occur immediately upon completion of the first draft of the physical model. Consider conducting the first review as denormalization tasks near completion within the first subject area. While denormalization tasks are underway, the physical model is likely to experience substantial change. On the other hand, waiting until the physical model is complete can be an expensive delay that might result in extensive rework. Problems that could have been corrected with little effort early in the process might mean the physical model is built upon errors that compound into maintenance and integration nightmares.

The final physical model review should be conducted in time to allow the modeling team and DBA to respond to recommendations from the reviewer. The reviewer should make every effort to remain close to the physical modeling effort and perform frequent reviews as the model nears completion. This arrangement prevents a flurry of activity that might mean a critical recommendation is overlooked, or worse, not implemented.

The reviewer, the modeling team, and the DBA should work together during the physical model review. Model reviews are most valuable when conducted by an expert architect who has considerable experience modeling a wide range of business functions and who is familiar with the RDBMS platform selected as the target server. The reviewer should also have a clear understanding of the technical architecture of the enterprise. An experienced reviewer should have no difficulty determining whether the physical model aligns with the strategic goals and objectives of the enterprise.

The reviewer works with the modeling team and DBA to establish the review frequency. The reviewer is responsible for assessing the physical model for accuracy and completeness in meeting the business objective, using the supporting documentation provided by the modeling team and the DBA.

> **TIP**
>
> The physical model reviewer should be intimately familiar with the RDBMS target server to determine whether the physical model leverages the strengths of the database platform.

The reviewer should also give advice on modeling practices and corporate standards as needed by the modeling team. The reviewer's findings should be documented along with the resolution approach devised in partnership with the modeling team. Although the responsibility for the quality of the review clearly rests with the reviewer, the modeling team and DBA play an essential role in providing the supporting documentation for the model and working with the reviewer to determine a resolution approach. Of course, the modeling team and DBA are also responsible for implementing the resolution approaches that are deemed appropriate.

Conducting an effective physical model review involves preparing the supporting documentation and delivering the documentation to the reviewer, who performs the physical review tasks. The sections that follow describe examples of supporting documentation and an introduction to physical model review tasks.

Preparing for the Physical Model Review

The reviewer prepares for the physical model review by conducting an initial meeting with the modeling team prior to beginning the review. The reviewer collects the latest supporting documentation and works with the team to establish the review schedule. The group should discuss any questions regarding the business objective, usage requirements, and database platform selection. It should also determine the process for communicating the review findings and working together to define resolution strategies.

To prepare for the review, the modeling team and the DBA prepare the documentation for the reviewer. Documentation for the review should include the following:

- Logical model diagram
- Information requirements and business rules
- Enterprise model (if available)
- Usage requirements and RDBMS platform decision
- Physical model diagram
- Decisions made during the translation from logical to physical
- Results of any previous physical model reviews

The information requirements and business rules were input for creating the logical model. The logical model, usage requirements, and RDBMS platform decision were input for creating the physical model. The enterprise model provides the architecture within which both models must reside.

The modeling team should also provide documentation for any business rules that are present in the logical model but are not represented in the physical model. The team should also include the results of previous reviews to prevent needless rehashing of decisions. The physical model review documentation should be provided to the reviewer prior to the physical model review session.

Physical Model Review Tasks

As in a logical model review, there is no quick, simple way to perform a physical model review. It takes time and demands close attention to detail. The reviewer performs a step-by-step examination of the physical objects to determine whether the proposed model accurately and completely meets the business objectives and usage requirements and leverages the features of the selected target database.

The following steps outline a process that organizes the physical model review into a series of high-level tasks:

1. Study the documentation of the business objective.
2. Study the logical model diagram and logical model review documentation.
4. Study the usage requirements.
5. Take a quick pass through the physical model diagram.
6. Study the business rules that are implemented in the logical model but are not implemented in the physical model.
7. Select a subject area for review.

8. Organize the subject area into data clusters using the same techniques described in the logical model review process in Chapter 12, "Reviewing the Logical Data Model."

9. Examine the independent tables and their columns, with particular attention to indexes, as well as the optionality and cardinality of foreign key columns.

10. Examine the dependent tables, columns, and relational integrity constraints.

11. Compare the physical objects to the usage requirements.

12. Document the review findings.

13. Present the review findings to the modeling team and work with the team to develop a resolution strategy.

14. Document the resolution action taken.

15. Schedule the next review.

Study the documentation of the business objectives to gain a clear understanding of the business function that the physical model is intended to support. Study the logical model, taking particular note of the data clusters used during the logical model review. Take a quick pass through the physical model diagram to gain an overall understanding of the translation from logical to physical, and review the documentation regarding business rules represented in the logical model that are not represented in the physical model.

The modeling team and DBA should identify areas of the physical model that are considered stable, as well as those that are expected to undergo significant change. The reviewer should study the documentation provided by the modeling team to understand the level of completeness of each subject area in the physical model, prior to selecting the initial model review area. At a minimum, tables and columns should be complete with standard abbreviated names and datatypes. Primary key, alternate key, and inversion entry indexes should be defined. The reviewer, the modeling team, and DBA work together to determine the order in which subject areas should be reviewed.

The model probably contains an area that is clearly the core or heart of the model. For some physical models, it might be best to begin by examining the core subject area. With other models, it might be best begin with a subject area that integrates with existing data structures. Frequently, the implementation schedule dictates which subject area should be the first reviewed. Data structures are often reviewed in the order in which they are scheduled for implementation.

After selecting a subject area for review, review the ERwin physical model reports to understand the tables, columns, and other database objects it contains. Group the physical model objects into data clusters using the techniques described in Chapter 12.

> **NOTE**
>
> The physical model data clusters might correspond to more than a single logical data cluster.

Analyze the independent tables and dependent tables according to the techniques in Chapter 12, with particular attention to the key indexes, as well as any indexes defined to support specific usage requirements.

Examine the role of the physical objects in the context of enterprise objects to ensure that concepts shared across the enterprise are modeled using consistent names and datatypes. Take particular note of integration with other physical data structures to identify opportunities to reuse existing data structures. Compare the physical model objects to the usage requirements to ensure that data can be delivered according to access requirements.

> **TIP**
>
> The important thing to remember is to review the physical model in manageable chunks.

After the Physical Model Review

After completing the physical model review, the reviewer will present the documentation of the review findings to the modeling team and DBA and then work with the team to develop a resolution strategy. The team should ask questions regarding the findings to ensure that everyone understands each issue or concern. The reviewer must be available to respond to questions from the modeling team and work with the team to develop resolutions. The team should document the resolution decisions and the timeframe in which the resolutions are scheduled for implementation.

> **NOTE**
>
> It is essential that every question or concern regarding the physical review findings be addressed and resolved. The reviewer and modeling team must also document and implement resolutions to produce a physical model that provides a solid foundation.

After documenting the physical review findings and working with the modeling team to define resolution strategies, the reviewer remains an integral part of the team and shares responsibility for delivering a physical model of the highest quality possible.

Summary

Physical model reviews should be an integral part of the data modeling process. The modeling team and the DBA prepare and deliver the necessary documentation to the reviewer. In addition to an in-depth understanding of the technical architecture of the enterprise, the reviewer should have extensive knowledge of the RDBMS selected as the target server.

The modeling team, DBA, and reviewer work together to determine the order in which to review the physical model subject areas. After selecting the first subject area, the reviewer groups it into data clusters and analyzes them according to the techniques described in Chapter 12. The data clusters defined in the logical model review process are guidelines for identifying physical data clusters, with the understanding that physical data clusters can correspond to more than a single logical data cluster.

The reviewer examines each physical data cluster to evaluate the extent to which it meets the information and usage requirements. He or she takes special note of business rules that are represented in the logical model but are not represented in the physical model. The reviewer also analyzes each key index, including additional keys intended to support specific usage requirements.

The reviewer documents issues or concerns about the physical model and reviews them with the modeling team and the DBA. The reviewer works with the team to determine a resolution strategy. The team is responsible for implementing any resolution that is deemed appropriate.

When the physical model review is complete and the resolution strategy has been implemented, the physical model is ready to be delivered. In the next chapter, I discuss ERwin's features for delivering the physical model and creating the physical data structures.

Delivering the Physical Data Model

In previous chapters of Part IV, "Creating the Physical Model," I described the process of denormalization as a way of meeting usage and access requirements and showed how the physical model can differ from the logical model. I also proposed using reviews to ensure that the physical data model is the highest quality possible. In this chapter, I discuss delivering the physical model in the following topics:

- Delivering the physical model documentation
- Organizing the physical model diagram
- Creating the physical database objects
- Creating an SQL script

After the physical model review process is complete and the resolution tasks performed, you're ready to deliver the physical model. Delivering the physical model has two parts, the physical model documentation and the data structures. ER*win*'s reporting features make delivering most of the documentation a simple matter of reporting. ER*win*'s forward engineering features make creating data structures as simple as creating an SQL script or connecting to the database and letting ER*win* create the database objects.

Physical Model Documentation

Providing good physical model documentation is as important as creating the data structures. Documentation is particularly important when extending or enhancing an existing model and when integrating information sources. I encourage modelers to include documentation tasks as an integral part of the modeling process.

Just in case your organization has not yet defined the documentation that should be produced, I include a list of physical model supporting documentation to provide examples of the *type* of supporting information that goes into producing a quality physical model. The list is not all-inclusive. For our purposes, this documentation consists of two types:

- Documentation that is produced outside ER*win*
- Documentation that is produced within ER*win*

Documentation produced outside of ER*win* provides the information that documents the physical data model. Examples of supporting documentation produced outside of ER*win* are

- Usage requirements and target server specifications
- Session notes and meeting minutes
- Issue resolutions and documentation on the decisions made by the modeling team
- Results and responses to physical model reviews
- Business rules represented in the logical model that are not represented in the physical model

TIP

The form of the model documentation can vary from a good-sized ring binder to publishing on a Web site. The form of the documentation is not nearly as important as the content. Take care to provide documentation that is easy to understand.

The usage requirements and database platform (target server) selection should clearly and concisely document *how* the users will use the data. In Chapter 15, "Developing the Physical Model," I provided some examples of usage requirements. Be sure to include session notes and meeting minutes, as well as the results and responses to physical model reviews along with any other documentation that records the issue resolutions and design decisions made by the modeling team.

Sometimes, in the process of translating from the logical to the physical model, business rules that were present in the logical model do not get represented in the physical model. For example, in the model for Betty's Ice Cream Shop, the logical model has data structures and relationships representing the business rules that hot fudge sundaes have two servings of ice cream and banana splits have three. In the physical model, I use a single table to contain sundaes and a single table to contain the ice cream selections for each sundae. The relationship that represented the business rules for the number of ice cream servings for sundae types must be implemented elsewhere. To ensure that all business rules are implemented appropriately, be sure to provide documentation for the team responsible for getting the data into the data structures.

Documentation produced within ER*win* provides details of the physical model objects produced in support of the usage requirements and the target server. ER*win* has facilities to produce the following supporting documentation of the physical model:

- Physical model diagram
- Report containing the details of any database object
- Physical model validation reports
- Volumetrics estimates report
- DDL (Data Definition Language) or SQL scripts
- Schema generation log file

ER*win* provides features that allow you to print the physical model diagram along with robust reporting capabilities to provide details for all diagram objects. ER*win* does a good job of creating DDL using the correct syntax for the target server and automatically creates a log file during schema generation.

Delivering the Physical Data Model Diagram

You might need to organize a large model into several subject areas in addition to the main subject area, and each subject area might need additional stored displays. Remember that subject areas span both the logical model and physical model. Logical subject areas can represent business views. In the physical model, you can use subject areas to represent the implementation schedule or to assist in the physical model reviews. For Betty's, I created a subject area for the OLTP enhancements and another for the data structures that support the tracking of campaigns and ice cream flavor selections.

TIP

Use subject areas to organize the model into data clusters during the model reviews.

ERwin (for the most part) prints a diagram WYSIWYG, "what you see is what you get." That is, the current display of the current subject area is printed. To print a physical model diagram, be sure you are in physical mode and select File, Print. See Chapter 13, "Delivering the Logical Data Model," for instructions on printing options and the Print Setup dialog.

Delivering ERwin Physical Model Reports

The ERwin Report Browser is a flexible, customizable tool for creating and running reports on ERwin diagrams. ERwin provides a set of predefined report types. Each report type has options that allow you to include or exclude diagram objects in the report. Some reports have built-in filtering and sorting options. You can select a report category and use it to create a customized report that includes specific options. Once you create the report, it is displayed under the appropriate folder on the left side of the main Report Browser window.

To run a report, double-click the report icon. The Report Browser displays the result in the Result Set panel on the right side of the window. A result set icon is added to the tree control under the appropriate report icon. You can then use the Report Browser's features to further customize the content and change the appearance of the result set. See Chapter 7, "Reverse Engineering and Report Generation in ERwin," for instructions on changing the appearance of a report in the Report Browser.

The Report Browser includes a set of standard ERwin reports that you can use to report on the physical model. The standard report set includes reports on all the diagram objects. You can exclude logical diagram objects to produce physical object reports or select reports based on physical objects, such as table reports, stored procedure reports, and view reports. ERwin includes a special set of reports called model validation reports, covered in the next section.

Using ERwin's Model Validation Reports

ERwin's model validation reports are designed to help you make sure the physical model is complete, prior to generating the physical database objects. Model validation reports list inconsistencies or missing information in the physical (or logical) model.

The model validation reports for physical model objects include

- Indexes without columns
- Columns without comments
- Redundant indexes
- Tables without primary keys (PK)
- Tables without columns
- Tables without comments

- Columns with different foreign key (FK) datatypes
- Columns with default datatypes

In addition to the standard model validation reports, you can create a new physical model validation report by selecting File, New ER*win* Report option or clicking the New Report icon and then selecting ER*win* Report as the new object. Either of these actions launches the Report Editor, shown in Figure 19.1. Select Physical to display the list of report categories (report types) available for physical model objects.

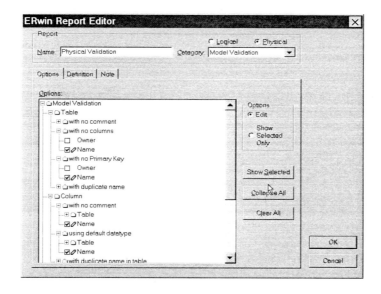

FIGURE 19.1
The Report Editor allows you to create customized reports for both the logical and physical models.

After you create the new physical model validation report, the report name and icon appear under the Model Validation Reports folder in the Report Browser. Use the Report Browser to generate the report just as you do other ER*win* reports, by double-clicking the report name. After generating a result set for a report, use the Report Browser to further customize the content and appearance of the result set.

The Report Editor allows you to

- Name the report. Remember to use good names that are indicative of what is contained in the report.
- Select a category for the report. Place the report in an appropriate category or create a new category using the New Folder option on the File menu or the Folder new object option on the New icon.

- Select the Logical or Physical option to filter the categories to show the appropriate reports.

The ERwin Report Editor also includes tabs that allow you to specify properties for the report:

- The Options tab allows you to select the database objects to be included in the report.
- The Definition tab allows you to enter or edit a definition for the report.
- The Note tab allows you to enter or edit a note for the report.

ERwin's reporting features make delivering the physical model documentation and validation reports simple. Use the validation reports to ensure the physical model is complete before using ERwin's forward-engineering features to create the database objects.

Forward Engineering the Physical Model

In ERwin, the process of creating the physical data structures from the physical data model is called *forward engineering*. Forward engineering means creating the physical database schema. The Forward Engineer/Schema Generation option on the Tasks menu allows you to create the database schema, including tables, triggers, stored procedures, and other database objects.

ERwin allows you to generate the database objects two ways:

- Creating a DDL or SQL script.
- Connecting ERwin to the target server and generating the database objects directly in the database.

Selecting the Forward Engineer/Schema Generation option from the Tasks menu launches the Schema Generation Editor, shown in Figure 19.2. It is customized to contain options appropriate for the target server. Note that ERwin includes the target server in the name: Access Schema Generation. ERwin also includes the current subject area name—OLTP Collection 17.1—which contains the database objects that can be included or excluded in the schema generation.

The Schema Generation Editor allows you to select which ERwin physical objects, such as tables, indexes, and stored procedures, to include in the generated schema. You can also create different schema generation option sets to generate schema to match the implementation schedule.

Click the Preview button to open the Schema Generation Preview dialog and view the schema report onscreen. Preview display is limited to 32KB; you can preview larger models by clicking Report to create a DDL file that you can read using any text editor or word processor. After previewing the schema report, you can create the database objects by clicking the Generate button.

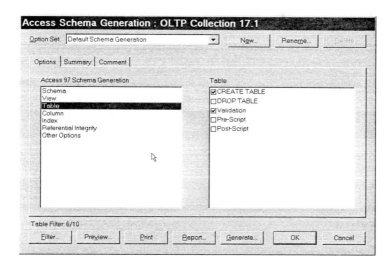

FIGURE 19.2
ERwin customizes the Schema Generation Editor to contain the options appropriate for the target server you selected.

The Schema Generation Editor contains three tabs:

- Options—Set the schema options for forward engineering. Read more on setting options in the next section.
- Summary—View all selected schema options. Show Selected Only is the default. Select Edit Options allows you to modify the selected options and enables buttons that allow you to clear all options.
- Comment—Enter a comment for the current option set.

The Option Set drop-down list displays the name of the current option set. To use a different schema option set, select it from the list. You can create a new option set by selecting the options you want to use and then selecting the New button to save the option set with a new name.

Setting the Schema Generation Options

The left panel of the Options tab displays a list of database object classes (see Table 19.1). Select a class to see the database object options in the right panel to control the database objects generated.

TABLE 19.1   Database Object Classes and the Related Options for Schema Generation in Access

Database Object Class	Schema Generation Option
Schema	Pre-script, post-script
View	Create view, drop view, pre-script, post-script
Table	Create table, drop table, validation, pre-script, post-script
Column	Validation, caption, physical order, DEFAULT value
Index	Create index, primary key, label, alternate key, foreign key, inversion entry
Referential integrity	Create relation, delete relation
Other options	Comment

If you are creating new database objects, you do not need the drop statements. Including the drop statements for database objects that do not exist causes an error message to be generated by the RDBMS. Don't include statements such as pre-script or post-script if you haven't defined them.

TIP

Examine the default options for the target server you selected. Some options don't include the creation of all indexes. Missing indexes, particularly foreign key indexes, can create a painful experience.

Use ER*win*'s preview feature to review a sample of the schema generation report. It can be a real time-saver.

Additional options are available for database objects supported by other target servers. If you're not sure which options to select, use the default options selected by ER*win*. Remember to check the schema generation for unnecessary or absent options.

Filtering the Schema Generation

In addition to providing the options that let you specify the database objects to be included in schema generation, ER*win* allows you to filter the tables that are created when you forward engineer database objects. The Report Filter Editor, shown in Figure 19.3, allows you to exclude tables in the subject area from forward engineering. Using the Display Names options, you can select whether to display logical or physical table names. To open the Report Filter Editor, click the Filter button in the Schema Generation Editor.

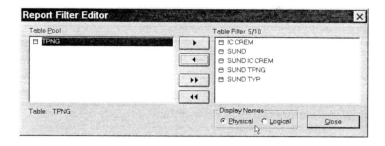

FIGURE 19.3
Use the Report Filter Editor to select which tables in the current subject area to forward engineer.

You can use ER*win*'s filtering feature when using the Schema Generation Report Editor or when using ER*win*'s Alter Database or Complete Compare. (I discuss Alter Database and Complete Compare in Chapter 20, "Advanced Features for the Physical Model.")

By default, all the tables in the current subject area are selected for forward engineering schema generation. The tables that ER*win* will forward engineer are listed in the Table Filter list box. Use the controls on the Report Filter Editor to move tables to be excluded from the Table Filter list box to the Table Pool list box.

TIP

When you are generating schema using only some of the tables in the model, take care to handle dangling relationships. Dangling relationships are relationships to tables that are not included in the schema generation.

To remove dangling relationships, select the Filter Dangling Relationships from Schema Gen option on the Subject Area Editor's General tab.

You can also select one or more tables in the physical model prior to selecting Forward Engineer/Schema Generation. ER*win* asks whether you want to use the current diagram selections and tells you the number of tables you have selected. Clicking the Yes button moves the selected tables to the Table Filter list box and moves all other tables to the Table Pool list box. This is a nice feature that I use frequently.

Creating a DDL Script

A DDL (Data Definition Language) script is a file that contains the SQL statements for creating the database objects. Creating a DDL script does not create the database objects. The script must be executed on the server to generate the database objects. ERwin lets you generate the DDL script and save it as a text (.txt) file. You can open the .txt file with any word processing application, such as Microsoft Word, Notepad, or WordPad. The file can be executed by any database utility that can interpret SQL scripts, such as SPUFI for DB2, ISQL for SQL Server, or SQL*DBA for ORACLE.

To create a DDL script, press the Report button in the Schema Generation Editor to launch the Generate SQL Schema Report dialog.

NOTE

The Generate SQL Schema dialog offers you two file extensions (.ers and .sql) to use with the name you provide for the script file. The .ers extension is ERwin's own. Use the .sql extension to help database utilities recognize the file as DDL.

Add a filename, select the drive and directory where you want the file to be saved, and click the OK button. It's as simple as that!

Creating Database Objects Directly in the Database

To create the database objects directly in the database, click the Generate button on the Schema Generation Editor to start the schema generation process. ERwin first displays the Target Server Connection dialog, which allows you to log on to the target server and connect ERwin to the system catalog in the target database. To connect ERwin to the target server, the appropriate client connectivity software for the target server must be installed on your computer. Some databases require an ODBC data source in order to generate schema. I discuss creating an ODBC data source in Chapter 20. For the examples in this text, Access is the target server.

NOTE

If you elect to generate both DROP and CREATE statements for database objects, ERwin executes the DROP command first and then executes the CREATE command.

ERwin creates an active connection to the system catalog when you log onto the target server. This connection allows ERwin to forward engineer a schema directly to the target database catalog. ERwin executes the DDL script automatically. While executing the DDL script, ERwin displays the Generate Database Schema dialog, as shown in Figure 19.4, allowing you to view the results as each statement is executed.

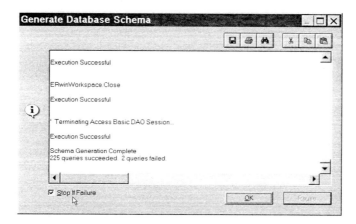

FIGURE 19.4

ERwin's Generate Database Schema dialog displays a log file that records the results of creating each physical database object.

The Generate Database Schema dialog contains editing icons that enable you to save, print, and search (as well as cut, copy, and paste) the log file created during schema generation. Select the Stop If Failure check box (shown in Figure 19.4) to have ER*win* pause the process of generating the database objects if problems are encountered in the DDL. In addition to pausing in generating schema, ER*win* displays a message in the dialog window describing the problem. You have the option of stopping the generation by clicking the Abort button or clicking Continue to continue generating the database objects.

If you choose to abort, ER*win* stops processing the file. However, all statements that executed successfully before the failure generate database objects. All statements after the problem statement are not processed. Clear the Stop If Failure box if you do not want ER*win* to pause each time a statement fails to execute. ER*win* writes a description of the problem and continues to generate the database objects.

ER*win* also allows you to halt schema generation at any time by clicking the Pause button. If you use the Pause button to stop the process, you can click Continue to continue generating schema or Abort to stop.

> **CAUTION**
>
> Although ERwin is good at generating the DDL using the correct syntax for the target server, it is not perfect. In addition, some database objects you create in ERwin require you to understand the syntax as well.
>
> Closely examine the log file of the database object creation. Test the data structures thoroughly to ensure they are complete and correct.

ERwin generates a log file during the schema generation process. It is important to keep this log as part of the generation process documentation. Any problems with the script should be resolved and documented.

Summary

Delivering the physical model has two parts, delivering the physical model documentation and creating the physical database objects. The documentation for the physical model is as important as creating the database objects.

The physical model documentation is divided into that produced outside of ERwin and that produced within ERwin. Examples of documentation produced outside of ERwin are usage requirements and database platform (target server) selection, session notes and meeting minutes, the results and responses to physical model reviews, and any documentation that records the design decisions made by the modeling team. Of particular importance is documentation on any business rules represented in the logical model that are not present in the physical model. You might need to implement these business rules elsewhere.

Examples of documentation produced within ERwin are

- The physical model diagram
- Reports on physical model objects
- Model validation reports
- Volumetrics estimates
- DDL scripts
- Schema generation log files

ERwin provides a set of standard reports that you can run. You can customize the result set's content and appearance, as well as create new custom reports using the Report Editor. ERwin's validation reports are a good way to review the model prior to generating schema.

ER*win* allows you to create a DDL (Data Definition Language) script file or to generate the database objects by connecting directly to the target server. Creating the DDL script does not generate the schema. The script must be run using a utility that can execute SQL statements. To generate the database objects directly in the target server, ER*win* requires a connection to the server. You can instruct ER*win* to pause the schema generation process if it encounters problems with the DDL. ER*win* halts the schema generation and writes a description of the problem to the log file. ER*win* is good at creating DDL, but it's not perfect. Study the log file carefully and test the database objects for completeness and correctness.

In the next and final chapter, I provide an overview of ODBC (Open Database Connectivity), including creating an ODBC data source, connecting to Access, and generating the schema for Betty's Ice Cream Shop. I conclude with an introduction to some of ER*win*'s advanced physical modeling features: Alter Model, Alter Database, and Complete Compare.

Advanced Features for the Physical Model

The greatest portion of this part of the book addressed building a physical model in ER*win*, culminating in Chapter 19, "Delivering the Physical Data Model," with delivering the physical model documentation and creating the database objects. In this chapter, I provide an overview of ODBC connections and an introduction to some of ER*win*'s advanced features for the physical model.

In the sections that follow, I cover

- An overview of ODBC
- Generating schema in Microsoft Access
- Using ER*win*'s Alter Model and Alter Database features
- Using ER*win*'s Complete Compare

Given a direct connection to a database, ER*win* has features that allow you to update the physical database to reflect changes made in the model, as well as update the physical model to capture changes made directly to the database. The synchronization process allows you to compare differences between an ER*win* data model and a physical database, between a data model and an SQL script file, or between two ER*win* models. You can use ER*win*'s list of changes to update the current ER*win* data model, the current database, or both. To connect to some target servers, ER*win* requires an ODBC connection to create database objects.

Understanding ODBC Connections

ODBC (Open Database Connectivity) allows you to connect a specific target database to ER*win*. An ODBC connection requires that you have

- The appropriate ODBC driver on your computer
- An ODBC data source

An ODBC database driver is a dynamic link library that translates communications to and from the database into the appropriate syntax. Check the documentation for your target server for ODBC drivers. An ODBC data source associates the appropriate ODBC driver with a particular database. You use an ODBC data source recognized by the ODBC Data Source Administrator on your computer or create a new one.

Creating an ODBC Data Source

You can launch the ODBC Data Source Administrator from the Windows Control Panel. Click the Windows Start button and select Settings, Control Panel. You might need to scroll around to find the ODBC Data Sources (32-bit) icon, shown in Figure 20.1. ODBC Data Sources can be 16-bit or 32-bit. Your Control Panel might have icons for both. If you're not sure which to use, choose the 32-bit version.

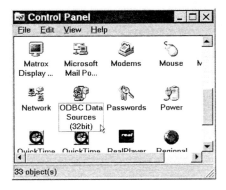

FIGURE 20.1

The ODBC Data Sources icon appears in the Windows Control Panel.

Double-click the icon to launch the ODBC Data Source Administrator, shown in Figure 20.2.

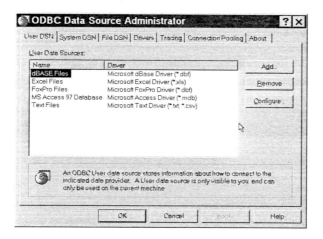

Figure 20.2

The ODBC Data Source Administrator allows you to associate the appropriate ODBC driver with a particular database.

The ODBC Data Source Administrator has several tabs:

- User DSN—User data sources are local to a computer and can only be used by the current user.

- System DSN—System data sources are local to a computer but can be used by any authorized user or system.

- File DSN—File-based data sources can be shared among all users who have the same drivers installed, and need not be dedicated to a user or local to a computer.

- Drivers—Displays information about the ODBC drivers installed on the computer. The ODBC Drivers list shows the drivers already installed on your computer. You install new drivers using their own installation packages.

- Tracing—You can specify how the ODBC Driver Manager traces calls to ODBC functions.

- Connection Pooling—Change the time period for connection retry wait and connection timeout for a driver that is using connection pooling. You can also enable or disable Performance Monitoring, a facility that records connection statistics.

- About—Displays information about the ODBC core components, such as the driver manager and cursor library.

Creating a data source to a database is fairly straightforward. For the most part, you only use one or two of the tabs, User DSN and System DSN.

To create a user DSN for a Access database, follow these steps:

1. Click the Add button on the User DSN tab to open the Create New Data Source window so you can select the appropriate driver.

2. Select the Microsoft Access Driver (*.mdb) and press the Finish button to open the ODBC Microsoft Access Setup dialog, shown in Figure 20.3.

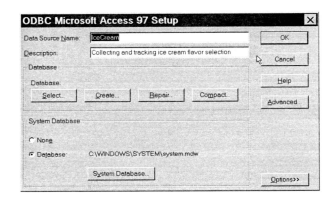

FIGURE 20.3

The ODBC Microsoft Access Setup dialog allows you to set the properties for the data source. You can repair and compact as well as select or create an Access database.

3. Enter a descriptive name for the data source. Although the Setup dialog allows you to enter a description, the description is not displayed when you close and reopen the data source.

4. Click the Select button to navigate to, and select, an Access database as the data source.

CAUTION

I was not successful in my attempts to use the Create button to create a new database. Although a message indicated the database had been successfully created and I could see the database using Windows Explorer, Access could not open the database. Therefore, I recommend that you create the database first, using Access.

5. In the System Database options, None is the default selection. Select Database instead, and then click the System Database button to locate the system.mdw file. (In Windows 95 or Windows 98, the file is in the Windows\system directory. For Windows NT, the file is in the Windows\system32 directory.)

6. Click the OK button, after which the new data source appears in the User DSN list. You can change the properties of any data source by selecting the data source and then clicking the Configure button.

You create a system DSN using exactly the same steps. If you share the computer where the database is located, consider creating a data source that can be reused by other authorized users.

Generic ODBC

ERwin supports generic open database connectivity (ODBC) to extend its target server support. Using generic ODBC allows ERwin to connect to a target server using an ODBC data source. If the target server supports a generic ODBC driver, you can select ODBC as the target server in ERwin. ERwin queries the database to determine the physical properties such as standard datatypes.

After you select ODBC as the target server, ERwin immediately prompts you to connect to the database. If you connect to the database, ERwin determines the datatypes and displays them in the editors. Allowing ERwin to connect to the database replaces generic datatypes with those supported by the database. This might help you avoid schema-generation errors for invalid datatypes when forward engineering the physical model.

If you do not connect to the database, the physical model editors display generic datatypes to assign to the data model objects. Using the generic properties instead of those supported by your database can cause schema-generation errors for invalid datatypes when the physical model is forward engineered.

TIP

I performed a couple of quick comparisons creating an Access database using a direct connection and using an ODBC data source. Using the same physical model, the ODBC data source produced more errors and did not create all the database objects. I recommend using a direct connection to the database when possible.

Creating Database Objects in Access

Betty's Ice Cream Shop selected Access as the target server. In this section, I discuss the steps for creating the database objects defined in the ER*win* model in an Access database.

To create the database objects for Betty's Ice Cream Shop, you must first create an empty Access database (*.mdb).

1. Launch Access.
2. Select File, New Database or click the New icon on the toolbar.
3. Select the Blank Database icon on the General tab.
4. Select the location to store the database and give it a name. I used "iceCream" as the name for the example.

Of course, you need to launch ER*win* and open the physical model diagram that contains the subject area with the database objects you want to create. In this example, I use the DSS Campaign Management subject area.

To create the database objects, select the Forward Engineer/Schema Generation option from the Tasks menu. If the option is dimmed, make sure the diagram is in physical mode. ER*win* opens the Access Schema Generation Editor to allow you to select the database objects to be included in the schema generation.

Because this is a new database, there is no need to select the drop statements. I did not define any pre-scripts or post-scripts, so there is no need to select them as options. For this example, I create database objects by selecting these options:

- Schema: None
- View: Create view
- Table: Create table, validation
- Column: Validation, caption, physical order, DEFAULT value
- Index: Create index, primary key (PK), alternate key (AK), foreign key (FK), inversion entry (IE)
- Referential integrity: Create relation
- Other options: Comment

You can review your selections using the Summary tab and check the DDL using the Preview button. I will not use the Filter button to exclude tables, so I am ready to click the Generate button to begin schema generation.

ERwin will not present a connection dialog if it is already connected to a database. ERwin automatically creates the database objects in the target server to which it is connected. You should verify that you are connected to the correct database by selecting the *Target Server* Connection item in the Server menu before generating schema (by clicking the Generate button).

Note that in Figure 20.4 in the following section, the item is called Access Connection. ERwin customizes the menu items by including the name of the target server you selected.

Connecting to Access and Generating the Schema

If you are not already connected to Access, ER*win* presents the Access Connection dialog shown in Figure 20.4.

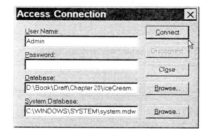

FIGURE 20.4

The Access Connection dialog allows you to specify the location and name of the database in which ERwin will create the database objects.

The Access Connection dialog requires you to enter some information:

- User Name—You need admin privileges to create objects in the database. Simply enter the name as shown in Figure 20.4.

- Password—If you created a password for your database, you need to enter it here. In the example, I do not need one, so the password is blank in Figure 20.4.

- Database—Enter the location and name of the database. Use the Browse button to navigate to the database you built in the previous section.

- System Database—Enter the location of the system.mdw file for Access. Use the Browse button to navigate to the location of the file.

After entering the information, click the Connect button to connect ER*win* to the database.

> **TIP**
>
> Finding the `system.mdw` file is simple. If you are using Windows 95 or 98, the file is located in the `Windows\System` directory. If you are using Windows NT, it appears in the `Windows\System32` directory.
>
> If the file is not in one of these locations, use the Find option on the Windows Start button. Select Files or Folders and enter `system.mdw` as the name. Windows will find the file for you.

After setting the Schema Generation options and connecting to the Access database, you create the database objects by clicking the Generate button in the Access Schema Generation Editor.

When you click the Generate button, ER*win* begins executing the DDL to create the database objects. A log file records the outcome of executing each statement in the DDL. ER*win* automatically creates the database objects for which it encounters no errors. See Chapter 19 for tips on resolving errors.

Synchronizing Models and Databases

All databases eventually need to change. No matter how well the original database was designed, you need to update the model and alter the database at some point to meet newly defined information and usage requirements. When the business objectives change, you need to reflect the change in the data model and the physical database.

ER*win* automatically performs tasks that you ordinarily have to perform manually, such as unloading and reloading database tables to prevent loss of data. ER*win* generates the code to unload data to a temporary table at the time the update DDL script for the database is created. ER*win* can also reverse engineer the database, allowing you to import database changes to the model.

ER*win*'s synchronization features allow you to

- Update the current ER*win* data model using Update Model.
- Update the database directly or by generating a script using Alter Database.
- Update both the database and the model using Complete Compare.

> **NOTE**
>
> ER*win* does not compare or synchronize index physical properties, table physical properties, or synonyms.

ER*win* detects and reports the differences in tables, columns, views, and other database objects. You then have the option to

- Selectively undo changes.
- Document changes by printing a report that lists the differences.
- Update the current model or database based on the changes.

The Update Model option on the Tasks menu only updates the open model. No changes are made to the database, DDL script file, or ER*win* model used in the comparison. The Alter Database option only updates the database. If you want to synchronize both the model and the database, DDL script, or ER*win* model, you should use ER*win*'s Complete Compare.

Setting the Options

Selecting Update Model, Alter Database, or Complete Compare from the Tasks menu displays the appropriate Set Options dialog. Figure 20.5 shows the Update Model - Set Options dialog, which enables you to select the database, file, or ER*win* model for comparison. The same options are available for Complete Compare and (with the exception of the Case Conversion of Physical Names) Alter Database. Use the Filter button to exclude tables from update or alter processes.

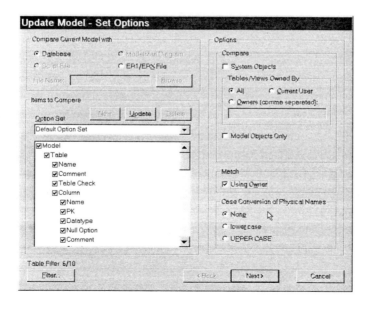

FIGURE 20.5
The Update Model – Set Options dialog allows you to specify which objects ERwin will compare.

The Set Options dialog contains several groups of options you can set.

Compare Current Model allows you to compare the physical model to the following:

- Database—Select to compare the current model with an existing database.
- ModelMart Diagram—Select to compare the current model or database with a model stored in ModelMart. This option is not available unless you are logged on to ModelMart.
- Script File—Select to compare the current model with a DDL script file. This option is not available for Access, Clipper, dBASE, FoxPro, and Paradox.
- ER1/ERX File—Select to compare the current model with an ERwin model file (*.er1) or a model that has been exported as an ERX file.

If you select a ModelMart diagram, DDL script, or another ERwin model, you can use the Browse button to navigate to it. Remember that not all options are available for all target servers.

The Items to Compare group box allows you to select a different option set from the drop-down list, update the selections for the current option set, or create a new option set. The Option Set list box displays a list of the database objects supported by the target server. Select the boxes in front of database objects ERwin should compare, and clear the boxes for database objects that should not be compared.

> **NOTE**
>
> ERwin only uses these Option Set selections to create the display list in the Resolve Differences dialog. It does not use them to filter items for import or export.

The Compare options allow you to specify which tables should participate in the compare. ERwin uses these settings to create the database objects displayed in the Resolve Differences list and to determine the database objects that ERwin attempts to synchronize. The Compare options you can select are

- System Objects—Select this option to compare your model with both system and user tables.
- Tables/Views Owned By—Select one of the options to filter the tables used in the comparison based on owner. You can select All, enter Current User, or enter a list of Owners, separated by commas.
- Model Objects Only—Select this option to have ERwin disregard new objects in the target. ERwin detects new objects if this option is not selected.

The Match option available for Access, Using Owner, tells ER*win* to match database objects in the physical model with the source based on the owner name and other standard matching criteria. To match database objects using only standard matching criteria, clear the box. Note that ER*win* automatically assigns ownership for tables using the name entered in the User Name text box on the Target Server Connection dialog.

The Set Options dialog for Update Model and Complete Compare contains a set of options (none, lowercase, uppercase) allowing the case conversion of physical names. These options are not available in the Set Options for Alter Database.

Update Model, Alter Database, and Complete Compare all let you use the Filter button to exclude tables from the comparison process.

When all options are set, click the Next button in the Set Options dialog. ER*win* reads the target database objects selected for comparison and attempts to match the source database objects to the target database objects. After the matching is complete, ER*win* displays the Resolve Differences dialog.

Resolving Differences

The Resolve Differences dialog displays the differences between the source (model or database) on the left and the target database, script, or model on the right. Database objects matched automatically by ER*win* are displayed on the same line.

The buttons on the right of the Resolve Differences dialog allow you to assign an action to the objects in the list. A button is unavailable (dimmed) if it is not a valid action for the selected object. The buttons allow you to assign actions to

- IMPORT/EXPORT—IMPORT implements the change to the model and EXPORT implements the change to database.

- IGNORE—This allows you to select objects to be ignored during the Update Model or Alter Database process.

- DELETE—Mark one or more selected objects for deletion. ER*win* deletes the object during import or export.

- MATCH—You can manually match two objects that were not automatically matched by ER*win*. When you select the Match Tool, the cursor changes to a double-ended arrow. Click an object in the list on the left side, and then click an object on the right side. ER*win* aligns the objects on the same line.

- UNMATCH—Break the match between an object in the source and an object in the target database, DDL script, ModelMart diagram, or ER*win* file. Select the row with the items that do not match and click the Unmatch Tool. ER*win* moves the objects to different lines.

If you select Update Model, ER*win* automatically sets the action for all differences in the target database, script, or model that are not in the open physical model to IMPORT. If ER*win* finds a database object in the target database or file that has no corresponding database object in the model, ER*win* automatically sets the action for that item to IGNORE.

If you select Alter Database, ER*win* automatically sets the action for all differences in the open physical model that are not in the target database or file to EXPORT. If ER*win* finds a database object in the target database or file that has no corresponding database object in the open model, ER*win* automatically sets the action for that item to IGNORE.

If you select Complete Compare, ER*win* automatically sets the action for all differences to IGNORE. You can set the action for each difference to either IMPORT the change to the model or EXPORT the change to the database, as well as IGNORE or DELETE the change.

The Resolve Differences dialog also includes an action bar in the center of the differences list. Each object in the differences list is associated with an action symbol on the action bar that indicates the action for that object. In addition to the actions that ER*win* sets automatically are mixed actions and delete actions. Other options in the Resolve Differences dialog allow you to

- Show Only Differences—Select this option to have ER*win* list only the differences between the source and the target.
- Report—Click to open the Comparison Report Options dialog.

To resolve differences between the source model and the database, observe the following guidelines:

- If you are using a user-defined subject area (any subject area other than main), make sure you select the Filter Dangling Relationships option.
- Resolve many-to-many relationships. Even if the relationships are defined as logical only, ER*win*'s automatic resolution produces database objects.
- Verify that all database objects that should not be generated are defined as logical only.

Updating the Model

After you resolve the differences listed in the Update Model - Resolve Differences dialog, click the Next button to display the Update Model - Import Changes dialog, shown in Figure 20.6.

The Case Conversion of Logical Names allows you to select how ER*win* handles the creation of logical names. I recommend the Mixed Case option, unless your organization's naming conventions indicate otherwise.

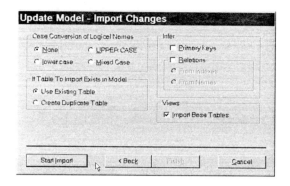

FIGURE 20.6

The Update Model – Import Changes dialog allows you to set options for how the changes are implemented in the updated model.

The If Table to Import Exists in Model options allow you to select how ER*win* handles importing a table that exists in the main subject area into a new subject area. You can elect to

- Use Existing Table—Select this option to allow the table in the new subject area to be a reference to the table in main.

- Create Duplicate Table—Select this option to create a duplicate table in the new subject area and add the table to main as well.

The Infer options allow you to infer primary keys and relations from names or indexes. Selecting the From Names option tells ER*win* to infer a relationship between two tables if all of the primary key columns of the parent are in the child table. Selecting the From Indexes option tells ER*win* to infer a relationship between two tables only if the primary key columns of the parent table are an index in the child table.

NOTE

Because most databases support primary key and foreign key declarations, you probably do not need to use the Infer options.

The Views option allows you to tell ER*win* whether to import the base tables referenced by a view. Selecting this option causes ER*win* to parse the DDL statements for each view and automatically create a view relationship to each referenced table in the updated model. ER*win* stores the details of the referenced tables, and if you import one or more of the referenced tables later, it creates the view relationships to the referenced tables.

Click the Start Import button to begin importing objects and definitions into the source model from the target. ER*win* displays messages about successful and unsuccessful import actions during the import process. You can click the View Results button to open the Import Summary dialog and view, print, or save the import message log.

Click the Back button to return to the Resolve Differences dialog.

Implementing Changes in the Database

After you resolve the differences listed in the Alter Database - Resolve Differences dialog, click the Next button to display the Alter Database - Export Changes dialog, shown in Figure 20.7.

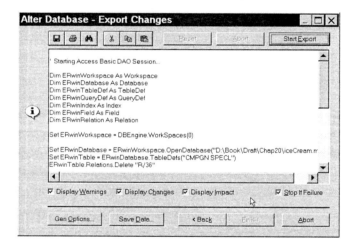

FIGURE 20.7

The Alter Database – Export Changes dialog allows you to set options for how the changes are implemented in the database.

ER*win* displays the DDL script in the dialog window. You can preview and edit the script. You can also use the tools at the top of the dialog to save, print, and edit the DDL change script. The Alter Database - Export Changes dialog contains a set of options that allow you to specify the messages that ER*win* should record in the log file:

- Display Warnings—Select this option to have ER*win* include warning messages.
- Display Changes—Select this option to have ER*win* include change messages.
- Display Impact—Select this option to have ER*win* include impact analysis information.

Select the Stop If Failure option to have ER*win* pause the export process if an action is unsuccessful. Clear the option to have ER*win* continue the export without pausing at each error.

Click the Gen Options button to open the Schema Generation Editor and specify database objects and properties ER*win* should apply when creating the new database objects.

Click the Save Data button to open the Data Preservation Options dialog. This button is only available when statements in the DDL script are potentially destructive to data. For example, a statement that changes a column datatype from character to date could potentially destroy the data contained in the column.

Click the Start Export button to begin exporting database objects from the source to the target. ER*win* displays messages about successful and unsuccessful export actions during the export process in the log file. You can print or save the log after the export is complete.

Click the Back button to return to the Alter Database - Resolve Differences dialog.

Importing and Exporting Changes

After you resolve the differences listed in the Complete Compare - Resolve Differences dialog, click the Next button to continue. Because ER*win*'s Complete Compare combines the functionality of Update Model and Alter Database, it uses the same dialogs. If you select at least one import action, ER*win* displays the Complete Compare - Import Changes dialog. If you also select at least one export action, ER*win* displays the Complete Compare - Export Changes dialog.

Summary

For some target servers, ER*win* requires an ODBC connection to the database. An ODBC connection requires the appropriate ODBC driver and an ODBC data source. There are several sources for ODBC drivers; check the documentation for your target server for recommendations. You create an ODBC data source using the ODBC Data Source Administrator. To create an ODBC data source, follow these steps:

1. Select the User DSN or System DSN tab.
2. Click the Add button and select the appropriate ODBC driver from the list.
3. Name the data source.
4. Select the database.
5. Click OK to create the data source.

To create the database objects for Betty's Ice Cream Shop in Access, use Access to create an empty database. Then using ER*win*'s Access Connection dialog, enter the connection information and click the Connect button to connect to the database. After connecting to the database, select Forward Engineering/Schema Generation from the Tasks menu. Set the schema generation options using the Schema Generation Editor, and then click Generate to begin creating the database objects. ER*win* produces a log file that records the outcome of the execution of each DDL statement. Take note of problems with the execution of any statement and resolve as necessary.

Every database needs to change over time. As business needs expand, you need to reflect the new information requirements and usage requirements in both the model and the database. ER*win* provides three powerful features for synchronizing the model and the database:

- Update Model allows you to import changes from a database, DDL script, or another model to the current model.
- Alter Database allows you to export changes from the current model to a database, DDL script, or another model.
- Complete Compare allows you to make changes in both the model and database during the same process.

ER*win* provides an additional facility, the Data Preservation Options Dialog, to produce the code for unloading and reloading data when the proposed changes to the database might cause data to be lost.

ER*win*'s online documentation contains information specific to the target servers it supports. I encourage you to examine documentation for additional information about specific database platform support.

References

Date, C.J. *Relational Database: Selected Writings*. Reading, Massachusetts: Addison-Wesley, 1986.

————. *An Introduction to Database Systems, Volume I*. Reading, Massachusetts: Addison-Wesley, 1986.

Finklestein, Clive. *An Introduction to Information Engineering: From Strategic Planning to Information Systems*. Reading, Massachusetts: Addison-Wesley, 1989.

————. *Information Engineering: Strategic Systems Development*. Reading, Massachusetts: Addison-Wesley, 1992.

Martin, James. *Information Engineering, Book II: Planning and Analysis*. Upper Saddle River, New Jersey: Prentice Hall, 1989.

————. *Managing the Database Environment*. Upper Saddle River, New Jersey: Prentice Hall, 1983.

Reingruber, Michael C., and William W. Gregory. *The Data Modeling Handbook*. New York: John Wiley & Sons, 1984.

INDEX

Other Related Titles

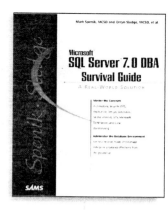

Microsoft SQL Server 7 DBA Survival Guide
Mark Spenik and Orryn Sledge
0-672-31226-3
$49.99 USA/$74.95 CAN

DB2 Developer's Guide, Third Edition
Craig Mullins
0-672-31168-2
$59.99 USA/$84.95 CAN

Sams Teach Yourself DB2 Universal Database in 21 Days
Susan Visser
0-672-31278-6
$49.99 USA/$71.95 CAN

Oracle8 Server Unleashed
Joe Greene
0-672-31207-7
$49.99 USA/$71.95 CAN

Microsoft SQL Server 7.0 Unleashed
Simon Gallagher, Sharon Bjeletich, et al.
0-672-31227-1
$49.99 USA/$74.95 CAN

Microsoft OLAP Unleashed
Timothy Peterson, Jim Pinkelman, and Russell Darroch
0-672-31671-4
$49.99 USA/$74.95 CAN

Building Enterprise Solutions with Visual Studio 6
G.A. Sullivan, Don Benage, and Azam A. Mirza
0-672-31489-4
$49.99 USA/$74.95 CAN

Creating Microsoft Access 2000 Solutions: A Power Users' Guide
Gordon Padwick
0-672-31894-6
$39.99 USA/$59.95 CAN

Oracle Development Unleashed, Third Edition
Advanced Information Systems, Inc.
0-672-31575-0
$49.99 USA/$74.95 CAN

Sams Teach Yourself UML in 24 Hours
Joseph Schmuller
0-672-31636-6
$24.99 USA/$37.95 CAN

SAMS

www.samspublishing.com

All prices are subject to change.